Management Development

Alan Mumford's experience in management development has been exceptionally wide. It includes periods with John Laing & Sons, IPC Magazines, International Computers Ltd and the Chloride Group. He was also Deputy Chief Training Adviser at the Department of Employment.

In 1983, he was appointed Professor of Management Development at International Management Centres, and is now Visiting Professor there. His main work is on improving management performance, especially through effective learning processes. He has worked with senior managers and directors and developers in a variety of organisations including Ford of Europe, Pilkington, Brooke Bond, the Post Office and Unison (the UK's largest trade union). He has also worked with organisations in Australia, South Africa and the United States.

He has published numerous articles and books on management development.

The Institute of Personnel and Development is the leading publisher of books and reports for personnel and training professionals and students and for all those concerned with the effective management and development of people at work. For full details of all our titles please telephone the Publishing Department on 0181 263 3387.

Management Development

Strategies for Action

Alan Mumford

Third Edition

INSTITUTE OF PERSONNEL
AND DEVELOPMENT

First published 1989
Second edition 1993
Reprinted 1993
Third edition 1997

Phototypeset by Fakenham Photosetting Ltd
and printed in Great Britain by
Short Run Press Ltd, Exeter, Devon.

British Library Cataloguing in Publication Data
A catalogue record for this book is available from the British Library

ISBN 0 85292 689 8

**INSTITUTE OF PERSONNEL
AND DEVELOPMENT**

IPD House, Camp Road, London SW19 4UX
Tel: 0181 971 9000   Fax: 0181 263 3333
Registered office as above. Registered Charity No. 1038333
A company limited by guarantee. Registered in England No. 2931892

Contents

Figures

Acknowledgements

The then Manpower Services Commission, sponsored a research project 'Learning to learn for managers' and two projects on the development of directors. I am grateful to them for having given me the opportunity to do the research, publish it and use it in other books, especially *Developing Top Managers.*

I am also grateful to Gower, the publishers of *Developing Top Managers,* for agreeing that I could use some of the charts and figures from that book here; and to *Personnel Management,* for permission to reprint (in adapted form) the exercise which appears at the end of Chapter 9.

This book makes use of a wide variety of experiences with different employers and a large number of managers. John Laing and, particularly, Don Stradling gave me my first opportunities in management development. My subsequent work has been built on the sound base of this early experience. I was given opportunity, challenge, sensitively conducted review processes – and sent on some good courses. If this book helps others to have similarly good experiences, then part of my early debt to John Laing will be repaid.

Finally, my thanks to Richard Wright for his help in improving the book.

Introduction

The IPD has led the way in continuous learning, and in fulfilling the need to integrate formal and informal development, through its ABCD campaign, the book *Continuous Development* and finally its encouragement to members – 'Continuing Professional Development'. I was delighted to be asked to write this present work since my own ideas relate so clearly to those themes.

Two earlier books of mine, *Making Experience Pay* and *Developing Top Managers*, gave considerable attention to informal learning. The first was written to challenge the focus on formal management development of most other books on the subject, while the second is a research-based analysis aimed particularly at the top levels of management. These books do not, therefore, cover the formal aspects of management development in enough detail to offer a comprehensive view of the topic which is suitable for managers at all levels. This the present book sets out to do, while sharing with my two earlier books a belief that learning is the central issue; it is not inputs which define the success of management development, but output.

I have attempted to write a book which is innovative without being fanciful; its ideas are not wholly untested. They are based on 30 years of experience in management development, for most of which time I was employed as an in-company management development adviser. My later experience at an innovative business school, International Management Centres, has provided me with the opportunity to carry out research on the learning and development processes of managers and directors.

I believe that the combination of these two different kinds of experience has enabled me to write a better book than I would otherwise have written. Up till then I had had the experience of sitting with the top five executives of my company and helping them make decisions about whether a senior manager should go on a course at the London Business School, and whether another manager should be sent to run a new company in South-East Asia or should be given a new role co-ordinating marketing in Europe. My research experiences since then enabled me not only to collect different views on the ways in which such problems should be approached in planning formal management development, but to understand better why such decisions are not often made as part of a coolly reflective, long-term planning process.

Two prime strategies

In Chapter 1 I present my definition of management development, and my personal discovery that whereas most authors have seen management development wholly as a formal process of structured learning, I have come to understand that we need also to embrace accidental and informal processes of development. Formal approaches to development represent a very explicit strategy of identifying needs and providing learning activities to meet those needs. It may seem odd to describe the second – accidental and informal learning – as a strategy at all. My justification for describing this as a second strategy is that management developers need to recognise how they can convert informal, accidental and often unrecognised learning into an organisational and personal strategy of learning through the accidental and unplanned realities of managerial life. These ideas may be captured as:

Strategy 1

Management development achieved through analysis, diagnosis and the delivery of planned learning experiences (both off the job and on the job).

Strategy 2

An approach that gives greater emphasis to seizing learning opportunities as they emerge from the hectic reality of managerial life – an opportunistic approach not necessarily derived from a previous analysis of needs or competence requirements.

Strategy 1 is, of course, much more within the control of management developers, management educators or trainers. The formal diagnostic approach it engenders is seen in a particularly powerful form in the competence approach presented through the Management Charter Initiative (MCI). A fundamental feature of this is that it is geared, through a definition of 'levels' of manager, to a series of generic statements of competence, and is matched to National Vocational Qualifications (NVQs). Some of the arguments for and against the use of competences are presented in Chapter 6. Here, it is appropriate to develop the consequences of an MCI national qualification approach to a strategy for management development. It represents a continuing belief in the generic nature of management, and thus flies in the face of management research which shows instead the contingent situational nature of management. It proclaims a view of management as a profession, which should therefore have examinations or other processes for determining membership; and membership by qualification implies that each individual should satisfy general national standards. Ironically, given that a fundamental feature of competence is the ability to do things, evaluation of competence is largely driven by the written word, since it is far too expensive and anecdotal for the evidence of competence to be acquired through personal observation.

I should emphasise that I think a strategy within any organisation of using a carefully created schedule of skills and knowledge – or competence – requirements can be an entirely appropriate route. What I want to emphasise is that, in my view, management development advisers may need to think hard before they adopt a national competence approach which is geared to the justification of qualifications, rather than an organisationally based competency approach geared to specific organisational needs.

Interestingly, two other aspects of the MCI approach provide potential links to Strategy 2. The emphasis on the need to understand and develop an individual's capacity to learn, and the idea of 'Crediting Competence' (Accrediting Prior Experience and Learning) brings Strategy 2 into play. The plea I make is that management developers should think in terms of both these strategies.

Definitions

The terms and processes of 'manager development', 'management development' and 'organisation development' merge into one another both in understanding and practice. In this introduction it is only necessary to say that I use management development to describe the total process by which managers learn and grow in effectiveness; I do not regard it merely as the third leg of a tripod (the other two being management education and management training). Those concerned with the development of directors and senior professional people should find the principles described here also relevant to them.

The chapter sequence

The chapters follow one another in a logical sequence. However, this sequence reflects my own views of where we need to start in order to understand and implement management development processes. Some readers may arrive at the book with different ideas about what is significant and important, which may influence where they want to start.

I recommend that everyone starts with Chapter 1. Those who are initially particularly interested in formal management development processes could then choose to read Chapter 2, followed by Chapters 4–8. Readers who are in the first instance more interested in informal processes may prefer to follow Chapter 1 with Chapters 3, 9 and 11.

However, since it is my opinion that we need to draw informal and formal processes together, the book makes most sense if read in the sequence in which it is written.

Catering for differences

One of the major challenges in management development is coping with individual differences: differences in needs, differences in preferred approaches to learning, differences between men and women. I have already tried to show that I intend to practise what I preach in this book by offering suggestions about the different sequences the reader might choose.

Another of the book's themes is that development most frequently occurs as a result of managers actually taking action. Most modern management development advisers would also subscribe to the view that development is something you undertake and achieve for yourself; it is not something 'done to' you. It is therefore appropriate that in many parts of the book I shall be suggesting development activities that advisers can test out on themselves; there can after all be no better recommendation when offering these processes to managers!

Further reading

I make a number of references to my own books and articles, not out of egotism but because they develop the case I am making. Chapter 13 provides balance by listing not only additional material on the points made in the book, but also references to views that differ from my own.

1

 Starting from Where You Are

A paradox in management development

- Managers often say 'I learned to be a manager from experience'.
- Managers quite often lack the skills and knowledge necessary to do their jobs fully effectively.

It is to fill the gap between these two statements that formal management development processes have been designed – to widen the range of experience, to give specific training in particular skills and to provide knowledge of the context in which the manager operates. The paradox is that managers continue to think of learning and development as being essentially and primarily about the work experiences they have had, whereas personnel and management development advisers think about management development mainly in terms of planned processes of job rotation, succession planning and courses.

A second paradox is that while personnel directors will often talk about formal processes of development to others, their own personal development experiences have often, just like managers', been informal and accidental.

Personal experiences of development

You can test how far you believe these paradoxes to be true, first for yourself and then for others. Here is an exercise – see page 3.

Figure 1.1

Methods of Learning off the Job

Books	Business games
Lectures	Simulations
Programmed learning	T groups
Interactive video	Demonstration and practice
Films	Role plays
Group discussion	Outdoor
Case study	Discovery
In tray	Diagnostic instruments

Figure 1.2

Learning Opportunities

The opportunities identified here are not necessarily separate. You may, for example, think of something first in terms of something happening at a meeting – or you may think of the way in which one of your colleagues achieved success at a meeting.

Situations within the organisation	*Processes*
Meetings	Coaching
Task – familiar	Counselling
– unfamiliar	Listening
Task force	Modelling
Customer visit	Problem-solving
Visit to plant/office	Observing
Managing a change	Questioning
Social occasions	Reading
Foreign travel	Negotiating
Acquisitions/mergers	Mentoring
Closing something down	Public speaking
	Reviewing/auditing
	Clarifying responsibilities
Situations outside your organisation	Walking the floor
	Visioning
Voluntary work	Strategic planning
Domestic life	Problem diagnosis
Industry committee	Decision-making
Professional meetings	Selling
Sports club	
	People
	Boss
	Mentor
	Network contacts
	Peers
	Consultants
	Subordinates

Exercise

1 Look back over your professional and managerial career and identify:
   - your two most significant/important/helpful learning experiences
   - your two least significant/important/helpful learning experiences

Or perhaps you would prefer a less specifically focused exercise.

2 Look back at your life and pick out the major events in it which have helped to make you the person you are. Assess each event by defining:
   - your feelings about it then/your feelings about it now
   - what you think you learnt from that experience at that time?
   - whether you have learnt something new or different by looking at it now.

When you have completed either or both of these exercises, consider your response to the paradoxes stated at the beginning of this section.

3 How far have the best and worst of your experiences been planned/formal/structured, as compared with informal experiences within and around your work?
4 Think about the managerial group with which you have the closest connections. How far have they been developed through formal processes and how far through informal processes?

You may want some assistance in checking and clarifying your answers both for yourself and for your colleagues. Figure 1.1 may jog your memory, especially about some of the formal processes to which you have been exposed. Figure 1.2 illustrates situations or people from which you may have learned within and around the job.

Here are two examples of replies to this exercise.

> My boss took time in joint problem-solving to let me reach my own conclusions, coaching me as necessary through my thinking processes. Sometimes this led to outcomes which he probably anticipated. He was able to think laterally and find answers to questions which sometimes seemed impossible to solve. In those situations he coached me in the techniques he favoured.

This was from a man in his mid-20s.

The next example is from a senior director.

> I did an MBA after five years' work experience. It was my initiative to go on it. I have found the jobs I have done, and the movement between different functions, very interesting. What I did not understand was how things really worked, who pulled things together, and what it was all about in terms of principle rather than detail. I wanted to know how things fitted together into a conceptual framework. The MBA gave me that framework, a base for continued intellectual stimulus, and an assurance that problems were actually analysable even though they were not necessarily always soluble.

These two examples illustrate the difference between informal and formal development processes. They also bring up the issue of the different development needs of different individuals and the different opportunities of meeting those needs. The two managers were roughly the same age when they had these two different, significant learning experiences. A second important point is that although the first manager recognised in retrospect what he had learned, the processes of 'joint problem-solving' and 'coaching' were not offered by his boss as part of a formal management development scheme. They were just things he did as part of his normal managerial work.

In reviewing your own experiences, and looking at those of people around you, you are likely to have found a variety of good and bad experiences. You may find either for yourself or for the majority of your colleagues that their careers and successes have been significantly stimulated by planned job moves or excellent courses. You may alternatively find, as I frequently did in my research with directors,[1] that you or your colleagues' most significant learning experiences were not derived from careful planning and structure, but from the accidents of working with particular bosses in particular situations and of meeting changing challenges and opportunities.

One major finding of that research was not simply that so many directors identified informal, not formal, experiences. It was how much more frequently informal experiences were quoted even where the individuals concerned had been exposed to courses or worked in organisations with planned job moves. When I talked in my introduction about a 'balanced view of management development' I meant that we have to consider management development as a total process which embraces the informal and accidental as well as the formal.

Definition of management development

We have to take account of both formal and informal processes for the following reasons:

- Everyone will agree that we learn through informal processes, although the proportion of formal and informal will vary.
- If we apply the term management development only to formal processes we are excluding a large part of common experience.
- If we exclude a large part of common experience from our definition, and more especially our understanding, of management development, we are doing something more than being potentially illogical: we are being unhelpful to managers by dismissing that part of their learning and development which many of them will recognise most readily and which in their own ways they use most effectively.

This separation of formal management development and informal learning is something which existed for me until relatively recently. I used to use a shorter version of a definition of management development produced by the Training Services Agency in 1977: 'an attempt to improve managerial effectiveness through a planned and deliberate learning process'. Yet a great deal of my work had increasingly been on the ways in which managers could learn from opportunities at work in an unplanned, though admittedly thoughtful, way. In *Making Experience Pay*[2] I described many of these opportunities, but did not sort out in my own mind, let alone offer to other people, a view of whether these processes of learning from practical work experiences could really be included under the kind of definition of management development used by myself and many others.

Of course, it would not matter very much if I, or others, were confused about the scope of management development if this did not affect action. But the fact is that both the definition of management development, and the working practices aimed at meeting that definition, have emphasised formal, planned and deliberate processes which originate from, and are often monitored and controlled by, people and forces other than the individual manager involved.

As your review of your own learning experiences, and your review of the likely answers of others, may well have shown, a great deal of management development is not 'planned and deliberate' – and, even more significantly, probably cannot be. So my revised view of a definition is 'an attempt to improve managerial effectiveness through a learning process' (see pages 24 to 29 for a more extended argument on this point).

The next chapter gives more detail on why the nature of managerial work will always require us to embrace informal and accidental processes of learning in our definition, if we want to tackle the reality of the managerial world rather than to separate ourselves from it. Alternative definitions include Lees'[3]: 'that entire system of corporate activities with the espoused goal of improving the managerial stock in the context of organisational and environmental change'.

Is learning different from development?

Until relatively recently the debate, such as it was, about the possibly different meaning of these two words was really about 'current' versus 'future'. Some people thought that activities directed at performing your current job well involved 'learning', whereas activities aimed at a job or tasks you might do later were really 'development'. More recently an attempt has been made to differentiate the two more on the basis of the content of the experience rather than the present or future application of it. Chris Argyris[4] introduced the idea that the learning necessary to use present processes to meet current job requirements could be closely specified and developed. He saw this as 'single-loop learning', as compared with the process of challenging the nature of the problems, redefining them and perhaps transforming the organisation and its values, a process he called 'double-loop learning'.

Pedler and Boydell[5] distinguish explicitly between learning and development. They see learning as more concerned with an increase in knowledge or a higher degree of an existing skill, whereas development is, in their view, a move towards a different state of being or functioning.

Other authors have argued for the concept of different 'levels' of learning. It is a readily acceptable idea that some things are relatively easy to accept and implement, while others require a greater degree of personal commitment and understanding. Whereas these authors highlight several interesting issues, the most important seem to me to be discussions of the objectives of development processes. The purpose of development or learning is to encourage challenge and debate, either about the nature of the organisation or the individual. Do those who offer such opportunities accept the dangers and risks involved, and do they make those to whom they are offering the opportunity aware of those dangers and risks? I do not think that differentiating between 'learning' and 'development' necessarily helps clarify these issues, especially in discussion with managers.

In many ways, it is much more important to note that 'learning' and 'development' are both more relevant terms than 'training' or 'education'. They both say more about output – about results – than input and activity. This last point connects with something Winston Churchill is supposed to have said. 'I am always ready to learn, but I did not always like being taught.' This again says something to us about the likely response of many managers to formal processes, particularly courses. It also takes us, finally, back to the point about management development being essentially a process done *by* you rather than done *to* you. The movement towards self-development as a philosophy and process has been, with action learning, one of the two major changes in understanding about management development in this country in the last 20 years.

Your organisation's experience of management development

Personnel and management development advisers normally believe in formal management development processes. Providing opportunities for these is often, of course, a stated part of their job description. Their oral comments, written statements and policies, and their actions all suggest they have the following beliefs:

- Managers are not born, they are not made, but they can be developed.
- Most managers do not carry out their responsibility for the development of other managers properly; if left to themselves, not much of value would happen.
- It is therefore necessary to set up systems for management development through which the processes of developing managers are organised and planned.
- The effectiveness of such systems depends to a very large degree on the commitment of top management; that commitment is often difficult to obtain.
- Managers cannot be expected to enjoy the formal disciplines involved in planned development.
- The results achieved by planned management development are so obvious that there is no need to set clear objectives and monitor results.

Not all organisations have a personnel director or management development adviser with a clear responsibility for the development of managers. Some small organisations may certainly have an administration director or company secretary who has some interest in, and perhaps responsibility for, formal management development. In a few organisations the lead will be taken not only in principle but in detail by the chief executive. Whatever the job title, however, the beliefs of people trying to initiate or review formal management development processes are likely to be similar to those given above. You can test yourself:

Exercise

How far on a scale 0 = low, 10 = high, do I agree with the statements made above?

If we move from beliefs about the desirability of formal management development processes to actuality, you can look next at how far your organisation goes in providing formal management development. Some organisations offer absolutely nothing – no individual reviews, no plans for individual development, no annual review of succession, no nominations for courses. Others provide a full range of formal opportunities. Inevitably a lot are in the middle, providing something but not everything, or providing for lower-level managers but not for the most senior. The phrase 'management development' has probably existed in the UK only since 1951. While some commercial and industrial organisations have been carrying out at least some of the processes identified below for even longer than that, formal management development has been put in place much more recently in most organisations.

Elements of formal management development

Formal management development will normally include the following items:

- a statement of the purpose of management development, such as

    to ensure that executives are developed or recruited and trained in sufficient numbers to sufficient standards to meet the specialist and general management requirements of the group in the short and the long term.

(See Figure 1.3 on page 11 for a more extended version.)

Some organisations will have set and sustained an objective that all top management appointments should be filled from within, from people developed by the organisation itself. Others will have set some target figure for recruitment from outside, or will in practice operate a modification whereby senior functional jobs are filled from outside (eg finance or personnel).

Even some organisations which have dedicated attention and resources to formal management development do not necessarily have a policy about it. This may be because the organisations concerned have such a well-established series of procedures and processes that there is no need to give the attention and focus that the production of a formal policy might achieve. Others have found that the production of a policy document has been valuable precisely because it provides the opportunity for drawing attention to the issue and at least stating what the organisation believes

- a statement about the processes to be used in identifying and developing managers. Characteristically, such a statement will refer to individual performance review or appraisal, to the identification of individual training and development needs, the planning and review processes applying to these individual assessments and perhaps to the decision-making powers of those involved in making job-movement or development decisions.
- appraisal processes and procedures, which will be identified, perhaps with some guidance given in written form – possibly

Figure 1.3
Management Development Policy

Effective management is clearly vital to the success and continuing prosperity of the group, and to the security and quality of employment and morale of its staff.

We accept that it is the group's responsibility to:
- provide every manager with the opportunity to develop his ability and potential so that he does his existing job effectively
- ensure that there is an adequate supply of trained staff who are competent for promotion to meet the future managerial needs of the group.

We believe:
- that people derive more satisfaction from working when they themselves have helped to establish and are committed to the objective of their jobs.
- that people should be encouraged to develop their own creative roles, exercise initiative and demonstrate self-discipline within the agreed limits of their jobs.

Application
The policy requires that through the divisions:
- we create an environment in which all managers contribute to the objectives of the business to their maximum ability
- we give all managers the scope for exercising initiative by allocating responsibility with authority down the line and see that decisions are taken at the lowest appropriate level
- we ensure that every manager participates with his superior in determining the basic responsibilities of his job, and the results that can be reasonably expected of him, and accepts full responsibility for achieving those results
- we appraise every manager's performance against his expected results, for the purpose of helping him to develop his skills and improve his performance
- we assess every manager's potential on the quality of his performance
- we encourage and train all managers to adopt a similar policy in the management of their subordinates.

Context
We have undertaken to support this policy by:
- providing an organisational structure within which the responsibilities of each manager are clearly defined
- providing and implementing consistent personnel policies covering recruitment, salaries and promotion
- providing appropriate training and development programmes.

Expectations
We expect that increasing the influence and scope for initiative and self-motivation of managers and their subordinates will lead to increasing job satisfaction and to direct improvement in the group's commercial performance and efficiency.

supplemented by training – on how to carry out the review and development task with individuals.

- the range of development processes which might be considered; these may be indicated either on an appraisal form or in a guidance booklet.

Formal development processes

The following processes, normally arranged through the intervention of someone other than the manager and his or her boss, and designed explicitly with a development objective, are 'planned and deliberate learning processes'. All of these might form part of the armoury of any formal management development system, in the sense that they could be considered, recommended or applied by advisers, bosses or by individuals themselves.

Changes in job and job content

- promotion to a new job
- movement to a job at a similar level but in a different function, product or activity (job rotation)
- stretching the boundaries of a job by allocating additional responsibilities or tasks
- secondment, ie (in my definition) movement outside the employing organisation to a different job
- special projects, ie (in my definition) being given responsibility for a special project outside the normal routines of current job
- committees or task groups where the content of what was being studied would normally be within the current experience and competence of the manager involved; sometimes the content would, however, be outside his current job in terms of level or function
- junior boards, set up to 'preview' decisions required by the board proper.

Development processes within the job   Formal development interventions include:

- coaching, ie being deliberately taken through problems and issues with the explicit intention of developing the recipient (this is usually carried out by the boss)
- counselling, often carried out in the context of an appraisal or performance review, and involving either specific counselling and advice about a particular aspect of performance, or occasionally personality or longer-term career guidance (again usually carried out by the boss)
- monitoring and feedback by boss
- mentoring, (in my definition) undertaken by someone other than the manager's direct boss. This is an advisory relationship between a manager and, usually, a respected senior individual who provides guidance and advice on processes, organisational policies and the way to do things generally. It may involve a respected senior presenting the case for a candidate for a particular job.

Activities external to the job   These include:

- internal courses
- external courses
- work on external committees, associations, voluntary or charity organisations
- reading.

Development activities planned by the individual

- modelling on boss, colleagues or outsiders
- reading
- participation in groups of managers from different organisations.

Where are you?

Exercise

You can assess your organisation on each of the elements
and each of the processes. Which of them exist or are used?
Again, you can use a scale of 0 = low, 10 = high.

You may, of course, work for an organisation with relatively autonomous units, some of which may achieve a high score on this
analysis and others a low score. You might therefore like to consider
these questions for different units.

You may wish to take your analysis further by considering the
reasons for the scores you have given, whether for your organisation
as a whole or for particular units. Sometimes an organisation has
simply not considered some part of the formal opportunities that
exist or can be created. Sometimes it has tried the process, or a version of it, in the past and found that it did not work. Sometimes the
opportunities simply cannot be created.

Finally, it may be worth carrying out your analysis according to
some definition of the levels of manager who might be involved. It
is frequently the case, for example, that courses are more readily
made available to lower levels of management, and certainly that
senior levels go on external courses only, if they go on courses at all.
We found in our research with directors, which confirmed our own
working experience, that the senior levels of an organisation are
much less likely to be subject to appraisal as a formal process than
are middle and lower levels.

What benefits – and to whom?

Management developers may be asked to justify either a general increase in management development in their organisations, or a particular aspect of it. The following list of potential benefits may be
helpful:

Benefits of management development to the organisation

- improvement in the effectiveness of managers in their existing jobs
- improvement in the potential effectiveness of managers in future jobs
- building from 'learning from experience', which may be recognised as inadequate in current jobs
- building from 'learning from experience', which may be recognised as inadequate for future changes
- meeting specific concerns about individuals or groups where performance has been lacking – 'felt hurt'
- responding to a general belief of senior managers from personal experience that development improves effectiveness, bottom-line results
- meets the results of a benchmarking exercise – 'What other organisations like us do.'

Managers responsible for developing others
Managers may have an interest in developing others:

- They pursue the resolution of problems and, in the process, accidentally aid the development of others.
- They believe that improving the performance of others will reflect favourably on their own performance and perhaps also create more space for their own managerial interest and ambitions.
- They derive personal satisfaction from helping someone to grow.
- They develop their own skills, knowledge and insight as a result of sharing experiences with others.
- Their organisation demands that they develop others, through formal systems such as appraisal and succession plans.

(From *How Managers Can Develop Managers*, A. Mumford, Aldershot, Gower 1994.)

Individuals and development
Individuals may see benefits from management development in response to:

- a concern about personal performance in their current job
- a concern about becoming better equipped to perform effectively in a future job.

They may also wish:

- to acquire the knowledge through the formal feedback necessary for either of the previous two points
- to acquire understanding of and some actions on issues of personal growth, not necessary related to performance
- to ensure that personal ambitions about promotion or career development are catered for
- to be identified on a fast track for development
- to stay on terms with other people who are being developed
- to gain personal satisfaction from achievements in learning and development.

The learning culture of an organisation

The list of formal processes you have considered is fairly clear cut. Responses can be based on hard facts. It is also possible to measure the extent to which an organisation encourages learning – see the discussion of 'the learning organisation' in Chapter 12 and also Figure 1.4 on page 20.

An organisation can be said to encourage learning when:

- it encourages managers to identify their own learning needs
- it provides a regular review of performance and learning for the individual
- it encourages managers to set challenging learning goals for themselves
- it provides feedback at the time on both performance and achieved learning
- it reviews the performance of managers in helping to develop others
- it assists managers to see learning opportunities on the job
- it seeks to provide new experiences from which managers can learn

- it provides or facilitates the use of training on the job
- it tolerates some mistakes, provided managers try to learn from them
- it encourages managers to review, conclude and plan learning activities
- it encourages managers to challenge the traditional ways of doing things.

Exercise

Review each of the factors listed on pages 16–17 for your organisation and mark on a scale 0 = low, 10 = high the extent to which you believe the criteria to be currently met.

Where are we? – a company case

I was asked to carry out a review of the management development policies and processes of a large, UK-based company. It had been active in formal management development for 30 years. I reviewed the documents, plans, processes and brochures available from its files and interviewed a number of personnel staff. I generated the following questions, which I discussed with 20 senior managers and directors.

Exercise

1 What do you believe to be the purpose of the company's management development policies? How effective have they been for yourself and for the managers reporting to you?
2 How helpful has the appraisal process been in defining the effectiveness of individual managers and their development needs?
3 Do you use other processes for reviewing performance and development?
4 Do you believe that the processes for collecting and reviewing individual potential have worked satisfactorily, eg succession planning?

5 What contribution has been made by processes such as
   job rotation, and internal or external courses?
6 Can you quote cases of managers who are more effective as a result of these management development processes?

What would the answers be in your organisation?

Who thinks what?

The last case study enabled me to carry out, at much greater depth
and with a much larger number of people, the process which I had
employed in my original research with directors. We were able to
compare what the organisation said it had been trying to do with
what it was perceived to have achieved by the respondent managers
and directors. The organisational view was normally given by the
chief executive or, in larger organisations, by the personnel director
and management development adviser, as in the case quoted above.
The comparisons we were able to make between these two sources
of evidence were powerful and disturbing.

The question of ownership raises one of the most significant
issues. It is normally part of the stated values of the modern personnel practitioner that desirable management practices, in this case a
management development scheme, should be 'owned' by line managers rather than by personnel. In fact, while personnel people certainly want line management to 'own' the management development
scheme, they frequently have great difficulty in actually securing a
transfer. They commonly ascribe this to the failure of line managers
to recognise how important such issues are.

In a sense the personnel people are right – line managers often do
not want to participate in the disciplines of the formal management
development process. However, you might benefit from asking
yourself the following questions.

Exercise

1 Who really 'owns' our management development scheme? How do they demonstrate their ownership?
2 If we in personnel are really the initiators, proponents and monitors of the management development scheme, why has this happened?
3 Could it be that line managers do not own the scheme because they do not see it as dealing with their major business concerns? Could it be that they see the scheme as being about some expensive technique called 'management development', rather than about how managers learn?

These latter stages in your self-analysis should help you to focus on two important aspects of knowing where you are starting from. It is quite likely that both you and your managers have currently considered only 'planned and deliberate learning processes' as proper management development. Understandably, these processes are considered by both personnel and line managers to be the appropriate responsibility of the people seen to be professional in 'planned and deliberate learning processes'. If these formal processes are the only things on which you and your organisational clients want to concentrate, then you should find my check-lists on formal issues mentioned above helpful. You may also find that you want to move from this chapter to those chapters which deal explicitly with the formal processes, especially Chapters 6, 7 and 8.

The beliefs of chief executives

The review of the beliefs of personnel people on pages 8–9 included a statement about the importance of commitment by top management. The bad news is that such commitment is difficult to obtain; all too frequently lip-service is paid at best. For example, chief executives are much more likely to sign the annual letter starting the round of appraisals than they are actually to appraise their own direct

Figure 1.4

Reported Major Influences on Chief Executives

Rank order	Statements	Score out of 100
1	Ability to work with a wide variety of people	78.4
2	Early overall responsibility for important tasks	74.8
3	A need to achieve results	74.8
4	Leadership experience early in career	73.6
5	Wide experience in many functions before 35	67.6
6	An ability to do deals and negotiate	66.4
7	Willingness to take risks	62.8
8	Having more ideas than other colleagues	61.6
9	Being stretched by immediate bosses	60.4
10	An ability to change managerial style to suit occasion	58.8
11	A desire to seek new opportunities	56.8
12	Becoming visible to top management before 30	56.0
13	Family support (spouse/parents)	55.2
14	Having a sound technical training	54.8
15	Having a manager early in your career who acted as a model (from whom you learnt a lot)	52.0
16	Overseas managerial/work experience	41.2
17	Experience of leadership in armed forces (peacetime/wartime)	40.4
18	Having special 'off the job' management training	32.8

subordinates. The good news is that a great deal of effective management development can be achieved without the direct help of the chief executive. In terms of testing where you are, however, it might well be helpful to look at the beliefs of your chief executive or relevant head of your organisational unit. We are fortunate in being able to compare individual chief executive opinions with those found by Charles Margerison in the UK. His study was replicated with very similar results in the United States.[6] The research asked chief executives to identify the major influences which had helped them develop as managers. The results are given in Figure 1.4.

As a starting proposition we could conclude that if these are the beliefs that chief executives had about what influenced their progress, they might be likely to apply those beliefs to the development of their subordinate managers. In analysing your own organisational level it could be valuable to make your assessment of where your chief executive stands on this list. Would you place things in the same order of priority?

Two cautionary comments are desirable. The process used for collecting this information – questionnaires – is different from that used in my own research through live interviews. It may be that individuals respond differently to questionnaires from the way they do to interviews. If you were thinking of getting your own chief executive to fill in such a chart, you might have to balance the apparent ease and speed of that kind of process with the advantages of a biographical discussion. Secondly, there is a risk in the statement with which I started this section. It may seem reasonable to assume that the actions or views of chief executives would reflect their beliefs about management development processes. There are, however, two good reasons for supposing this may not be true. The first is one to which I have already referred in relation to personnel people themselves. People often have values that they do not actually adhere to in practice. Anyone whose experience inclines them to disbelieve this statement is referred to the marvellous case study given by Chris Argyris on appraisal.[7]

The second reason for looking closely at this list takes us back to the point of doing it in the first place. My suggestion was that you should analyse a particular chief executive – indeed, that you might ask a chief executive to do it for him- or herself. You want to establish the actual position of your own chief executive, which may differ from the general views of this sample. You want to know whether your particular chief executive favours 'early overall responsibility for important tasks'.

With all these qualifications, Charles Margerison's list provides a potentially helpful aid to establishing where you are.

Some final questions

I have included a number of exercises and questions in the body of the chapter. Here are some more questions and some suggestions for action.

The final question on where you are is directed at those organisations which have a personnel specialist, particularly a management development adviser. The attention which organisations pay to management development is doubly related to the organisational position of those who advise on management development. If the organisation is serious then status will follow – but of course if you do not have status it is difficult to persuade the organisation to be serious! It is easy to blame it for having low status management development advisers; but may the low status not be a reflection of the processes that they try to sell?

Exercise

1 What have I learnt about myself as a learner? What conclusions do I draw for myself and in relation to others?
2 What has been the balance of formal as compared with informal processes for myself? How has this influenced what I offer the organisation?
3 Where do I stand on the lists of beliefs about formal management development given on pages 8–9? Is there anything in this chapter which causes me to change those views?
4 Could I use one of the organisational audit check-lists? Several? How?
5 How could I compare my own answers on any of these exercises with those of:
   ● another person in my own function within my own organisation
   ● a line manager in my own organisation
   ● a friendly outsider?
6 What definition of management development did I hold before reading this chapter? Has this reading changed it? If so, what kind of action might I take?
7 Do I see management development as concerned with remedying weaknesses, developing potential or both? Would my answers be the same for everyone or different for different managers?
8 If asked to assess the success of formal management development processes in my organisation, what answer would I give?
9 To what would I attribute the level of success on formal management development processes:

- the enthusiasm and commitment of top management
- the content of the scheme
- my own involvement and influence
- the involvement and influence of my predecessor?

References

1 MUMFORD A. *Developing Top Managers*. Aldershot, Gower, 1988.
2 MUMFORD A. *Making Experience Pay*. Maidenhead, McGraw-Hill, 1980.
3 LEES S. 'Ten faces of management development'. *Management Education and Development*. Vol. 23, Part 2, 1992.
4 ARGYRIS C. 'Double loop learning in organisations'. *Harvard Business Review*. September/October 1977.
5 PEDLER M. *and* BOYDELL T. *Managing Yourself*. London, Fontana, 1985.
6 MARGERISON C. 'How chief executives succeed'. *Journal of European Industrial Training*. Vol. 4, No. 5, 1980, MARGERISON, C. *and* KAKABADSE, A. *How American Executives Succeed*. American Management Association, 1984.
7 ARGYRIS C. *Reasoning, Learning and Action*. San Francisco, CA, Jossey-Bass, 1982.

Further reading relevant to this chapter is shown in Chapter 13.

2

 Management Development Models

Current definitions of management development, and much of the formal practice in response, have been flawed. An overemphasis on the 'planned and deliberate' has excluded many of the experiences which are particularly real for managers. The exclusion of those preponderant and powerful experiences is not only illogical but leads to a diminished persuasiveness in talking to managers about development. We have therefore reached a position in which the reality of management development is reversed, so that the minority pursuits of carefully planned and deliberate development experiences have become the only ones recognised as management development! This creates an *Alice in Wonderland* situation, where Humpty Dumpty says 'Words mean what I say they mean.'

This unreal position has been arrived at for entirely understandable and laudable reasons. Explicit, powerful, relevant, realistic – these are all appropriate words to use about the unplanned experiences which managers so often quote as the main source of their development. Yet the same experiences are fragmentary, insufficient, inefficient, only partially understood and subject to the winds of circumstance.

It is also understandable that personnel and management development advisers intervene on what they feel themselves able to deal with. It is quite understandable that they put aside those uncontrolled, day-by-day, accidental and frenetic activities from which managers claim to learn. It is quite logical for them to prefer to deal rather with processes and exercises over which they have influence and indeed often power, which they can claim to understand and rationalise and which represent a defined area of their own territory. However, one of the consequences is that they then set up a game which is different from the one managers normally play in and in which personnel and management development people use rules that are also quite different from those which obtain in normal managerial work.

There are a number of reasons formal management development processes have not worked successfully in many organisations. Here

24

it is necessary to establish only that formal management development processes, often owned by personnel people and not line managers, have not become part of managers' own understanding of
learning and development.

It is also true that personnel people have been insufficiently attached to the reality of managerial work. For 30 years formal management training and education has sought to improve the reality of
its products. It has moved from lectures by more or less authoritative
people to syndicate discussions in which groups of managers exchange comments and experiences. When these discussions were
found to be lacking in both reality and intellectual stimulus – so that
the syndicates could be defined as groups gathered together to exchange ignorance – they were replaced by case studies on the
Harvard method. When case studies were found to be productive of
analytical thought but lacking the tensions of immediate cut and
thrust (except when conducted by a charismatic tutor), increased emphasis was given to a variety of simulations. In these processes,
whether building bridges or towers in Lego bricks, constructing
paper planes, doing computerised business exercises or engaging in
the latest fashion for outdoor training, the basic intention was normally to reproduce the tensions created by the pressures of time,
conflicting priorities and not always helpful colleagues. In developing courses there has been a continuing search for techniques that
could be employed to improve the reality of the process.

It took the coincidence of a series of events connecting the creation of Manchester Business School, the departure of Reg Revans
and his creation of the first major action learning programme in
Belgium, and Lord Weinstock having 'flu and watching television,
for the major breakthrough of action learning to be achieved and
recognised. Revans developed the proposition that managers preferred to work on and discuss real issues rather than participate in
traditional courses. In essence his process not only uses the recognition that managers learn most from working on real management
problems, but faces management educators and trainers with the
proposition that the construction of neat separate boxes of learning
experiences, even simulations, is unnecessary.

Revans is the extreme manifestation of the desire to take management development back into the reality of management. The separation of learning experiences from work experiences is:

- illogical
- unreal
- unhelpful
- unnecessary.

I have confessed that I managed to work on both formal and informal aspects of management development without fully recognising the necessity of drawing them together. I have come to recognise, however, that it is not appropriate to operate powerfully and apparently effectively in one area unless this can be integrated with the other. Although, as I will show, it is highly desirable that formal processes deal confidently and explicitly with the reality of managerial life rather than with some academic view of what it ought to be, the incoherent and barely recognised learning that people achieve from *ad hoc* work experiences is disastrously insufficient. We must have an understanding of management development which provides a complete model of the total process, not only the formal part of it. Just as we need to increase the reality of formal off-the-job development, so we need to increase the capacity to learn from informal experiences at work.

Defining reality in management

So we ought to incorporate both formal and informal processes in any definition of, and practical work towards, improved management development. I have so far made the case purely in terms of the fact that managers learn in a variety of informal and often unconscious ways. The attempt to concentrate entirely on the formal processes, although initially understandable in terms of the obvious inefficiencies of informal development, has been misconceived for another reason.

The separation of formal management development from informal processes literally takes management development away from the reality of on-the-job managerial work. The planning of job moves for development purposes, or the development and implementation of training and education, are divorced in terms of time, mental application and even physical circumstances from managers' normal activities. Although this is done for the apparently best of motivations – the hit-and-miss nature and inefficiency of on-the-job learning processes – the result has been the construction of management development processes and activities that are not seen by managers as part of their real world.

In addition to the failure to identify and make use of the full range of development processes, both on the job and off the job, another reason why the balance of attention has been fixed so firmly on the formal derives from inappropriate and obsolete models of what managers actually do. We can only be surprised and saddened by the continuing apparent failure of many authors, business schools and management training centres to define and implement their offerings in terms of what managers actually do. Rosemary Stewart's fundamental work[1] has, it seems, been adopted neither by management developers nor by management educators and trainers. Henry Mintzberg's[2] analysis of managerial roles appears rather more frequently on courses; but again the fundamental features of managerial life which he identified have not apparently affected the philosophy or major substance of development programmes or courses. At best his chart has been used to provide an interesting session. Nor has the work of John Kotter,[3] similarly powerful in exhibiting the realities of what top managers do, influenced management developers as yet.

The results of these research studies are developed in Chapter 6, which looks in more detail at the things managers have to do well as the necessary focus of development activities. Here the fundamental point is that all the research on what managers actually do points in the same direction. Their work is carried out at a hectic pace, it is fragmented, it is more likely to be intuitive and responsive than rational and reflective. Perhaps most important of all, what managers actually need to be able to do is more likely to be specific and contingent than easily generalisable.

Although there are common aspects to managerial jobs, it is the particularities that often represent the greater challenge. The view that a good manager can manage anything is not a good prescription either for career development or for the construction of management development schemes. There are elements of managerial effectiveness in common between the work of a reseach manager and that of a sales manager; but the reality of effective development for these two jobs is likely to be very different. This is true not only for the obvious professional and functional differences. It is even true for something which may seem to be appropriately generalisable. Since one of the characteristics of a manager is that he or she manages people, one of the more generalisable aspects would seem to be the process of delegation. Yet if we take sales and research managers, the probability is that effective delegation in these two jobs would be quite different, not only in terms of what is delegated but perhaps even more importantly, how it is delegated.

Management development ought, then, to be based on:

- a wide view of development processes, accepting the reality of the ways in which managers will learn
- the relatively disorganised reality of managerial work, as compared with the neatness of classical management theory
- the particulars of what managers have to do in specific jobs within different kinds of organisations.

The argument is not that it is inappropriate to help managers to be more systematic, better organised or more reflective. It is a very appropriate purpose of management development to challenge and stimulate improvement even among managers who work relatively effectively, let alone among that considerable number who work very ineffectively. The case is rather that management development must recognise and make use of the relatively chaotic and unplanned nature of a great deal of management, instead of ignoring it or attempting to replace it with formal management development alone.

One final implication emerges from the research and from my own and others' experience over the years. Managers are people who actually do things and get others to do things. Their prime concern is normally to implement effective action rather than to collect knowledge for its own sake. The understandable tendency of management academics and theorists and, indeed, of some managerial authors, is to create neat boxes, clear statements, to distinguish one kind of action, one function, one form of behaviour from another. As an analytical process this is understandable and, up to a point, useful. But most managers operate as if they were multi-programmed. They do not concentrate on one thing at a time, applying the knowledge that they have acquired in a discrete way. They work on a complex tangle of issues and their prime purpose is to achieve a result. What they achieve may occasionally surprise them as much as it may bewilder others. The important point is that they *do* achieve things. A development process that is focused on the acquisition of knowledge (however seductively organised the knowledge-gathering process is) is therefore likely to be less helpful than one that emphasises what managers have to do in order to be effective, and how they do it.

As a concrete illustration of this point, consider the implications of one of the most important findings of the three researchers mentioned above. One of the major factors contributing to the effectiveness of managers is their use of networks. It would therefore be logical if management development processes were geared to helping managers identify and use those networks successfully, for example through identifying the kind of behaviours in which they need to engage. One of the more familiar traditional management development objectives is to give managers knowledge about other functions. Traditional management development, for example, exposes production managers to a knowledge of marketing processes. It is believed that the acquisition of such knowledge will somehow improve relationships between them. A management development process that focused on effectiveness would instead deal with the issue of the systems through which these two departments interact, the basis of relationships between the two departments in pursuing their objectives and how these could be improved. Although it may undoubtedly at some level be a useful piece of knowledge for the production manager to know how the marketing manager produces a marketing plan, in real managerial life the more important issue is how the production manager and marketing manager develop a process for managing the consequences of the plan.

Effectiveness in learning processes

There is a third major input to the creation of effective management
development. Even if our conceptual understanding, and our practical application of our management development scheme, were to include the widest variety of development processes and focus clearly
on what managers really do, we would not have provided all that is
necessary for effective development. To expose managers to a variety of developmental opportunities, and to base more of them in different ways on real managerial processes, is certainly likely to raise
the general level of achievement. On their own, however, these two
processes will not transform traditional understanding about management development. A third element is the process of learning and
development itself. The fundamental point here is that past generalisation about how managers learn has been found to be as badly
flawed as some of the other generalisations we have been examin-
ing. Over a 30-year period there has been a fairly consistent search
for activities that can be seen not only as real, but that in some sense
'involve' managers and require them to 'participate'. The grotesque
ineffectiveness of the lecture process, and the vociferous feedback of
many managers bored with being its victims, has led to the development of a variety of teaching methods, and particularly of active
simulations. In the course context this has meant that most course
designers have tried to provide a variety of processes. This was
partly because variety was seen as a good thing in itself, since managers would be more likely to remain interested if they were offered
a varied process. But it also stemmed from partial recognition of a
much more fundamental point.

More aware tutors frequently find themselves faced with conflicting feedback. A session marked very highly by some managers will
be marked poorly by others. A process found particularly stimulating by some will be put down as wholly unreal by others. A charismatic lecturer will be marked as the highlight of a course by some
managers and rejected by others as having had 'nothing concrete to
say about my kind of organisation'. The result of conflicting feedback of this kind over years of experience has led at least some tutors to provide 'the catholic menu'. This means providing a variety

of experiences, because you know that some participants will enjoy one form of learning whereas others will not. The catholic menu provides the course designer with a basic protection: not all participants will be bored all of the time.

It ought to come as no surprise at all that managers differ in their likely response to any particular learning process. Not only is this our common experience within the formal learning environment; it is also observably true that managers differ in their ability to learn from particular kinds of opportunity on the job. We face a remarkably self-evident conclusion. People differ in their preferences for opera and pop music, for different kinds of sporting activity, in their enjoyment of different holidays. Closer to home, in management development terms we know that managers differ substantially in terms of managerial style. Some are hard-edged, directive, forceful autocrats, some are reflective and listening people who prefer to consult before making a decision. So it should be no surprise to us that people differ in their preferred approach to learning. The question for management development is what you are prepared to do about such differences.

The answer to that question has often been a sort of unfocused general provision where it is hoped that the offer of a wide range of different kinds of opportunity or process will mean that successes are balanced by failures. A really effective management development model can, and should, go much further than this. The stimulus to my own thinking beyond 'people learn differently' was provided when I first encountered the work of David Kolb. At the theoretical and conceptual level his ideas are available in his major book.[4] He would not, I think, claim that his concept of the learning cycle was wholly new. His startling and most useful innovation was to show that it is possible to use a diagnostic instrument to identify which people were likely to have a preference for which kind of learning activity within the learning cycle.

Peter Honey and I took Kolb's original concepts and developed a different questionnaire and improved processes for making use of the results. The full detail of our work on learning styles is available elsewhere.[5] A brief summary of our major conclusions, and of the impact of these on the design of effective management development, is now necessary.

Figure 2.1
Honey and Mumford's Learning Cycle

The learning cycle

All managerial learning involves all stages of the cycle (see Figure 2.1); the emphasis will differ for particular kinds of activity. Reading a book is having an experience; but so is working on a major business project for six months.

While the emphasis given to parts of the cycle may differ according to the nature of the experience, they may also observably differ not because of the objective nature of the activity but because of the personal preference and ability of the learner. The anecdotal discovery that individuals differ in terms of their receptiveness to particular kinds of learning process can be explained in terms of their relative preference for, or rejection of, a particular stage on the learning cycle. Four major styles are identifiable not only through the Learning Styles Questionnaire but by observation and by self-analysis and perception.

Activists:

- try anything once
- tend to revel in short-term crises, firefighting
- tend to thrive on the challenge of new experiences
- are relatively bored with implementation and longer-term consolidation
- constantly involve themselves with other people.

Reflectors:

- like to stand back and review experiences from different perspectives
- collect data and analyse it before coming to conclusions
- like to consider all possible angles and implications before making a move
- tend to be cautious
- actually enjoy observing other people in action
- often take a back seat at meetings.

Theorists:

- are keen on basic assumptions, principles, theories, models and
systems thinking
- prize rationality and logic
- tend to be detached and analytical
- are unhappy with subjective or ambiguous experiences
- like to make things tidy and fit them into rational schemes.

Pragmatists:

- positively search out new ideas or techniques which might apply
in their situation
- take the first opportunity to experiment with applications
- respond to problems and opportunities 'as a challenge'
- are keen to use ideas from management courses
- like to get on with things with clear purpose.

The detailed application of this kind of knowledge is covered in later
chapters, which deal, for example, with the issue of how far you can
go in providing different learning processes for individuals with different preferences. From the perspective of this chapter, the important point to emphasise is that only 20 per cent of managers emerged
with three strong preferences, ie could be seen as potentially good
all-round learners. In contrast, 35 per cent of managers had one
strong preference. An effective management development scheme

must take account of the fact that individuals will respond differently to the same kind of learning opportunity, whether part of a real task or a course.

The triangle of effectiveness

The three issues I have been discussing so far all provide for effectiveness. Three points can be usefully presented visually, as in Figure 2.2. The point, literally, of the triangle is that the purpose of management development is not to have a particular kind of development, nor even to provide an effective learning process, but that these two both focus on and are pointed towards effective managerial behaviour.

Figure 2.2
Effectiveness Triangle in Management Development

Virtuous and vicious learning sequences

Modern motivational theory tells us that behaviour which is not rewarded is not willingly repeated. Clearly, some managers have had useful management training or educational experiences and subsequently repeat these experiences. There are at least an equivalent number who have had bad experiences which have put them off formal management training or education.

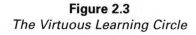

Figure 2.3
The Virtuous Learning Circle

What we have just been looking at in terms of the reality of management affects specifically the effectiveness of any learning experience. It can be shown diagramatically in Figures 2.3 and 2.4. The virtuous learning circle helps us to understand the most powerful and significant statement about management development in the 1970s, made by Reg Revans in *Action Learning*.[6] Revans himself has never attempted to provide a single statement which encompasses all his views about action learning. From a review of his many books and papers and those of other followers I have generated the summary that follows.

A review of action learning

- Learning for managers should mean learning to take effective action. Acquiring information, and becoming more capable in diagnosis or analysis have been overvalued in management learning.
- Learning to take action necessarily involves actually taking action, not recommending action or undertaking analyses of someone else's problem.
- The best form of action for learning is work on a defined problem

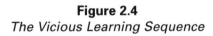

Figure 2.4
The Vicious Learning Sequence

Generalised knowledge/skills

Transfer to own situation

Difficulty in application

Absence of rewards for
learned processes

Full stop

of reality and significance to managers themselves. The problem should involve implementation as well as analysis and recommendation.

- While managers should have responsibility for their own achievements on their own projects, the learning process is a social one: managers learn best with and from each other.
- The social process is achieved and managed through regular meetings of managers to discuss their individual projects; the group is usually called a 'set'. The managers are 'comrades in adversity'.
- The role of people providing help for the members of the set is essentially and crucially different from that of the normal management teacher. Their role is not to teach (whether through lecture, case or simulation) but to help managers learn from exposure to problems and to each other. As Revans says, action learning attacks 'the inveterate hankering of the teacher to be the centre of attention'.

Although Revans is primarily associated with action learning, he produced a neat equation describing the total potential managerial learning process, $L = P + Q$. Learning, L, was produced as the result of both programmed knowledge, P, and Q, which is the pursuit of hitherto unresolved questions and problems (the action learning element). Despite his trumpet blasts against the walls of the traditional management development establishment, Revans is not opposed in principle to the virtues of programmed knowledge. He is indeed contemptuous about some aspects of both content and delivery, and certainly about issues of priority. It is obviously true for him that the Q element is both objectively more important and subjectively more attractive to real working managers.

It was probably inevitable that Revans's major contribution would be abused and misused. The crucial point for this chapter is to be found in his focus on learning from doing real work, but doing so in a relatively structured learning environment. The idea of using projects as learning vehicles may well have pre-dated Revans, but the idea existed previously in a significantly different form. The use of a project where a manager operates as a consultant to another organisation, or the creation of a project essentially as a simulation exercise within a course context – for example asking course members to 'produce a corporate strategy for the year 1998' – is actually quite different from action learning. To achieve full experiential reality the project must carry real management responsibility and involvement in implementation. This is absolutely fundamental. Some people have been seduced into offering projects that are not 'real work' as I define it. Some are seduced in the opposite direction to offer projects that do involve real work but pay little attention to the learning process. Action learning is not itself a model of management development and can certainly be misused even as a partial answer to some important issues in management development. The Revans equation $L = P + Q$ is a complete model, but is obviously somewhat lacking in detail.

The Mumford model of management development

My research on how directors learnt, the obligation to write a report on it and then the opportunity to write a book helped to sharpen my own conceptual grasp of the totality of management development. Formal management development processes are important but by definition, in the managerial world, insufficient. They are also often inefficiently provided. Informal processes are both insufficient and inefficient, because managers have often lacked the skills to make the most of them as learning experiences. Professionals from the management development world have compounded this failure by paying too little attention to the opportunities informal experiences provide. What we found in our research was that the process of actually asking people about their learning experiences achieved two things (other than contributing factual data to our research): for the people with whom we were having discussions, it brought out the content of, and the processes in, their actual learning experiences; and these discussions and revelations about content and process were the equivalent of a cartoon lightbulb shining over the head. If people could clarify their learning experiences in discussion with us, and could identify future potential experiences for themselves and others, was there not some other way of achieving this apart from an accidental visit from a researcher?

I was therefore persuaded of more than the need for a conceptual model of management development which included both informal and formal learning experiences. It was brought home to me that my own writing about better development on the job by a more considered process in fact represented a major third element in such a model. Instead of seeing things simply as either brought about by formal management development processes, or by accidental, informal, not very effective learning, we should see management development as including improved learning on the job, where the improvement was initiated and sustained by the managers themselves, not by management development professionals. This was the origin of the model in Figure 2.5. Type 1 learning is likely to be most effective because it is drawn directly from managerial performance. However, from a learning point of view, the emphasis in learning-cycle terms is almost always on the 'having an experience' stage, omitting, certainly as far as conscious processes are concerned, the 'reviewing' stage. Managers subsequently act, so they have in a sense passed through the concluding and planning stages, but all too

Figure 2.5
Model of Types of Management Development

Type 1 Informal managerial – accidental processes

Characteristics   Occur within managerial activities
Explicit intention is task performance
No clear development objectives
Unstructured in development terms
Not planned in advance
Owned by managers

Development
consequences   Learning is real, direct, unconscious, insufficient

Type 2 Integrated managerial – opportunistic processes

Characteristics   Occur within managerial activities
Explicit intention both task performance and
    development
Clear development objectives
Structured for development by boss and subordinate
Planned beforehand or reviewed subsequently as
    learning experiences
Owned by managers

Development
consequences   Learning is real, direct, conscious, more substantial

Type 3 Formal management development – planned processes

Characteristics   Often away from normal managerial activities
Explicit intention is development
Clear development objectives
Structured for development by developers
Planned beforehand and reviewed subsequently as
    learning experiences
Owned more by developers than managers

Development   Learning may be real (through a job) or detached
consequences   (through a course)
Is more likely to be conscious, relatively infrequent

---

often experiences which have not been reviewed are not even partially developed as achieved learning.

Nor have the formal development experiences of Type 3 often encouraged or facilitated full learning cycles. Some emphasise altogether too much the delivery of conclusions from other people's experience – lectures, books, case studies. Some supposedly planned management development experiences – such as job rotation – stick at the top of the cycle, again simply offering an experience with no opportunity to reflect on, for example, what working in a different department actually involves. Some formal training courses have, in the pursuit of apparent participation and activity, emphasised the experience stage but really done nothing to facilitate the other three parts of the cycle. In what sense has success or failure in building a tower of Lego bricks been assimilated as a learning experience rather than enjoyed as an active time-filler?

In learning-cycle terms Type 2 attempts to provide precisely that opportunity to review, conclude, plan, act again, review and plan, which we know managers do not normally undertake.

Levers for success, causes of failure

The first question to ask in considering whether management development is successful or otherwise in your organisation is what that term means to you. If you see management development wholly in terms of its formal aspects, then you will want to measure it against criteria appropriate to that definition; if you take the broader view offered here then you will have additional criteria. If you accept my arguments, your chances of success will be increased by the increased reality of what you do.

It is explicit in my view of success that management development is actually about improved managerial performance. This may well be difficult to assess because a lot of other variables will also affect managerial performance. The crucial point is that management development should aim directly at managerial effectiveness and be dedicated in terms of priorities and clear intentions to that end. This is different from dedication to, and an attempt to measure, *systems* of management development. The difference becomes clear when you consider alternative answers in discussions I have had with management development advisers. Both the following comments arose in response to my question to advisers on how they measured the success of their Management Development schemes.

Case 1

We have very clear processes set up here. There is Annual Appraisal, and we monitor whether the forms have been completed and returned to us. Then we put a lot of effort into reviewing the training and development suggestions included in those forms. For example we decide how many courses we will run on particular subjects from this analysis. We chase up the laggards, but we do not have very many. We also insist that there is some comment in each division's annual business plan on management development. If the plan does not include something it is sent back to them. We send round a catalogue of courses each year, and we also make recommendations about which external courses are appropriate for which levels. We have a written management development policy which says that all managers should be given the opportunity to go on a relevant management training event, and we have recently added a specific target of five days' management training a year.

Case 2

We provide formal encouragement. There is a written policy, and every manager should have a Performance and Development Review at least once a year. But really most of the important work is done by discussion that comes out of our involvement with business plans and problems. Of course it is a good thing to stimulate a general review of management development issues at least once a year at the same time as the Business Plan. But we find most of our real work is done outside that. We try to get managers to think about development opportunities for themselves and for other people at the time they are making their ongoing business decisions. It does not work with all managers, but most actually do work quite well on using the opportunities that emerge from real work problems. A lot of managers prefer to work that way, rather than having theoretical discussions about problems or projects that might come up in the future. But we do not treat them as alternatives – we have a go at both. In fact working successfully through current problems tends to encourage managers then to think about ways in which they can plan ahead a bit. The main thing is to try and stimulate the discussion through the things they are doing already, rather than trying to put in a logical process of thoughtful analysis which they see as separate and not much to do with their real priorities.

Our director research enabled us to compare what the organisation was trying to do with what it was perceived as achieving by those involved. I then compared the results of our research with the considerable literature on management development, and of course also related it to my own detailed working experience in half-a-dozen different organisations. The result of all this was the two charts that follow in Figures 2.6 and 2.7. I use these charts as a way of getting people to review their own organisations. You may like to undertake the exercise below for yourself.

Figure 2.6
Management Development: Levers for Success

- Clear appropriate job objectives
- Effective selection for the job
- Driven by business opportunities/problems
- Ownership shared
  — hierarchically
  — by individual self-development
  — by personnel
- Shared diagnosis
  — of individual needs
  — of group needs
- Development activities are
  — appropriate to need
  — appropriate to individual
  — based on management reality
- Development processes are linked
- Learning processes are identified and worked on
- Outputs are identified and measured

Exercise

1 Consider each of the criteria in the two charts. Assess your own organisation, in terms of how strongly you feel the criterion applies to it, on a scale 0 = low, 10 = high.
2 What are the reasons for any very high or very low scores on each of these charts? (Remember that the

meaning of high or low is reversed, since a high score on
a lever for success means that you believe you will be
doing well, whereas a high score on the cause of failure
suggests you will not be doing so well.)

Figure 2.7
Management Development: Causes of Failure

- Purposes — unclear
              — unsupported by managers
- Poor diagnosis of culture and business requirements
- Poor analysis of individual needs
- Development processes
    — unconvincing to managers
    — inappropriate to need
    — unreal
    — unacceptable to individual
- Overemphasis on
    — formal
    — general
    — off the job
    — future 'succession planning'
    — mechanics
    — one-off experiences
- Flavour of the month
- Owned by personnel

When you have carried out this review yourself, you may like to
consider using it with a wider audience: you can give it to your chief
executive or to your management development committee, if you
have one. Perhaps you will just want to use it with colleagues either
in the personnel department or in line management. One of the most
valuable potential results of having a variety of people fill it in is to
see the kind of differences that emerge. I had a very interesting experience of exactly this kind, where the chief executive's view was
different from the general view of several line managers; both sets
of views again differed in some significant respects from the personnel director's views.

It may be worth re-emphasising that the validity of the criteria
suggested in these figures is something that you have to determine for
yourself. The intentions and objectives of your scheme, as I said in

the first paragraph in this section, may make some of the criteria irrelevant from your point of view. These irrelevant criteria can, however, stimulate, both in your mind and in the minds of others who may complete the exercise above, a useful discussion on exactly what kind of management development you are pursuing: in other words what your model of management development actually is.

Charles Margerison[7] offers two lists indicating ways of achieving success in management development. He does not present them as a model, but it is convenient and appropriate to consider them here.

Achieving success in management development

Success

Success can be facilitated by:

- selecting high-achieving managers
- enthusiastic managerial support
- involving key people in diagnosing management development needs
- designing active work-related activities
- pressing hard for outputs
- providing early leadership experience
- letting each person appraise himself
- following up with workshops
- making line managers be accountable for management development.

Failure

Failure is likely to arise when:

- there is no clear policy
- there is no top management support
- management development is not related to business plans
- there are inadequate diagnoses and *ad hoc* solutions

- political issues are ignored
- pay/promotion is unfair
- line support is low
- the buck is passed to the training department
- people are kept in jobs too long
- there is no regular follow-up.

Here again you can conduct a similar exercise for yourself on your view, and others' views, of management development in your own organisation. In fact, you can use the same process of marking and involvement of others suggested for the earlier exercise.

One of the interesting differences between my lists and Margerison's is that he has included lack of top management support as a cause of failure. While such support is undoubtedly desirable, my research and experience show that it is not, in fact, an absolute requirement. I have encountered organisations where management development has proceeded very satisfactorily despite the fact that the chief executive and several of his main board colleagues were known to be uninterested. However, absence of top-level support is an undeniable constraint and a limitation on what can be achieved. If management development is generally a failure it will be because there is no significant managerial support at any level.

Burgoyne's model

Professor John Burgoyne[8] has been one of the most stimulating thinkers in the UK on management development (and I have encountered no equivalent in the United States). In conjunction with his co-authors, Mike Pedler and Tom Boydell, he has had a formidable impact on the creation of the ideas about self-development and the learning organisation referred to later in this book. He has also made one of the few attempts to produce an explicit model of management development (Figure 2.8). The model emerged from a re-analysis of 14 years' pure and applied research and development work at the Centre for the Study of Management Learning at

Figure 2.8
Levels of Maturity of Organisational Management Development

1 *No systematic management development*	2 *Isolated tactical management development*	3 *Integrated and co-ordinated structural and development tactics*	4 *A management development strategy to implement corporate policy*	5 *Management development strategy input to corporate policy formation*	6 *Strategic development of the management of corporate policy*
No systematic or deliberate management development in structural or developmental sense, total reliance on natural, *laissez-faire* uncontrived processes of management development.	There are isolated and *ad hoc* tactical management development activities, of either structural or developmental kinds, or both, in response to local problems, crises, or sporadically identified general problems.	The specific management development tactics that impinge directly on the individual manager, of career structure management, and of assisting learning, are integrated and co-ordinated.	A management development strategy plays its part in implementing corporate policies through managerial human resource planning, and providing a strategic framework and direction for the tactics of career structure management and of learning, education and training.	Management development processes feed information into corporate policy decision-making processes on the organisation's managerial assets, strengths, weaknesses and potential, and contribute to the forecasting and analysis of the manageability of proposed projects, ventures, changes.	Management development processes enhance the nature and quality of corporate policy-forming processes, which they also inform and help implement.

Lancaster University. It aims to show what is involved 'in becoming a mature organisation in terms of management development'.

The first point to note is that Burgoyne defines management development as 'the management of managerial careers in an organisational context', and managerial careers as 'the biography of a person's managerial worklife'. He says that processes of 'natural' management development happen, they are not deliberately planned or contrived for management development. They are inevitable, usually good, and destined always to be the major provider of management development. However, in most situations he says they are not enough. In particular he sees these processes as essentially effective in new entrepreneurial firms, usually small in size. As such organisations need to cope with increasing scale and complexity, natural career structuring and learning alone are not sufficient, so the journey to what he calls 'organisational Management Development maturity' begins. As will be seen, all five levels of maturity after this first are variants of what I have called formal management development, Type 3.

In Burgoyne's view, possibly the majority of organisations are at levels 1 and 2. Levels 3 and 4 describe the limits of current best practice achieved 'with any consistency or thoroughness by what I would regard as the best organisations in these terms'. Levels 5 and 6 apparently exist as 'occasional achievements often precariously achieved and lost, and often only occurring in some relatively autonomous part of large organisations'.

Burgoyne has offered what seems to me a very recognisable and usable statement about the formal processes of management development. Understandably they follow from his definition of management development. Readers will have immediately noticed the difference of definition between us. The application of that difference can also be seen, in that what he describes as 'natural' management development processes and as 'usually good and destined always to be the major provider of management development', disappear from his model after level 1. It may be that he means to imply that such natural processes continue at all levels, but in fact no further attention is paid to them in the article. However, as a model of formal management development processes this seems to me an

excellent formulation and one that could well be applied in reviewing your own position. You may wish to do so either in preference
to the model I have suggested, because you wish to focus entirely on
formal processes; or you may wish to use Burgoyne's model as an
additional means of getting at the formal processes. Here is an exercise for you.

Exercise

1 Compare Burgoyne's definition of management development with Mumford's. Which do you propose to use in
   reviewing your own management development processes?
2 At what level of maturity do you believe your own organisation to be, in terms of Burgoyne's model?
3 What steps would need to be taken by you, and by
   others, to move your organisation upwards in terms of
   the levels described?

There is one other item not mentioned explicitly in my lists. One
cause of failure can be that the whole process is driven by fads.
Organisations get overwhelmed by the latest approach to appraisal,
or decide to send all their top people to Harvard, or send everyone
on an outdoor training course. My argument here would be that such
fads emerge from more basic failures of the kind I have indicated.
They arise when management development is not driven by business
needs but by someone's idea of clever processes and when development activities are not appropriate either to needs or to individuals.

Exercise

1 What model of management development have I been
   using so far?
2 Have my views been changed by reading this chapter?
3 What has been the model, or demonstrated beliefs and
   values, of my organisation?
4 Is there a difference between our beliefs about management development and what we actually do and

achieve? (One example would be a theoretical model that says managers are responsible for their own development, and a system that provides for all the initiatives to be taken by the organisation and the managerial hierarchy.)

5 What conclusions do I draw from my answers to these questions? What actions should I, and what actions could I, undertake as a result?

References

1 STEWART R. *Choices for the Manager.* Maidenhead, McGraw-Hill, 1982.
2 MINTZBERG H. *The Nature of Managerial Work.* Hemel Hempstead, Prentice-Hall, 1973.
3 KOTTER J. P. *The General Manager.* London, Macmillan, 1982.
4 KOLB D. *Experiential Learning.* Hemel Hempstead, Prentice-Hall, 1983.
5 HONEY P. *and* MUMFORD A. *Manual of Learning Styles.* 3rd edn. Honey, 1992.
6 REVANS R. W. *Action Learning.* Blond and Briggs, 1980.
7 MARGERISON C. 'Delivering success in management development'. *Journal of Management Development.* Vol. 3, 1982.
8 BURGOYNE J. 'Management development for the individual and the organisation'. *Personnel Management.* June 1988.

Further reading relevant to this chapter is shown in Chapter 13.

3

 Informal Management Development

The case for informal development

In Chapter 1 the frequency and impact of informal learning experiences were identified by inviting readers to think about their own personal experiences and then to consider the position elsewhere in their organisations. Chapter 2 gave the reasons so much managerial learning is unplanned and unstructured, though often very powerful: this is the nature of managerial work. Informal managerial learning is a by-product of the variety of managerial tasks, the dynamic nature of managerial priorities, changes in the working environment, and changes in colleagues and bosses, which all provide new opportunities and stimuli. So the clearest reason for including informal processes in our definition and models of management development is that excluding them takes us away from reality and eliminates from conscious consideration a number of potential opportunities for learning. This chapter shows how to improve those informal processes.

Informal learning is often seen by managers themselves as actually preferable to various forms of planned management development. Even if individuals work in organisations that have attempted various kinds of formal management development, they often none the less rate their informal experiences as much more significant.

Since at least the mid-1960s, with the push given to management education in the UK by the launch of the first major business schools and by the existence of Industrial Training Boards, attempts have been made to emphasise the importance of formal management development. Yet the reports by Professor Charles Handy[1] and Professor John Constable[2] again made the point that there is insufficient formal provision for the development of managers. In terms of needs as expressed by these latter reports, and by comparative judgements against the development of managers in other countries (Handy), insufficient is done. The research of Professor Mangham, looking at the management training component, further supports that view.[3] That research, and Mangham's subsequent contribution to the

Constable Report, showed that the majority of British managers received no formal management training at all and that 20 per cent of
companies employing more than 1,000 people had no provision for
training their managers in 1985. Ten years later Thomson[4] found a
more encouraging picture. Now only 4 per cent of the larger organisations and 20 per cent of the small reported doing no training. He
found (a very important issue as described in my introduction in relation to Strategy 1 and Strategy 2) that there was a reasonably equal
balance between formal and informal methods of training.

No equivalent figure is available for the totality of formal management development, describing the extent to which other aspects
such as planned personal development, job rotation or career planning are offered by organisations. It is probable that the figure for
'no action' organisations is higher. There are organisations that
make use of courses in an unplanned way, but that lack any overall
development scheme.

Particularly as far as courses are concerned, there are clear
reasons why managers often find informal processes more effective
than formal ones. These are:

- the content of development programmes, especially courses,
  which is experienced as unreal, irrelevant to the manager's priorities, or difficult to transfer from a course to a managerial job
- processes of learning that too often reflect the interests of course
  designers and tutors rather than managers
- processes that do not take into account different individual learning preferences.

When I make the point to personnel directors and management development advisers that formal management development processes
are often less effective than their providers perceive them to be, it is
understandable that some of them seek to show that my evidence is
flawed. The most frequently offered comment is that it is inevitable
that managers will downgrade the importance of planned processes
because they are unwilling to present themselves as needing to learn.
The problem with accepting this defence is why it should apply to,
for example, courses but not to other kinds of learning experience.

Managers who said they had learnt little of significance from courses were quite prepared to illustrate learning from informal processes. It is not at all clear why a manager's ego should prevent him from saying he has learnt from a course but does not prevent him from saying that he has learnt from a colleague, from a boss – or even from a subordinate!

The conclusion is not that formal management development should not be attempted, but rather that it should be improved. Chapters 4 to 8 set out ways of doing this. However, in terms of the balance of effort in management development, it would surely be sensible to pay attention to the messages that have been sent to us for many years now by managers themselves. In addition to whatever we should do to improve formal processes, we need to help managers to identify and make more effective use of the informal experiences that they so often highlight. (The book by McCall *et al*[5] has particularly good illustrations of powerful informal learning experiences.)

Examples of informal accidental learning

Problem-solving

> I was a shift manager on a new production line in our plant. The line involved quite a bit of new technology and we had a number of problems with it. My immediate boss was a very ingenious guy with an engineering background. Every problem that came up he seemed to have an answer for, but the problems kept coming up. His boss, the Production Director, called all three shift managers and our boss to his office. He had two flip charts; one he marked 'Problems', the other he divided into two columns: 'Causes apparent' and 'Causes deeper?' After 40 minutes with him we did not come out with a single answer, whereas five minutes with our boss always produced an answer. The difference was we came out with the questions we needed to pursue in order to produce really effective answers. I learnt two things – one was about looking deeper into problems, and the other was about how to make the best use of the intelligence of five people working together.

Project

Our research people came up with a major technological break-through. The issue was to convert it into several products, and to get them onto the market before any of our competitors found out what we were doing. I was put in charge of the whole exercise – production, finance, marketing. My company had never tried a really integrated approach to managing the intro-duction of new products before. All the barons had looked after their own territory, which meant all the decisions got pushed up to the Management Committee. As a result it was assumed that everybody had to fight for their own resources, argue with each other about the best way to do things, and particularly to make sure that the other guy got blamed when things went wrong. I showed it could be done differently and better. I suppose that was learning both for me and for the organisation.

Presentation

I had always thought I was pretty good at putting my ideas over. Right from university days I found I could argue clearly but pleasantly, and influence people. I had found the same in my early years in management in business. Most people were so relieved to find someone who could put over an idea clearly in a few sentences instead of in pages that I got quite a repu-tation for it. Then I was moved from my then department to an area I did not know very well. I was faced with having to make a presentation to a visiting American director. I got my new subordinates to brief me beforehand and then I launched into the presentation with some nice slides, some good specifics and a few jokes. I was absolutely self-confident about it. I was jabbed to death by the Director – he wanted to know a lot more than I knew. We went off to lunch and when I saw him coming towards me I thought I was in for another going-over. I was as-tonished when he told me that my summary at the beginning was excellent. Then he added the comment which really rein-forced what I had gone through. 'It is practically never worth-while pretending you know more than you do.' Experience has since confirmed what I learnt that day.

Redundancy

We had to make some supervisors redundant. I should think we made every mistake in the book. We did not have individual packages properly prepared. We actually allowed rumours to go out beforehand, because we thought it would soften the blow. We saw them first thing in the morning and then let them stay on the plant, instead of telling them in mid-afternoon and sending them home. We made a lot of mistakes including, now I think of it, the fairly basic one of not finding out what other people's experience was. It was awful. But we did do it better next time.

Selling

We had built our company from selling professional services on a day-rate basis. We managed to negotiate contracts so that there was no prior agreement on the total that would be involved in any project. The basis for this was that neither we nor the client usually knew what the total cost could be, even in terms of the likely numbers of days. Then we were faced with a really major project for a client who wanted to change the basis of the contract to a fixed price. The project and the client were both great opportunities for us. But actually negotiating on a quite different basis really stretched us. The real problem was not negotiation skills. It was understanding the different objectives and priorities of the client. It took us a long time to understand why they wanted it differently. It was a basic selling message really. The customer is always right, but we wasted a lot of time trying to persuade him he was wrong.

Committee meeting

I attended a meeting with my boss and five other colleagues at the same level as myself. It was our formal annual review with his boss and his staff supports. My boss was shown up in the worst way. What his boss did was to get the rest of us to challenge each other's budgets and priorities. He really worked on us, and pushed our boss to one side. I think all of us lost in that situation. Although we didn't recognise it at the time, I think the five of us lost out because it was clear we were not a team. Our boss lost out because his boss put him down. I expect the top guy thought he was the winner, but he was not really. None of us respected him for what he had done, because we saw what kind of game he was playing.

Business visit

We acquired a new company in the United States. I was sent over with a colleague with a brief that we should look at some issues about how they managed their business, what sort of controls they used and what sort of review processes they had. There were actually some useful things I learnt there in terms of the different ways in which they did things. Looking back on it, however, I can see I learnt some more subtle things as well. As much as anything else, the differences were about what you saw the job of managers to be and how they behaved in a company which had great similarities to our own, and in which the only major difference was that they were American.

Observing

I was made assistant to a manager who was temporarily running two different jobs. They just threw me at him as a bright young resource who might be able to help him. He was so busy that he could never sit down with me to sort out what he wanted me to do. So a lot of the time I was underemployed. I volunteered to go round with him and make notes at meetings he had, and particularly to go with him on some visits he had to make to some old customers. I certainly did give him some useful notes, but I made a hell of a lot more that I kept for myself. The main thing I learnt was the obvious, that if you want to manage your time better, you have to invest some time to do it – *he* never did. Otherwise I learnt a lot of things actually about his skills in particular situations. He was extraordinarily good at not only listening but showing that he was listening. His whole body leaned towards the speaker, and on top of that he would summarise what the other chap had said – often actually expressing his view better than it had been delivered.

What these examples mean

These examples are the tip of an iceberg – in two senses. First, they are a tiny proportion of the full range of incidents from managerial work that provide learning experiences. Second, they are the tip of an iceberg for any particular individual. In both senses there are far more examples than are:

- identified in general as possible opportunities for learning
- identified, used and reviewed as learning experiences by any individual

So we return to one of our early propositions. Informal, accidental experiences are widely present but often badly identified and, in consequence, inefficiently used. When managers are asked to review their stimulating learning experiences they will often quote cases like those just given. However, many of them also recognise that they did not make the most of these experiences or even recognise them unassisted. The best of all possible news is precisely that managers do recognise that these often powerfully experienced managerial processes are also learning experiences, *but that as learning experiences they could be improved*, with significant benefit to themselves and their organisation.

It is sensible to answer some of the questions that may arise, particularly with people who see the concept of management development as being about formal processes. Learning from experience, although ever present, is for many purposes not only inefficient but insufficient. It is just possible that managers, if not management development advisers, will become so excited by the possibilities that follow in the next section that they will decide that formal management development processes are really quite unnecessary. Since this book is promoting the idea of a balance, using both informal and formal, I would clearly not subscribe to abandoning formal processes. There are some very major deficiencies in a total reliance on informal processes.

They include:

- *idealisation* – attitudes and behaviours which say that past ex-perience is so valued and appropriate that it is all that is necess-ary. Effective learning involves building successfully on properly understood past experience, not treating it as the only process of merit.
- *narrowness* – it is possible for a manager's work experience to be extremely narrow in terms of jobs, functions, kinds of organis-ation and sizes of organisation. While effective management de-velopment is more likely to focus on the specific than the general, this does not mean that a manager in retail needs to know nothing about, for instance, production processes.
- *obsolescence* – painful and perhaps carefully acquired exper-ience of how to do a managerial job may well become out of date. The appropriate attitudes and behaviour of managers in public-service utilities who change to meet the new demands of privatised business are a case in point. As a director said rather ruefully, 'I reached the top of this organisation by being better than most at managing a centralized bureaucratic business. Now I am here, I have to manage newly created profit centres with managers who want a decision yesterday.' If you learn only from what you encounter in the normal and natural processes of work at a particular level, this may mean that you will not be exposed to those activities or opportunities which you will actually need in future.
- In addition to the particular nature of the organisation, there is the specific issue of the closest relationship of all, with bosses and colleagues. These may be excellent providers of advice and good models of effective behaviour – or they may be neither.
- Of course people develop skills from the 'natural' process of doing the job, and finding out whether the way they do it works. If it does they understandably assume that they have a skill. However, the skill they have acquired may be either inappropri-ate or at an insufficiently high performance level. At worst it may even be the wrong kind of skill. One example is the process of interviewing. The skills that many managers deploy in selection

interviewing have been acquired from the experience of being interviewed themselves, and then of interviewing others. Their level of skill is often, however, well below what they need to interview effectively.

Developing Type 2 learning

Type 2 learning is defined as the process of integrating learning and managerial work, so that both are given conscious attention. The best way to test the proposition, and then to show how normal managerial work can be used more effectively for learning purposes, is to start with the following exercise:

Exercise

1 Look back over your last four weeks of managerial work. Pick out the most crucial, highest priority, the most significant things with which you have been involved.
2 What results were achieved from the managerial work (by you or someone else)?
3 Have you learnt something from the results achieved, and/or from the process by which the results were achieved?

It will be noted that, in contrast to the learning biography exercise with which we started in Chapter 1, we start here with managerial activity rather than learning experience. There are several reasons for this. The first is that in my experience of using both these exercises, some managers have problems with the first, but very few with the second. On the first exercise, where we ask managers to identify significant learning experiences, some people have difficulty recognising a 'learning experience', and have to be helped with lists of possible opportunities – as indeed the reader may have found in Chapter 1. But managers do not have problems in thinking about managerial activities. Nor do they usually have much problem in identifying some achieved learning from at least one of these over a four-week period, though some of them do say in tones of surprise, 'So that's what you mean by learning!'

The other major reason for starting with managerial activities when we are trying to help people achieve Type 2 experiences is that we are actually proposing that they should work in that way in their real-life situation. We are not asking them to think about learning opportunities first, and then to work out how their managerial activities might be used or tailored to meet the learning need. Appropriate as this process can be, this is a Type 3 kind of process, where the development of the manager is the initiating and perhaps prime concern.

At this point the reader may be saying, 'But aren't you talking about exactly the same kind of experience? For example, you quoted a project experience as a Type 1 case earlier on, yet in my organisation we use projects very much as development tools – what you would call Type 3.' The need to answer this question, and the use of the project as an illustration, brings out a very important point. Management development advisers very often see projects as useful vehicles for development, most particularly in the action learning process. However, the main interest and focus of most managers, *even in a formal development process*, is usually to complete the project itself successfully, providing it is realistic and has not been invented simply for development purposes. The great virtue of projects within the action learning process is that they provide a balance between managerial work and learning from the managerial work. In terms of our clarification of Type 2, however, the crucial point is that here we are using a project as a Type 2 example, where the initiating force for the project is the line manager, not the person responsible for management development. The development programme may have a very careful and sophisticated process for choosing projects which are realistic in terms of commitment and felt accountability, and indeed fundamental, to the development of the organisation. However, the great difference from the projects which managers talk about as learning experiences is that they start from outside the normal managerial process. The great virtue of an exercise like this is that it starts from where managers are, rather than requiring an understanding about a different kind of process called 'learning'.

The second feature of the exercise – aside from its reality and the fact that it takes us straight into what we mean by Type 2 learning – is that it brings out a process that Peter Honey and I call 'retrospective learning'. Informal accidental managerial learning is usually only partially understood and recognised when it happens. It is also, by our definition, wholly unplanned. All the examples given earlier in this chapter were of unplanned accidental learning – Type 1. They became a form of retrospective learning simply because the managers who described them were recalling particular experiences and reviewing them for me. The wording of many of the narratives makes it clear that it was precisely the process of description and review that identified the learning experience as such. This process not only identified the fact of learning, but in many cases clarified what the learning had actually been. The managers involved:

- recognised more clearly what they had learnt
- (in some cases) produced a deeper analysis of what they had learnt
- (in some cases) increased their understanding of how they had learnt.

As with many other managerial activities, it is the provision of an opportunity to stand back mentally, review and analyse the results of the review that produces a useful result. And again, it is precisely the absence of the process of reviewing, rather than its presence, that is the norm.

So the first stage in any attempt to encourage Type 2 learning is to facilitate retrospective learning. This is the easiest thing for managers to grasp; it is very productive in terms of immediately accessible examples from their own experience, and does not involve the kind of hypothetical constructions about future activities that many of them initially find difficult.

The next stage, still concentrating on the retrospective process, may well be to widen managers' vision about the kind of activities that may have provided opportunities for learning. You may have already made use of the learning opportunities chart (Figure 1.2). If you have not done so, or you want to try this out with some managers, you could do the following exercise:

Exercise

1 Consider the list of learning opportunities. Have any of these been particularly important to you in your present job/in a past job?
2 Consider whether you learnt something significant from one of these activities.
3 Consider why you learnt.
4 Consider how you learnt.

There are a number of things that can be done either as exercises in the form just indicated, or simply with questions posed during relevant discussions with managers, which can bring them into a discussion of how they have *actually* learnt from past experience.

The other major element in Type 2 managerial learning is to move to the more difficult but very productive stage of 'prospective learning'. One of the great advantages of a considered discussion of retrospective learning is that it does not have to be left as a purely evocative review, collecting with hindsight useful information from the past. It can be linked to prospective learning simply by asking managers who have identified useful retrospective experiences whether they can see any similar or indeed different learning opportunities that may arise in the future. Again our emphasis in Type 2 is to deal with such opportunities primarily as managerial activities, not learning opportunities. The exercise is:

Can you think of some similar or different managerial activities with which you are going to be involved over, say, the next three or four weeks, from which you might think to acquire some new knowledge or understanding, or which might allow you to test out a skill?

The final stage in developing prospective learning opportunities is to build on any success you or others have had in identifying the opportunities. Simply recognising in advance that something represents an opportunity is better than not thinking about it at all. However, you can benefit even more from planning in a little more detail what your learning objectives will be and how you propose to set about taking advantage of the opportunity. This is admittedly the most difficult of the suggestions made so far. It may well be appropriate for many managers to stay, at least initially, at the level of identifying the opportunity, without being pressed too hard to develop plans on how to take full advantage of it.

A manager who has identified a prospective learning opportunity should subsequently review the extent to which he or she has taken advantage of it. (This incidentally bring us on to one of the issues that often arises with the kind of personal development plans which managers can adopt in a fit of enthusiasm at the end of a course. There is no process for reviewing the success or otherwise of the plan, and since it is often divorced from normal managerial activity it tends to stay in the development file after the Type 3 event that created it.) Since in Type 2 we are always working on real managerial activities, the likelihood that the prospective learning opportunity will be lost is reduced. It may disappear because the activity disappears; but so long as the activity actually happens there is a greater likelihood of both the activity and its derived learning opportunity being reviewed.

The retrospective and prospective learning approaches are illustrated in Figure 3.1. In many ways it would be useful to adopt an alternative design for the prospective learning opportunity. We could make use of a concept initially developed, for slightly different reasons, by Professor John Morris, who used a learning spiral rather than a learning circle. The idea is that retrospective learning experiences lead to the identification of prospective opportunities, which in turn lead to retrospective learning which in turn lead to ... Chapter 11 provides a further breakdown of different approaches to learning, introducing the idea of the intuitive and incidental approaches. We have emphasised retrospective and prospective approaches here because of their greater productivity in learning terms. The reader may ask at this point why I have provided such detailed

Figure 3.1
Retrospective and Prospective Learning

Retrospective				
Something has happened	→	It is reviewed	→	Conclusions are reached

Prospective						
Plan to learn from a managerial activity	→	Implement the plan	→	Review it	→	Reach conclusions

exercises rather than simply explaining the nature of Type 2 development and then providing a list of examples. The reader has been taken through the process of actually carrying out the exercise because the process is more likely to be understood and accepted if an individual has carried it out personally. The detailed working through of the exercises is necessary to secure understanding of an unfamiliar process. In terms of learning, it is more effective to involve the reader in actively doing something rather than passively looking at an interesting list of opportunities.

Quality in retrospective learning

The first series of examples I gave were Type 1, because they were unplanned and the manager involved did not consciously identify them as learning experiences. They illustrate what can be achieved in Type 2 because they were subsequently reviewed with me by the participant manager. Without such a discussion and review they would have remained disorganised, fragmentary and only partially remembered. Even a relatively short discussion with someone else can add depth and understanding to achieved learning; it is this which turns a Type 1 experience into a Type 2.

However, this is still a fairly low-level Type 2 experience: The list of examples is accidental and informal in origin, and the discussion about them was accidental too – it so happened that I came along and

acquired managers' statements (not always in the context of my trying to find out what managers had learnt – sometimes simply
through a discussion of other managerial problems and processes).
The essential quality of the Type 2 experience really resides in the
care and thought that go into it. As shown earlier, this can be entirely
dedicated to a good retrospective review or to a good analysis of
prospective experiences. The main point is that experiences should
cease to be seen as exclusively managerial, with some fringe learning tacked on. They are managerial activities from which some deliberate learning is derived through conscious thought and
discussion.

Lee Iacocca's original book[6] provides a number of excellent illustrations of how he applied things he had learnt at Ford to his new
situation at Chrysler. The descriptions of how he learnt from his
Ford experiences (partly by observing the failures of others) and of
what he should do as the new boss in Chrysler (for example, ensuring that he was not the only new man when he went there) are important, high-level illustrations. However, it is given to few of us to
move from being one of the three most powerful people in Ford to
becoming the most powerful person in Chrysler.

Here is another example, this time about a young manager in his
late twenties. He describes one of the people he had worked for:

> He would take time in joint problem-solving to let me reach my
> own conclusions, coaching me as necessary through my think-
> ing processes. Sometimes this led to outcomes which he prob-
> ably anticipated. On other occasions an unexpected solution
> emerged and he would say, 'That's interesting' and be prepared
> to develop it. He worked hard at problem-solving and thinking
> laterally, and coached me in the techniques he favoured.
>
> His coaching and encouragement extended beyond the im-
> mediate problem. He helped me use the organisation's political
> system to get scarce resources and prompted me to improve
> presentations.

Here we begin to face one of the associated issues. Whereas a great
deal of Type 1 learning is entirely solitary and is appreciated only by
the individual who claims the learning, Type 2 is much more likely
to involve other people. 'Involve' means that the learning is placed

on the table between at least two participants, probably a manager and the boss in most situations, or perhaps between a manager and one or more colleagues. Discussion of both options, prospective learning and achieved learning (retrospective learning), are likely to be enhanced by checking them out with other people. It is partly through this process of openness, sharing, and, to at least some extent, partnership that some of the weaknesses of learning from experience are reduced. It is much easier to remain in a self-satisfied cocoon about your achieved learning and performance if you keep your views of both to yourself. If you have to, or decide to, check them out with someone else then you are quite likely to get some information which confirms your view and some which challenges it.

This takes us into organisational learning, the process by which an organisation changes its nature, culture and direction. In another sense it takes us into the field of Chris Argyris, of double-loop learning, where received wisdom is challenged. Argyris[7] discusses some of the issues involved here, and in particular explains how the processes of single-loop learning and the correction of errors in itself militates against double-loop learning, where values and beliefs are actually challenged.

Who can help?

The chart which follows (Figure 3.2) indicates that there are essentially five types of people who can help an individual improve learning on the job. Since each of them can help him in both Type 2 and

Figure 3.2
Helpers with Type 2 Processes

Direct Manager (Boss)
Mentor
Peers (Colleagues)
Direct Reports (Subordinates)
Network contacts

Type 3 learning situations, I have drawn both processes together in Chapter 9 and will not duplicate the details here.

The main point here is to distinguish between the kind of initiative which may be taken. A boss or a mentor is more likely to take the initiative in discussing Type 2 experiences with a manager. Colleagues are likely to do so only at the initiative of another manager seeking help or because they themselves want help on one of their own learning opportunities. Subordinates are, of course, extremely unlikely to take the initiative in setting up a Type 2 learning experience from their boss; however, they can be very useful in providing feedback about particular experiences and observations of what has happened at meetings, and, if the relationship is particularly good, they may even offer comments about their boss's performance.

It will be noted that the personnel director or management development advisers do not appear. There is a paradox here. All the suggestions in this chapter are in the first place directed at exactly these people. Why then are they not shown as helpers? Because the Type 2 context is one owned by managers and their colleagues. We want them to identify their own opportunities from their own activities and their own experiences. The roles of personnel and management development advisers are entirely subsidiary. They may help to the extent of some informal discussions, perhaps offering some of the exercises indicated in this chapter. They might choose to help in a much more serious way through the various opportunities existing in the current formal management development processes. In this case we should finish with the irony that Type 2 processes may be stimulated by discussion of Type 3 processes. However, the ways in which that can be done will be left to the chapters where we talk about Type 3 processes, and to Chapter 9.

How does a manager start?

The manager creates Type 2 learning experiences by thinking about and reviewing normal managerial activities. These can be identified purely 'in the head'. Alternatively, they can be found by a review of various kinds of (mainly written) material:

- *a review of priorities and objectives*, which may indicate areas of significance or novelty
- *a job description* (if the manager has gone into a new job or responsibilities have recently been changed)
- *an activity list* of the kind many managers keep as a daily or weekly reminder of things to do, or a note on actions which have been set up and need to be followed through
- *a work diary* which may simply indicate some of the most important events on a daily basis, which again may highlight interesting activities either already undertaken or to be undertaken
- *a development plan*, perhaps produced through some Type 3 process such as appraisal or a course
- *a learning log*, where a manager deliberately keeps a review of learning experiences and opportunities
- *discussion with colleagues*, where one or more colleagues identify similar activities and experiences which may provide learning
- *individual discussion with boss*, where some specific activity is related to a learning opportunity
- *a Type 2 learning review* of the kind illustrated in this chapter.

Further discussion on how to create Type 2 learning is given in Chapter 9, and detailed guidance is provided in various books and articles.[8]

What stimulates learning on the job?

Some of the things which bring about individual learning are recognisable in the case studies quoted in this chapter. Davies and Easterby-Smith[9] say, as a result of their research, that:

> managers develop primarily through confrontations with novel situations and problems where their existing repertoire of behaviours are inadequate and where they have to develop new ways of dealing with these situations. In general it is unlikely that there will be any shortage of novel situations facing organisations in the future.

Figure 3.3
Learning Problems in Job Moves

Familiar	Same function, same organisation
Part familiar	Same function, different organisation
	Different function, same organisation
Unfamiliar	New job, new organisation

This statement is a little too strong: it depends what you mean by 'novel'. Many of the examples encountered in my own research would not fit a definition of 'novel', if this implied something totally new and different. However, the pressure for change, whether it is within an existing job or caused by taking up a new one, certainly forces recognition of both the need to learn and the occasion of learning. (See Chapter 11 for further discussion.)

The process of taking up a new job necessarily involves a degree of novelty and different stages and pressures of learning. These are well described by Gabarro[10] (see Chapter 7 for his views). My own view of the implications of job changes is shown in Figure 3.3.

A second pressure to learn on the job is the recognition of significant problems in relationships or performance. These may be indicated through a formal Type 3 process, but they are more often indicated by informal processes – unsuccessful attempts to influence others, a failure of others to respond to your initiatives, or a failure to meet managerial targets. These kinds of occasion can be variously described as a jolt, or as stronger psychological disturbances of pain or shock. A number of them are described in an interesting article by Snell[11] who has also described how to try to reduce the pain or discomfort. Kelleher *et al*,[12] in a somewhat confusing article, identify three factors in the work context. These are:

- freedom – the extent to which managers' activity contained opportunities for self-initiative
- support, including issues such as how far rewards, communication and feedback encourage learning
- structure – boundaries, limits and constraints which channel managerial effort and energy.

Stuart[13] brings out a very important point about language. He compares formal methods of training with everyday forms of managerial behaviour. He compares the formal case study with the everyday form 'You'll never guess what's happened to me. There I was, and she said: "What would you have done?"' Stuart is bringing out the important point that natural descriptions of normal behaviour are recognisable and acceptable to managers. By implication, the processes described in this chapter will be attractive precisely because they build on the kind of natural language he describes.

Exercise

1 How might I set about improving informal learning processes in my organisation?
2 Can I make use of the ideas of converting Type 1 to Type 2 managerial experiences?
3 Can I identify some good retrospective and perhaps even some good prospective learners in my organisation?
4 How might I use these individuals to help others to learn more effectively from informal processes?

References

1   HANDY C. *The Making of Managers*. London, NEDO, 1987.
2   CONSTABLE J. *The Making of British Managers*. London, BIM/NEDO, 1987.
3   MANGHAM I. *Management Training*. Bath, University of Bath, 1986.
4   THOMSON A. *A Portrait of Management Development*. London, Institute of Management, 1997.
5   McCALL M., LOMBARDO M. *and* MORRISON A. *The Lessons of Experience*. Lexington, 1988.
6   IACOCCA L. *Iacocca*. London, Sidgwick and Jackson, 1985.
7   ARGYRIS C. *Reasoning Learning and Action*. San Francisco, Jossey-Bass, 1982.

8   MUMFORD A. *Developing Top Managers.* Gower, 1988;
    MUMFORD A., HONEY P. *and* ROBINSON G. *Developing
    Directors: Making experience count,* London, IOD, 1990; and
    HONEY P. *and* MUMFORD A. *Manual of Learning Opportunities.*
    Honey, 1989.
9   DAVIES J. *and* EASTERBY-SMITH M. 'Learning and developing
    from managerial work experiences'. *Journal of Management
    Studies.* Vol. 21, No. 4, 1984.
10 GABARRO J. 'When a new manager takes charge'. *Harvard
    Business Review.* May–June 1985.
11 SNELL R. 'The emotional cost of learning at work'.
    Management Education and Development. Vol. 19, Pt 4, 1988.
12 KELLEHER D., FINESTONE P. *and* LOWRY A. 'Managerial learn-
    ing: first notes from an unstudied frontier'. *Organizational
    Studies.* Vol. 11, No. 3, 1986.
13 STUART R. 'Towards reestablishing naturalism in management
    training and development'. *Industrial and Commercial
    Training.* July 1984.

Further reading relevant to this chapter is shown in Chapter 13.

4

 Systems for Development – Appraisal

The number of books and articles on this subject shows how crucial it is in the formal system (see Further Reading). In many ways it is the Holy Grail of management development. In principle it deals with one of the major issues about improving performance; yet the practice is often profoundly unsatisfactory. The most useful guide is by Fletcher.[1]

The starting-point – the job itself

Planned development ought to be based on a clear, formal view of the content of the manager's job. At an individual level this means that there ought to be a job description and some statement of priorities, preferably drawn up on a three- to twelve-month cycle. To attempt to develop managers for jobs whose purpose and nature are unclear, where the constraints and opportunities are unspecified, and where the boundaries are undefined, is to risk losing both sharpness and commitment to any subsequent development process. Chapter 2 touched on the contingent nature of managerial work, and this is expanded in Chapter 6. The idea that 'everyone knows what managers need to be able to do', and the consequent argument 'all managers ought to be exposed to ...' is likely to be a cause of failure in formal development processes. The particular skills or competences required are covered in Chapter 6.

Clarity of job purpose and clarity about priorities would themselves be a considerable step forward in many organisations. They would help at least to address the issue of what kind of problems and circumstances the manager needs to be able to overcome and what the purpose of development activities might be.

This basic level of understanding is usefully supplemented in some organisations by further clarification. A list of priorities agreed on an informal basis, with perhaps only a note exchanged between boss and subordinate afterwards, can be extended. There might be a list of key result areas, or a formal process for agreeing objectives and priorities as part of a structured management system. Historically the management-by-objectives approach was introduced in part through management development schemes and to satisfy management development needs as much as management systems needs; this is still the case in some organisations.

In other organisations job clarification may extend to a much more detailed statement like the Hay job description process, which clearly draws out the issue of accountability. This can be very helpful not only for analysing the job itself, but for clarifying aspects of the job for current development (although not for future development needs). Fletcher[1] argues that Performance Management Systems place appraisal in a central role. However, PMSs are now seen as less advantageous than when he wrote.

Appraisal and performance review

This chapter deals with the *purpose* of reviewing individual performance and the problems that arise from attempting to do so. The *consequence* of the review is covered in Chapter 6.

A survey carried out in 1986 showed that 82 per cent of employers operate performance appraisal schemes.[2] It is not only small companies that do not use such schemes: public and local government organisations are less likely to have such schemes than commercial organisations of comparable size. But any organisation with formal management development, or proposing to develop it in the future, is likely to go in for some form of performance appraisal. The problems of appraisal have been consistent, and were already visible 25 years ago in the work of Macgregor, Drucker and Rowe. What we have had since is a constant rediscovery that *in principle* performance appraisal meets a genuine need both of individual managers in their real work processes and of a formal management development scheme. We know that it is frequently attempted, that organisations constantly rediscover familiar difficulties and that appraisal schemes are often perceived by managers as ineffective. We will now look at the main issues.

Objectives

Research on appraisal schemes, and general experience, shows that many of the problems in conducting effective appraisal start with confusion over objectives. The confusion may arise because the scheme may not make clear what the objectives are. Alternatively, an appraisal scheme may be designed to have a number of objectives – explicit or not – which in practice turn out to conflict with each other. Possible objectives for an appraisal scheme include:

- providing information for succession and resource planning
- providing a basis for improved communication between boss and subordinate
- identifying and recording performance weaknesses
- providing a basis for analysis of performance and identification of required standards and improvements
- identifying potential
- providing mutual feedback between boss and subordinate
- providing a basis for training and career counselling
- providing a basis for salary decision-making.

It is theoretically unlikely, and certainly so in practice, that a single appraisal scheme will meet all of these diverse objectives. Perhaps more important is the fact that some of the objectives actually conflict with each other. The most familiar instance is that appraisal related to salary decisions is generally found to be ineffective at providing realistic performance-improvement discussion or improved feedback between boss and subordinate. None the less, Long's survey[2] reported that 40 per cent of companies associate their appraisals with salary decisions. In a later IPD survey,[3] only 30 per cent reported such a link, but 65 per cent of appraisees said appraisals were used to identify training and development needs.

Methods of appraisal

Obviously enough, the methods chosen for an appraisal scheme or for individual appraisal discussions ought to relate to the objectives which have been set. An open, frank and free exchange about problems in performance is more feasible, and more likely to be attained, if the objectives are to improve immediate feedback between boss and subordinate and to identify performance issues relevant to both of them. If the appraisal is to be used for succession planning or salary determination, open, frank and free exchange is likely to be inhibited.

Similarly, the extent to which the subordinate is asked to contribute to the appraisal, perhaps through conducting a self-appraisal, is also influenced both in prospect and in actuality by the subordinate's knowledge of how the information will be used.

Recognition of benefits

The major advantage of appraisal is that people like to know what is expected of them, how they are measured and what their boss thinks of their performance. The normal day-to-day processes of managerial relationships do not satisfy these needs. Too often, however, appraisal schemes pursue sophisticated objectives but fail to meet basic needs.

For appraisal to be effective and useful at any level other than that of recording words for longer-range salary or succession-planning issues, those who conduct and participate in it both must see some positive benefits for themselves. All too often neither boss nor subordinate actually recognises such benefits. Bosses do not always recognise that benefits which may exist for them do not exist for their subordinates; equally, bosses and subordinates tend to have different perceptions about the potential benefits to each other.

Ownership

The question of who owns the appraisal scheme is actually associated with the last point. Appraisal schemes tend to be introduced, sold and maintained by personnel people, and are not owned in any real sense by the line managers. Line managers particularly will not feel they own the scheme if they have had no say in determining either the principle or the detailed procedures involved. Since the process tends to be difficult, and since the benefits tend not to be recognised by the individuals involved, it is understandable that line managers lack commitment.

The problem of securing their commitment is that the process of consulting all those who might feel they have the right to contribute to decisions on both principle and method is extremely time-consuming, and tends to be seen as unnecessary by the top people in an organisation who have been persuaded to accept appraisal. Desirable though it is to have such support at top level, this will not in itself secure involvement in the spirit of the appraisal system; it may simply lead to a grudging completion of forms rather than the genuine involvement which is necessary to achieve any of the potential objectives of appraisal.

This problem is particularly acute if the chosen objectives for appraisal include the identification of improved performance requirements and the improvement of feedback between boss and subordinate. These extremely difficult processes will not be undertaken successfully if bosses are 'doing' appraisal because they are required to rather than because they have been helped to see how it could benefit them.

Rewards

The perception of benefit by boss and subordinate, and preferably both, provides one kind of reward. If the boss believes that the appraisal process will actually help him secure more effective performance from an individual or department, then he will expect to receive a psychological reward. The reward may be positive – the feeling by himself or others that things are improving – or negative – the reduction of criticism and unpleasantness. The reward may be the purely personal one of having carried out a difficult managerial task well.

It is not easy to find examples of managers securing rewards from appraisal. In practice they get rewarded for their performance on

issues usually seen as more directly relevant to managerial effectiveness. A manager may be lucky enough to have a boss who is
interested in effective appraisal, but the organisation usually provides only a negative reward – the absence of nagging from personnel for not having completed the forms (which of course have little
to do with effective appraisal).

There is much more scope than is generally recognised for re-
warding managers for undertaking, and doing a good job on, appraisal. At the least, they can be helped to see how they can get
personal satisfaction out of doing it well. More ambitiously, the organisation could develop the processes by which managers are given
feedback on the quality and effectiveness of their appraisals.

Previous experience

Appraisal schemes nowadays rarely spring up as totally new activities in a company; previous experience either within the organisation
or with previous employers will obviously affect the enthusiasm
with which particular managers enter the scheme and influence the
way they behave.

Managerial style requirements

One of the difficulties for many bosses is that effective appraisal for
improvement and development purposes requires them to behave in
a way foreign to their normal managerial style. They are required to
be reflective and analytical and to be good listeners rather than authoritative, immediate decision-takers leading a discussion. Not
many managers have the flexibility to behave or, at least, to behave
credibly in this way. They need to be helped to recognise the behaviour which particular appraisal objectives require them to adopt.
Where they are unable to adapt their behaviour, they need help to
deal with the consequences of that inability.

Wider context

Although appraisal essentially has to do with the individual's contribution, appraisal discussions seem too rarely to take note of the fact that the individual is performing within a particular context. The results achieved may have been achieved more or less easily depending on factors in the general environment: the difficulties of staffing within a department and difficulties of relationships with outside agencies or departments. The absence of this kind of consideration explains why appraisals of particular individuals tend to slide up and down a scale of perceived achievement: not enough weight has been placed on the factors which have affected either good or bad performance or achievement of particular results. Most important of all, of course, is the contribution of the boss to the subordinate's own performance. It would be an unusual manager who registered this on a subordinate's appraisal form, which is why many appraisal systems use the 'grandfather' to introduce that kind of comment, usually through a special section on the form.

Appraisal bureaucracy and appraisal help

The comments above suggest that the help most appraisal schemes need from personnel is assistance in clarifying objectives and ensuring that the objectives chosen for an appraisal scheme are appropriate and valid. Individual managers also need help in dealing with particular appraisal circumstances. However, what most personnel departments provide is important but insufficient: persistence in the bureaucracy of appraisal through designing forms and monitoring how many of their staff particular managers have appraised.

Appraising potential

Some management development schemes emphasise development for future rather than current jobs. The identification of potential is often the least satisfactory part of the appraisal system and can appear as a misplaced symbolic gesture rather than an effective management process. It might well be better to separate it from the normal review – but most organisations do not. A manager capable of helping to identify performance issues with his subordinates is not necessarily equally capable of identifying the same person's potential for other jobs in the organisation, perhaps even for his own job. The discussion of potential and career planning between boss and subordinate has different psychological and control problems. A substantial section on potential and career planning follows in Chapter 5, with comments particularly on assessment centres. These have often been proposed to avoid the errors of judgement about potential mentioned above.

Drawing out development needs

It is also true that many managers find it difficult to switch from reviewing performance to talking about training and development; they give these issues far too little attention. It could therefore be sensible to separate them. Many firms do so on the form, but do not require the discussion to be held separately. It is difficult to get the manager to give time for both sets of review. There is a limit to the amount of time that a manager will spend on something which offers few rewards and has many difficulties.

Standards used in appraisal – performance or personality?

Many systems now concentrate on assessing against pre-agreed priorities or objectives or against the job description rather than against personality characteristics such as initiative, dependability or judgement. These characteristics are extremely difficult to define and measure.

Where appraisal schemes concentrate on results rather than characteristics, some of the problems of different standards, halo or skew rating become less crucial. The review by Long[2] says that 63 per cent of forms deal with results, but that 29 per cent have rating of personality traits – some forms cover both.

Some people have experimented with generalised views of managerial skills like the Fayol headings of planning, organising, motivating, leading and controlling. Although these appear better than the personality characteristics they are in practice very difficult to define in terms which are acceptable to both parties. Which two managers, for example, would agree on what is meant by being effective as a leader? The most difficult, but the best, approach is to identify the explicit managerial behaviour needed.

The form

Some managers will say that the best form is a blank sheet of paper; others prefer lots of leading questions which help them to identify the course of the appraisal discussion. Standard forms tend to be required not for discussion and feedback between manager and subordinate, but for some other reason – usually to contribute to the organisation's succession or resource plan.

The skills required

The failure of some appraisal processes has clearly been due in some instances to the absence of the required skills. Many managers are simply not capable without formal training (and some not even then) of conducting appraisal in a way which satisfactorily meets even one of the potential objectives, let alone many. Their capacity to make accurate judgements or to listen or give feedback which can be heard and acted on is all too often lacking. Even when managers have learnt the theory of effective appraisal processes, including the skills of listening and effective feedback, applying the theory away from the training course or the guidance booklet often causes difficulties. A fascinating example of this is to be found in the x and y case discussed by Argyris.[4] His experience is that even people (including personnel specialists) who have defined the problems and established what behaviour is desirable in advance, will revert to precisely those behaviours which they know in principle are negative and ineffective when reviewing an ineffective subordinate in a formal training context.

Individual results from appraisal

The extent to which this process actually improves performance, where that is one of the immediately desired outcomes, is more often demonstrated by anecdote than by research. The impact on the identification of appropriate development processes is often even more tenuous. This is in part because many appraisal forms have been designed with unhelpful headings or boxes in terms of identifying what those development needs and, more particularly, what the development solutions might be. Thus a form may include two very large but relatively empty boxes:

- What are the development needs?
- What solutions do you recommend?

Sometimes forms will include questions on whether a manager should attend a training course to remedy any weaknesses identified. When associated with the catalogue of training courses that some particularly large organisations produce, this kind of form design has the advantage of tending to produce more specific recommendations, but sometimes on a standardised basis not related to the real needs of different individuals.

Either as part of an assessment of potential, or perhaps more helpfully as part of the preparation of a general development programme, desirable job moves can sometimes be highlighted by the design of the form. This can be very helpful, providing again that it is related to the real needs of individuals rather than to some overgeneralised statement that all managers should be moved at intervals of 2.5 years.

Most helpful of all would be the introduction into these formal Type 3 processes of references to Type 2 opportunities and action plans. This relates very much to the last point about job moves, which will often be undertaken either as a result of a Type 3 analysis, but more frequently offer Type 1 learning experiences because the reasons for them are purely managerial. Most opportunities for learning from the job will be identified between a manager and the subordinate. There is no reason at all – in fact every reason to the contrary – to separate these from Type 3 processes. In addition to the normal requests for formal development processes such as courses, job moves, appointments to committees or task forces, the kind of opportunities spelled out in the previous chapter can at least be referred to in this formal appraisal process.

There is no need for a long list of Type 2 opportunities or recent events; but the appraisal process should facilitate the continuing identification of opportunities and actions throughout the year. A review of managerial performance should therefore include a review of the extent to which Type 2 opportunities have been identified and plans undertaken to take advantage of them during the year. The reality of the managerial learning provided by Type 2 could be identified again, since the appraisal would concern itself not simply with achieved direct managerial results, but with the extent to which the manager involved has learnt from success or failure. While this review should in the main be a day-by-day/week-by-week basis, it would be extremely valuable for it to be summarised, and perhaps planned, on a more forward-looking basis through the opportunity which a Type 3 appraisal process would provide.

Shifting the boundaries in appraisal

One of the undoubted shifts over recent years has been away from a purely downwards judgemental review and feedback by the boss to a more participative process where boss and subordinate share the appraisal. This involves the subordinate in conducting some kind of self-appraisal, sometimes by using the normal form and filling in the details for later comparison with the boss's views; sometimes the individual has a separate, deliberately designed self-appraisal form.

While there can be problems about the degree of frankness and openness – particularly in organisations where these are not other-wise encouraged – self-appraisal, although it calls for additional skills from boss and subordinate, can be much more productive than a purely top-down appraisal.

A rather more recent development is a formal process by which the subordinate appraises the boss. This can work only in certain kinds of organisation; some in which I have been employed would not have been able to cope. However, it can be very productive in its discussion of how realistic a boss's perceptions of his or her own performance are. Even more importantly, it can be helpful in secur-ing change by one or both parties.

There is the possibility of team appraisal. This was most fre-quently encountered in the 1970s through organisation development and process consultation, where teams reviewed their own perform-ance. It has been suggested by Margerison[5] that team appraisal can be complementary to individual appraisal. I have not encountered other references to this or seen examples of it in practice, but in prin-ciple it seems attractive. It can raise issues which individual ap-praisal does not and it has the advantage of recognising the reality that managerial work involves team as well as individual achieve-ment.

360-degree appraisal

This process takes further the idea of individuals acquiring more in-formation about performance than they receive from their direct managers. It provides for feedback from three sources: direct man-ager, colleagues and direct reports/subordinates. Some organisations are experimenting with the idea of getting information also from clients or customers, a potentially valuable concept within an organ-isation, but even more difficult to gain from outside the organisation.

Clearly this process provides more feedback – a representative sample, rather than a complete collection of colleagues and subordi-nates, would probably produce a minimum of eight people. However, the real point is that the feedback not only presents a wider picture, but often a more accurate one. Colleagues and subordinates in particular are more likely to present their real views through a structured questionnaire response than they would do face to face. The accuracy of the comments depends in part, of course, on the construction of the questionnaire, and also on guarantees to respondents of anonymity. The comparison of the views of others with a self-appraisal can produce surprising results, sometimes in a positive and sometimes in a disappointing direction.

The enormous potential of this process, particularly compared with standard downwards appraisal, has been described, for example, by Ward[6] and Jacobs.[7] These authors, however, also show the care and preparation that needs to go into both the general design of a 360-degree process, and to enabling participants to make effective use of it. Indeed, Ward talks about possible needs for trained facilitators. While this may indeed be the best way of getting the best results out of such a process, it does raise questions about the economics of the process, since facilitation, except for perhaps a few people at the most senior levels, would be too expensive for most organisations to contemplate. In an excellent article McCauley and Moxley[8] bring out some important points. First, there is the question of whether the emphasis is on performance or development – essentially, of course, the same issue as occurs on traditional appraisal schemes. As they also comment, while consistent feedback across many raters is difficult to ignore, the process can also bring out significant differences of view which may contain important lessons. Finally, they emphasise that the process is not, ultimately, just about assessment but about improvement, and therefore the whole approach must be geared to producing specific improvement goals.

Although the potential for this process, and its inherent legitimacy in terms of giving participants accurate and usable feedback, seem clear, a significant caution must be expressed. We are familiar with many management development processes over the years that have been proclaimed as major and exciting developments to remove many of our problems. So far there is no significant evaluation available on a long-term basis of the success of this method. We have glowing reports from relatively short-term benefits.

Different purposes, different answers

One of the difficulties is that different people have different needs for different appraisal information at different places in the organis- ation. An answer which encourages effective individual discussion between boss and subordinate is not equally useful to a personnel man who wants to make a more effective resource and succession plan. Given the inaccuracies inherent in the nature of the discussion itself, ie the extent to which boss and subordinate actually identify the appropriate issues, and the probable difficulties of accurately recording what was actually said, it makes more sense to give greater weight to objectives relating to the discussion itself rather than the data produced. This leads towards a view of appraisal as:

- a discussion about how and why the subordinate is presently per- forming in his job
- identifying how the subordinate might perform more effectively
- identifying ways in which he or she might set about performing more effectively
- occurring in a context which leaves the subordinate, boss and or- ganisation all satisfied that action is being taken to raise the level of individual performances.

I once had the experience of acquiring a new personnel director boss who was very bothered by the fact that different divisions and companies in our group had different appraisal forms. I had diffi- culty in persuading him that they might actually represent what dif- ferent divisions actually wanted or needed. He wanted consistency because he thought it would help him. In a context in which decen- tralisation and empowerment are constant organisational buzz- words, it seems likely that monolithic, one-version appraisal forms or systems will be seen as both undesirable and ineffective.

Measuring your current position

We have reviewed the major issues about appraisal. You might find it helpful to review your own position against each of the major headings identified. This is not an audit which can be satisfactorily achieved by giving yourself marks. The process might rather involve answering the following questions:

Exercise

1 On how many of these issues would I rate my current organisation's position as satisfactory?
2 On how many would I find my organisation's position unsatisfactory?
3 What major changes have occurred in our appraisal process over the last five years? What caused the changes?
4 How many explicit objectives do we have in our appraisal scheme? Do we have concealed or implicit objectives as well? Do they conflict with each other?
5 Who owns the appraisal scheme?
6 How far up the organisation does formal appraisal go? Does the chief executive appraise his or her direct reports?
7 What is our position on the relationship of appraisal and judgement on salaries?
8 Is our appraisal process based on personality characteristics, performance/results, behaviours/skills? What is the reason for whatever basis we have chosen?
9 If you are setting up an appraisal scheme for the first time, on which of the potential objectives for such a scheme do you intend to focus?

References

1 FLETCHER C. *Appraisal.* London, IPM, 1993.
2 LONG P. *Performance Appraisal Revisited.* London, IPM, 1986.
3 HARRIS RESEARCH CENTRE. *Appraisal Survey.* London, IPD, 1996.

4   ARGYRIS C. *Reasoning Learning and Action.* San Francisco, CA, Jossey-Bass, 1982.
5   MARGERISON C. 'Team appraisal – leadership and organisation'. *Development Journal.* Vol. 4, No. 2, 1983.
6   WARD P. 'A 360 degree turn for the better'. *People Management.* 9 February 1995.
7   JACOBS R. *and* FLOYD M. 'A bumper crop of insights'. *People Management.* 9 February 1995.
8   McCAULEY C. *and* MOXLEY R. 'Developmental 360 degree'. *Career Development International.* Vol. 1, No. 3, 1996.

Further reading relevant to this chapter is shown in Chapter 13.

Potential, Promotion and Evaluation

Potential and promotion

These are linked, but not synonymous, issues. An individual needs to have potential for growth to work successfully when promoted to a higher-level post. However, an employee can have potential for a range of different jobs, which do not involve promotion: a sales manager can move to a marketing manager's job which is evaluated as being at exactly the same level; for the move to be successful the manager involved needs to have the potential to acquire the skills necessary for effective performance in the new job.

There are, essentially, two factors involved:

- the capacity of the organisation to identify the skills, knowledge and experience necessary to perform well in the jobs it currently has, and (a very important issue in some companies) jobs of a different kind it believes it may have in the future
- the organisation's capacity to measure those aspects of individuals' current performance, and those capacities which they are thought to have, in a way which makes prediction about their future performances accurate.

It would be an understatement to say that both these requirements present major difficulties. Job performance requirements ought to be identified through up-to-date reviews of the managerial content of existing jobs. Where such statements do not exist, then the organisation is compounding its capacity for error. It will obviously have had little basis for assessing the performance of current job-holders, and it will have nothing against which to assess the current abilities and future potential of individuals to do those jobs in the future.

There are major problems in making accurate judgements about the performance of individuals in relation to jobs different from those they currently occupy. There are problems in establishing a sound basis for judgement about current performance; the problems multiply when those judgements are used to predict performance in a different job. At least performance in a current job is being assessed by someone who has a responsibility for it and has grounds (however confused) for saying, 'That is the performance I am looking for.' That same manager can also reasonably be expected to make a judgement about the potential of a subordinate to perform the manager's own job. But when a boss is asked to look further afield and to make predictions about performance further up the line, or in different functions, in different countries, in different divisions or in different sizes of organisations, judgement becomes extremely fallible.

For these reasons researchers and specialists often advise that the making of judgements about promotion and general potential should be separated from the normal appraisal process (Chapter 4). This is rarely done, because most managers regard the connection between reviewing current performance and making predictions about the future as entirely logical (which it ought to be); moreover, many managers would be most unwilling to double the amount of time they give to considering such issues.

If the normal appraisal process includes judgements about potential, more sophisticated organisations will provide questions which are intended to focus on different aspects of a manager's performance. The more specific the focus of the normal appraisal process, the more necessary it is to provide some guidance to managers on the kind of things which might indicate potential. For instance, a manager may be very good at problem-solving, but in the sense of solving tactical, operational – basically firefighting – problems. A section on promotion or potential might ask the reviewing manager to identify those aspects of problem-solving which indicate the potential to operate in a more strategic, forward-looking way.

Formal schemes now often include other processes no longer within the control of the reviewing manager or the reviewer plus grandfather. We will now look at the most widely used of these.

- Some *psychological tests* purport to measure particularly significant characteristics. They may be helpful in measuring such dimensions as creativity, problem-solving and adaptability. If these are deemed necessary characteristics for someone to be moved successfully into another job, and if the tests are valid, then the tests can make a contribution.

- *Panel or group interviews* are essentially similar to recruitment interviews, although they may deal with prospective potential rather than immediate appointments. Most research on these processes seems to indicate that they face most of the problems of normal selection interviewing, complicated by the difficulty of getting any group or panel actually to agree on criteria or on the process for the interview.
- *Informal identification processes* include asking line managers or staff advisers, particularly personnel people, to produce lists of people with potential. These lists can be generated by a review of existing appraisal information or by visits carried out by a personnel specialist charged with the responsibility of identifying 'high-flyers'. In any combination, this kind of process leads to accusations of 'the old boy network', subjectivity and unfairness.
- *Management simulation processes* derive largely from officer selection analogies. This kind of process involves putting people through exercises which simulate the conditions of a job different from that currently held. The simulation may be very close – a carefully designed in-tray exercise – or it may be very distant, as with so-called leadership exercises. These usually involve some version of physical outdoor activities, in which the performance of individuals in either individual pursuits such as canoeing or abseiling, or in a team activity, can be closely monitored and assessed. When carefully designed against properly established criteria, simulation processes of this kind carry a degree of surface validity and provide at least some objective evidence. However, the greater their specificity and, therefore, their potential validity, the greater the expense involved in actually running them. The temptation is to use one of the existing general exercises or someone else's in-tray exercise – which takes us back to the recurring problem of validity.
- *Assessment centres* usually combine in-tray and other simulation processes with group discussion, group tasks and interviews. Again if these are designed against clear criteria, and particularly if they are established specifically for individual organisations,

then they can provide useful objective evidence. The same qualification, namely that this is often an expensive process, applies.
The assessment centre process can be used purely for judging
potential, but it can also be used to establish development needs
and may indeed be called a development centre. It is therefore a
particularly powerful tool, but like many tools it is dangerous or
ineffective if improperly used. For that reason it is given a section
on its own later in this chapter.

- *Intuitive methods* essentially comprise a senior manager, after
  collecting a variety of data about an individual, deciding that he
  or she 'has what it takes'. As in other areas of their work, senior
  managers are sometimes right in their intuition. They tend to remember when they were right more often than when they were
  wrong. Whatever the merits of intuition, it is a process which
  leaves everyone, except the person with the intuition and the person about whom the intuition has been positive, unhappy and un-
  convinced.

- *Assignments and special responsibilities.* Situations in which individuals are put through particularly pressing or stressful new or
  additional responsibilities are a way of testing them for the future.
  These can include being sent to small units with no support, or
  being sent to a different country or involved in projects outside
  the normal range of experience. These are variants on using normal appraisal, ie achieved performance, as the basis for making
  judgements. The difference is that assignments can be specially
  identified as having a particular relevance to a future job.

  A particularly important example of this was seen when Reg
  Jones, the Chief Executive Officer at General Electric in the
  United States, set about planning his own succession. (This case
  is described in a little more detail on p. 105.) It essentially included giving stretching assignments and increased visibility to
  10 potential successors.

The evidence suggests that any organisation which relies on only
one of these possible methods is exposing itself to major risks in attempting to identify and plan for the movement of its individual
managers, whether sideways or upwards. The methods an organis-

ation chooses to use is, of course, related to its level of sophistication about management development and other aspects of organisational culture. The confidence of managers in their own ability to make judgements about potential and promotability is rarely affected by data showing how fallible they are. This is because organisations do not normally carry out reviews of predictions that were made even two years earlier – let alone those which were made five years earlier – to establish at least some objective measure of managerial judgement. One piece of American research showed that in two successive years there was a 50 per cent turnround in a list of judgements made about individuals with outstanding growth potential. One reason for this is that judgements made about an individual very early in a managerial career are particularly likely to be unfounded, since virginal, high-IQ people untouched by industrial experience may seem to have extraordinary potential. It was said of the Roman Emperor Galba that 'no one would have doubted his capacity as Emperor if he had never been placed in that position'.

The comments so far have all been made from the organisational perspective: how do organisations make the most successful judgements? But as Lee[1] shows, individuals themselves make major interventions in the process. They do so in part by their own decisions about whether they want to pursue jobs elsewhere in the organisation, whether by promotion or sideways moves. Some decide not to, but do not necessarily indicate this to their organisations. Management mythology tends to concentrate much more on those who deliberately set out to be promoted. Such individuals then make judgements about how they are to secure promotion. They look for hints and information about the kind of activities and behaviour which are seen to lead to the promotion of people to the sort of jobs they fancy. Such individuals will tend to make themselves highly visible, will be greatly concerned about internal politics and will seek to form relationships of influence and attachment to others whom they think will be useful. Lee observed things in one particular organisation which will be recognisable to many of us. Managers reviewing the question 'What do I have to do to get promotion?' saw three ways:

- a fairly large minority who believed they had to work hard at their narrow task
- a majority who believed they had to achieve at their narrow task, but also at other work-related activities
- a few who were concerned with other ways of creating the right impression in the right places.

Lee's essential proposition is that 'textbook theory of promotion processes is based on abstract ideas about how formal systems should operate. As in most areas of management, this proves a poor guide to reality.'

In a much larger-scale exercise conducted by London and Stumpf,[2] the dominant factor influencing choice was the decision-maker's personal knowledge of the candidate or of the person recommending a candidate. As they also say, motivated, astute managers even without formal career-planning programmes seek information about opportunities and make their interests known.

An additional dimension is given by the common requirement to identify 'high-flyers'. This concept is based on the idea that a small number of people have significantly different (greater) potential from the generality of managers, that they can be identified early and that the benefits of doing so are that they can be put through processes of management development more quickly. As Hirsch has found from her research,[3] high-flyer schemes seem to generate more problems than solutions. The basis for judgement of early potential is unsound. The allocation of particular distinction to a small group of people tends to create jealousies among others, not least because the criteria for such identification are either unknown or unrecognisable. All too often, being a high-flyer and being put on a 'fast track' tends to mean that people are moved around quickly in a way which encourages superficial rather than substantially effective performance.

Then there is the question of the extent to which the organisation can actually predict its future requirements. The process of quantitative planning, with replacement tables, succession plans and so on, is covered later in this chapter. Here we simply need to note the more qualitative difficulty of actually establishing what the needs are: for existing jobs, for jobs as they may need to be done in five years' time or, even more problematically, for jobs that do not yet exist but may need to exist in the future. Again it is possible to generalise about the skills and competences that will be required, and some ideas about the future are reviewed in the next chapter. Any attempt to get managers to envision the skills required for the future as a way of making more effective promotion decisions becomes very fraught. It is not an area in which most managers have much skill in assessment, and only a few have the intellectual curiosity to be interested in the attempt.

You may like to test your own organisation's procedures for identifying potential and promotion with an exercise:

Exercise

1 Which of the processes indicated above are used in my organisation?
2 Which are the most important in practice?
3 Have we recently tested the accuracy of our predictions?
4 What could we do to improve our processes?

It must finally be noted that the potential and promotion of ethnic minorities and women are a special issue. We will look at this in greater detail in Chapter 10; but it is important to say here that even apparently objective processes for decision-making can be invalidated in relation to these two groups by the often deeply held but inaccurate stereotypes of many managers.

Assessment centres and development centres

Assessment centres now have a relatively lengthy history. In principle they go back to the officer selection processes adopted in the UK during the 1939–45 war. Until the 1980s assessment centres were mainly used for selection; the initial focus on selection for an immediate current job was sometimes broadened to include identification of potential for appointment to different and probably more senior jobs. The feedback on perceived performance which was inherent in the design of effective selection-directed assessment centres was gradually recognised as identifying individual development needs. Evidence about the effectiveness of such feedback for developmental purposes was either thin or negative. The idea of assessment centres focusing explicitly, and perhaps even primarily, on development was a logical extension.

The essence of the traditional selection-based assessment centre process was the use of a variety of simulations, exercises, tests, discussions and interviews. These were all directed towards the 'objective' evaluation of the performance of candidates against a desired list of skills or characteristics. The essential principles are those of the measurement of observed behaviour which is related to desired skills (preferably organisation-specific), with judgements made by at least a proportion of independent assessors, and explicit feedback to participants.

The validity of this process for selection purposes, certainly when properly designed and implemented, is now well established (see Sackett and Ryan[4]) . The value for the purposes of individual development, as compared with immediate selection or the identification of longer-term potential, has, however, been less well studied. It does seem clear that attempts to double up on objectives by adding development purposes to basic selection are unsuccessful. This should be no surprise to anyone who has been involved in any form of management training, where a similar confusion of objectives over development and performance assessment leads to failure in both objectives. So a simple association between selection and development is unlikely to be productive. From a development point of view, much the most successful experiences have been achieved where the centre process has been explicitly aimed at identifying individual development, normally − and sensibly − associated with individual career plans. However, if the career-planning element becomes part of feedback into the organisation's formal career-planning process, this can create another confusion of objectives. Individuals who may be prepared to participate honestly in a centre whose objective is their personal development may be less prepared to do so when they think that the results of their performance may provide material for judgements against them later.

Most work on the use of assessment centres for the identification of potential has been done with young and very junior managers, dating back particularly to the massive studies done in the American company, AT & T.[5] Accurate feedback early in their working lives enables individuals to make better judgements about the jobs they choose to do. While the success of such programmes in predicting potential seems to have been well demonstrated, their success in practice in helping people to make career choices does not seem to have been well researched, no doubt because such research would be extremely difficult to do. Dulewicz[6] provides a tough set of criteria for assessment centres, including impact on career. Woodruffe[7] offers a good guide to design and implementation of assessment centres and emphasises the important issue of integrating them with other management development processes; Shuttleworth and Prescott[8] give specific company case examples.

Assessment centres which identify current performance levels, and consequently development needs, may be called career development workshops, or personal development centres. Perhaps because this development is relatively new, research so far seems to indicate that such workshops, though highly valued by many participants, have not yet been proved to be effective. Again assuming that the programme has been well designed, the careful and valid identification of performance issues can be achieved. Beyond that, such workshops offer a substantial period of time to work on the development needs, and allow those involved to produce their own plans for tackling these needs.

It is more difficult to show that they result in concrete action. Outside the positive and encouraging context of the workshop, back in managerial reality, the likelihood of plans being implemented will be significantly reduced. However, given the level of commitment actually generated by individuals on such programmes, it would seem unreasonable to presume that the failure rate would be as high as it is on normal management training programmes, where similar aspirations and plans might be developed. Because the workshop operates at a much more specific level, and probably at a greater level of detail than time usually allows on most courses, the success rate may actually be both quantitatively and qualitatively higher. How much higher it is, and at what cost in terms of resources, is something which needs to be assessed by the organisation using the process. It would also need to look at why plans were not activated, if this turned out to be the case, and the extent to which this was due to the unrealistically high level of optimism generated on a workshop or to the organisational environment.

Boehm[9] gives an excellent review of some of these issues. The weakness of her article is that it does not bring out sufficiently the confusion and conflict over objectives which we indicated earlier (though she does point out that assessment centres designed for development probably need to be twice as long as those adopted for selection). An interesting particular case, with a detailed timetable, is given by Griffiths and Allen,[10] and Goodge[11] provides some good illustrations of learning-centred issues. You may wish to clarify your understanding of assessment centres and their place in management development through the following exercise.

Exercise

1 Read the article by Boehm. Have you experienced the purposes she has described? Which might be applicable to your own organisation? What weaknesses in your current processes might be remedied?
2 Read the article by Griffiths and Allen. If you were a manager in the organisation described, what concerns would you have about your involvement in such a workshop? On the information given, would you see the workshop as being primarily about:
   ● the improved capacity of the organisation to meet its own objectives?
   ● having improved information on which to base your own career plan?
   ● the clear identification of personal development needs, and plans to meet them?
3 Would you see any conflict between these three in your own feelings about the workshop?

It should finally be noted that existing descriptions of development centres rarely indicate that attention is given to the individual learning processes of participants. Most descriptions produce statements about the identification of performance needs and the production of personal development plans 'using a variety of development processes'. Specific, direct and individual attention is rarely paid to the learning process involved in carrying out any of the planned activities, and the likely differences in learning styles between individuals. (The general point about differing individual approaches to learning is covered in more detail in Chapter 11.)

Career planning

This section concentrates on the organisational processes used to identify career stages and to plan managerial careers. Chapters 7 and 11 look in more detail at the ways in which organisational plans may be put into effect by individuals, and ways in which individuals can take their own initiatives about their own careers.

An organisation is usually concerned to arrange its managerial jobs in an ascending hierarchical ladder, with the planned progression of individuals up that ladder. Where an organisation has carried out the kind of detailed job reviews indicated in this chapter and in Chapter 6, it is possible to establish a developmental hierarchy based on significant changes of content. That hierarchy may conveniently coincide with a hierarchy drawn up for the purposes of job evaluation, with an organisation chart or with job values as reflected by salary. Not surprisingly, however, judgements made for these other purposes may not dovetail with career planning.

These significant stages, in a formal sense, will therefore vary with the nature and size of any particular organisation. The five stages in Figure 5.1 will be found in many organisations, although the detailed descriptions employed are appropriate to commercial business.

In the Civil Service, local government or the National Health Service, the stages listed in Figure 5.1 will not be different. Readers from such organisations should tackle the following exercise:

Exercise

What are the major stages of careers in my organisation, defined by significant changes in accountability and content of managerial jobs? Are they more, less, or much the same as the levels indicated in Figure 5.1?

Figure 5.1
Management Career Stages

Supervisory function – detailed control of 'direct' workers
Functional management – managing the work of a complete area such as sales or production, through supervisors or lower management
Cross-functional management – involving the management of a number of associated functions; examples could be a production director responsible for manufacture, safety, quality
Profit centre management – involving full accountability for all the functions and both revenue and cost
Plural profit centre management – often at director level, involving a number of profit centres, eg separate companies, in a division or in a total group

Formal management development can then be designed to meet the changing needs of these different career stages, and can also be designed to incorporate the wishes of individual managers within the organisation. When organisations talk about career planning, they are usually talking about taking people through different kinds of formal process which contribute to the development of individual careers, but are not necessarily linked to a formal career structure. From a practical point of view it is probably the case that effort is more sensibly directed at the particularities of jobs rather than grand statements about developing people for level 3 in a career plan. The more significant point is almost certainly the one we hinted at earlier: the organisation's career-planning process ought to be regarded as a complete system to do with managerial careers rather than just those aspects of it which are clearly addressed by development processes. An effective career plan will probably include issues outside the job responsibility of a management development adviser, but certainly the responsibility of a personnel director, and even more appropriately, the chief executive. The plan will include:

- *clear job descriptions* which, in addition to their basic managerial merits, also provide clarity for identifying potential career moves
- *a reward system* which provides both recognisably different financial and psychological satisfactions between levels
- *job selection processes* which provide equality of treatment between insiders and outsiders
- *blockage removal processes* which enable organisations to remove dead wood or live wood blocking the growth of even livelier wood.

Mayo[12] provides an excellent review of both organisational and personal aspects of career.

As Herriot[13] has argued, an increasing gap has developed between what an organisation can offer in terms of a career and what all individuals used to expect – long-term security. My research has shown how great the distance can be between what the organisation was attempting in planning careers and what individuals have experienced. Individuals' views about their desired careers may be quite different from the organisation's. Whatever the organisation deems desirable in terms of total career plans, it should incorporate processes for finding out individuals' own views. I remember a case in an organisation where I worked, in which our plans placed considerable emphasis on a move to be made by a functional manager into a profit centre management job (level 2 to level 4 on Figure 5.1). But the individual involved told me that not only did he not want to make the move, but that he had been quite unable to communicate this to his own boss, who kept insisting that it was 'the right move for you'.

The link between career planning and the previous sections on potential, promotion and assessment centres will no doubt be clear. If the processes you employ to determine achieved performance are not accurate, if your processes for reviewing potential are ineffective and if, as a consequence, your ability to help individuals improve their performance is flawed, then career planning collapses from the weight it places on these crumbling foundations. Even where these organisational aspects are well designed, appropriate and successfully geared to identifying performance, the individual and his or her personal career ambitions, and particularly issues of personal growth and development, will still affect the implementation of any career plan. All too often career planning would work very well if only people were not involved. Chapter 7 takes a number of these issues further.

There is then the question of the 'plateaued' manager. The career plan must look at the issue of whether, at any particular level, there are managers who are either ineffective or who are effective but hold back managers with higher potential. While hard decisions may be necessary, sensible career planning will take account of the fact that most organisations need managers who have settled at a particular point. They may be referred to as 'solid citizens' or a 'safe pair of hands', but the probability is that they provide the stability, experience and commitment to a job which ensures that the organisation survives. The needs of such managers, and the organisation's need of them, must be incorporated in the career plan. An article by Davies and Deighan[14] provides useful guidance on this subject.

Here is an exercise through which you can test your own current situation and views:

Exercise

How far do we have a fully integrated system for career planning? Does the integration include consideration of the non-management development aspects mentioned above?

Succession planning – or is it resource planning?

There are organisations in which no one thinks about who will fill managerial vacancies before they occur – but very few. There are many more in which managers say, 'Of course we give some

thought to it, but I could not say we have a plan as such.' If you pursue the 'as such' you find that what they mean is that from time to
time they have conversations about what might happen if X left job
Y, or someone confesses that he is going for a job interview with
another employer and managers then think about what they will do
if they have to replace him.

Sometimes there is a level of concern about the performance of an
existing job-holder, and there is again discussion about who might
take over if that particular manager is moved out.

Because such discussions are obviously loose, rarely address the
issues on a longer time-scale and are subject to the accident of who
is known by whom, they cannot properly be called succession planning. Yet maybe we have been too dismissive of this idea in the past.
It is certainly an inadequate process in most organisations. The idea
that an organisation will have to plan the replacement of capital
equipment well ahead, with careful identification of performance requirements, but that such a process is either unnecessary or impossible for managerial resources, should not be readily accepted. But
what we should do is build on what managers will be interested in
doing naturally, rather than ignoring it. If managers can be persuaded to take an interest in issues of succession through real problems as they occur, we should use that as the basis for an argument
in favour of planning to fill managerial positions.

My study of successful management development schemes shows
that in most, although not all, cases, the successful introduction of
planning has derived from what I call 'felt hurt'. (Indeed, this is also
true for formal management development in total.) Attempts to introduce succession planning 'because company X does it' or 'because companies of our size normally do this sort of thing' or
'because I have done a study of management development systems
in other companies, and this is an area of weakness for us' are less
likely to be effective. If we start from where managers are we are
more likely to engage their interest and attention even in formal
processes than if we start from our management development or
personnel professionalism which indicates what a company 'ought'
to do.

The basic concepts of succession planning are simple, which is no

Figure 5.2

Company X – Succession Plan

Job/Current holder	Succession within 2 yrs	Succession 2–5 yrs	Comments	Suggested action
Divisional chairman (David X)				
Divisional chairman (Derek Y)				
Finance director (Sydney G)				
Production director (John S)				
Sales director (Brian B)				
Personnel director (Paul M)				

doubt why they have been followed by a good many organisations. There are various ways of setting out what is involved and securing the information necessary. Figure 5.2 is a relatively simple one which I developed for one organisation.

Some organisations produce much more complex statements, with colour-coding indicating functional or product experience, age, and items like job-ranking or evaluation score.

To support this kind of plan (which without the action plan column completed is a statement of intention rather than a plan) a complementary document may be produced which takes people rather than jobs as its prime focus. This will, in fact, deal with the question of a career plan for individuals of the kind indicated in the previous section. An illustration, again deliberately in a relatively simple form, is given in Figure 5.3.

Figure 5.3
Company X – People Plan

	Career progression within 2 yrs	Career progression 2–5 years	Comments	Suggested action
David X				
Derek Y				
Sarah G				
John S				
Brian B				
Paul M				

Which jobs, which people?

An organisation may have to decide which jobs to consider and which people to consider for which jobs. An issue that tends to cause considerable debate is whether all the jobs at a particular level are considered in the succession-planning process: they normally are. The associated question is whether all the job-holders are considered as part of the plan; in other words whether the list of people for career progression is exactly the same as the list of job-holders. Here there are two problems. The first is that some job-holders may be considered to be 'plateaued' or even, indeed, beyond their peak and therefore not worthy of consideration in a succession-planning routine. The second problem is that there will be people with potential at levels beneath those covered by the jobs under consideration. This may in practice be covered by a separate list – known colloquially as the 'high-flyer' list, whatever formal title such as 'longer-term potential' it is given within the organisation.

The list of jobs to be considered in some organisations will be self-evident; some are small enough for the whole managerial population to be reviewed. In large multinationals with thousands of managers this is clearly impossible. Because of their huge size Unilever and BP make judgements about succession and career planning through committees which consider people at different levels. Perhaps the most characteristic phenomenon is that of an organis-

ation that reviews its top layer of jobs, which often seems to fall between 30 and 70. It will have a similar but not identical list of people
and it is by making decisions about these two groups that the tables
illustrated in Figures 5.2 and 5.3 are filled in.

The process by which the plan is produced and discussed varies
between organisations, but some fairly common elements are:

- collection of information from appraisals of the individuals concerned (where they exist)
- summarising that information, often by the personnel function
- alternatively, presenting the line manager with a chart empty of
  everything except the name of the job and job holder, and then
  asking him to insert his comments on the blank, or to talk through
  his comments with a personnel adviser
- collecting the information and putting it together in a file or
  binder to be presented to a decision-making group or to the chief
  executive alone
- the group or chief executive reviewing the comments made and
  making a final decision about the comments recorded on the succession plan
- the process by which the succession plan is eventually reviewed
  and adopted including either a special meeting of the board or
  management committee, or involving a special management development committee created for the purpose. In either case the
  significance of the process and the decision-making intensity are
  quite often registered by holding such a meeting off site, normally
  in a pleasant residential setting.

Sadly, for some organisations this is purely a paper exercise. In
spite of all the trouble that the organisation seems to have gone to,
the actual process of deciding succession frequently takes place as
if the succession plan had never been produced. I suspect that the
well-intentioned process of taking people away from their normal
workplace actually contributes to this, because it makes the whole
thing so different from normal managerial decision-making. Of
course the intention is to enable people to concentrate fully on this
very important issue, rather than being distracted by phone calls or

'the likelihood of our being forced to attend to normal business issues'.

Another reason for the relative ineffectiveness of many succession plans is that they are initially designed and drafted by personnel people. The question of ownership mentioned in Chapter 2 applies strongly here. Making succession plans is too often seen as a purely personnel activity, not one owned by line management. Paradoxically, the greater the level of influence and sophistication of personnel, the more likely it is that they will produce and carry out, for at least a period of time, a succession-planning process which line managers regard as too complicated. Wallum[15] makes this point well.

Of course some organisations are successful, but consideration of causes of failure will perhaps help others avoid error. My own experience is that the succession-planning process is in fact rather too easily adopted by some line managers. It is a great relief to be able to make hypothetical decisions, rather than to engage with the sordid reality of decisions which have immediate consequences.

One successful case is the experience of General Electric in the United States. Some years ago its then chief executive, Reg Jones, identified as one of his prime concerns that there should be an internal candidate identified and developed for his job before he retired. He himself described the process he went through. This involved first of all drawing up a list of 10 people with high potential. This was narrowed down to three before his eventual successor, Arthur Walsh, was chosen and put in place. One interesting point here is the number of potential people who were considered. (Another is that they were tested by stretching assignments.)

It is sensible here to repeat a familiar message: decisions will be only as good as the information on which they are based. Alternative sources of information are listed in the section on potential. My own experience has been that the collection of information from a variety of sources has helped make decisions more realistic, but that the sheer volume of papers can be unmanageable. As an adviser I therefore developed a process of producing shorter pen pictures of the individuals involved in a succession plan. These summarised all the information available, from appraisal, psychological assessment, personal development discussions, to even oral comments where these had been given by the individual's manager on some serious occasion (as compared with off-the-cuff comments made on a site visit).

A resource plan

In most organisations the real issue is not succession, or certainly not solely that. The real management development concern ought to be the performance of managers in their current jobs. It is more sensible to think in terms of a resource plan than a succession plan. The resource plan embraces a review of all current jobs and job holders and causes responsible managers to review whether current performance is satisfactory with a wide-angle lens rather than the narrow focus on a particular individual, which is the purpose of individual appraisal. The review is then directed neither at hypothetical succession needs – 'if X falls under a bus' – nor even at explicit age-based needs, but is directed at issues of immediate direct concern to senior managers. Making a resource plan is certainly a less comfortable process, because it is not about hypothetical decisions which may never need to be acted on. It requires managers to de-liver a verdict on the success or otherwise of managers in their current jobs. The great virtue of the process is precisely that it deals with reality. Although it is more uncomfortable, it is accepted by managers as more meaningful, providing there is an existing level of interest and concern about managers' current performance.

As with appraisal, we here pass over a vast volume of detail about alternative versions of succession plans or resource plans; see Further Reading for more. The main issue here is clarification of purpose; it is not really a question of whether we can design clever forms, but whether we can design and implement a process which provokes not only interest but effective action from line managers.

The following exercise may usefully test out your ideas on these issues:

Exercise

1 What do we have at the moment in terms of planning our future management succession?
2 If we have had formal plans, have we checked to see whether they are used when vacancies arise?
3 Do we have a clear plan at least for those jobs which will arise through retirement?
4 Is the concept of a succession plan attractive to my managers, or would they be more likely to respond to the challenge of a resource plan?

Recruitment and selection

When I went to talk to a general manager whom my company had recruited from outside about the development of his people, his response was brusque. 'I won't mention sows; but I will say that I can't make good products out of poor materials.' The section on career planning has indicated the significance of recruitment and selection policies: there is very little point in planning internal careers if that planning is thwarted by quite different recruitment and selection policies. In the context of this book, these are the crucial points about recruitment and selection. We do now recognise in management development that training and development can be the wrong answer to some managerial problems, which have nothing to do with the level of skill and a great deal to do with other sources of managerial failure. Similarly, formal management development processes may help to remedy weaknesses in managers once selected, but they cannot deal with a totally inappropriate selection.

Evaluating the system

Remarkably little work has been done on assessing whether the system works; even articles which set out to describe the system often turn out to be describing the effect of courses.

The fundamental questions to ask about the effectiveness of management development schemes are:

- Does the scheme achieve what it sets out to achieve? (Answering this question, particularly in relation to courses, has often been described as 'validation'.)
- Has the process produced results in terms of the demonstrated effectiveness of managers?

Our research on the development of directors took us into some very large organisations which had been carrying out management development for many years. At that time none of them had made a formal analysis of the effectiveness of their scheme, either overall or in terms of whether it provided for succession to the main board. One of the major reasons for this is contained in the first of the two questions above. Few of them had established any measurable objective for their schemes, or specified the particular achievements they desired from individual management development processes. Without such objectives it is very difficult to evaluate management development systems.

It is easier to assess particular parts of the system. Some organisations do this for courses, or the achievements of the formal appraisal scheme. Naturally enough, if the inputs, ie the elements of the system, have not been reviewed, then any claims that may be made about the system producing more effective managers (the second issue mentioned above) will be extremely suspect. Managers' effectiveness might have nothing at all to do with formal systems of management development; and indeed that was the burden of the evidence presented to us by a number of directors in our research.

The only other research in the UK was conducted by Easterby-Smith and his colleagues in the late 1970s.[16] Although the particular approach they described was lengthy and resource-consuming, it is perhaps surprising that the major principles used in their audit approach seem not to have been subsequently taken up by organisations. Their approach involved managers in the organisations reviewed assessing the extent to which management development systems were actually influencing development. A cynic might take the view that since their research showed, as mine did later, that systems were much less effective than the personnel owners believed, there is every reason for personnel people not to sponsor evaluation processes.

The questions used in my own study of systems were (excluding specifics about directors):

Exercise

1 Do you have a policy or statement about developing managers?
2 Have these policies or systems changed significantly over the last 15 years? If so, how?
3 What stimulated any changes?
4 Have there been partial or smaller-scale initiatives within the total system which have been important (eg a particular process or activity)?
5 Is there anything else about the history of management development in your organisation which will help us understand the comments we will receive?
6 How significant have formal processes been in developing managers as compared with informal processes?
7 Do you have any prospective changes to your management development processes in mind?
8 How do you evaluate your investment in management development?

You may work for an organisation which has already evaluated its management development system. If this has not in fact been done, then you could benefit from providing your own individual answers to the above questions.

You might then consider whether to set up a more substantial process of assessing your scheme either by a small-scale exercise conducted by yourself with a selected number of managers, or by conducting a more rigorous review probably involving an outside consultant, in order to be fully objective. As part of the process of deciding whether you want to undertake a more sophisticated review you should look at the book by Easterby-Smith already referred to, and also at his later publication.[17]

The main focus of this section so far has been on meeting the first purpose of evaluation: does the system actually operate in the way intended? The second issue is clearly whether it secures desirable results. There are some problems about what is meant by results. Here is a list of a number of things which might be intended, and actually produced:

- improved competence in the existing job
- competence developed in advance of a future job
- more effective career decisions
- turnover of managers at the level desired by the organisation (which might be nil or 50 per cent)
- enhanced commitment to the purposes of the organisation
- reduction of frustration within individual jobs
- increased satisfaction within individual jobs.

As far as most line managers are concerned, the real question is whether formal management development processes affect desired organisational performance; this is referred to in commercial organisations as 'the bottom line'. The evidence on this is again extremely scanty. Although *In Search of Excellence*,[18] for instance, says that excellent companies give more attention to management training and development, they do not show any direct correlation between excellence and management development. This is also true of the 15 excellent companies identified by Kotter,[19] who gives rather more detail on the management development processes the companies actually use; again his research seems to show a coincidence rather than a correlation between good management development practices and excellent company performance.

We turn finally to national reports on management development. These have usually become attached to the names of the prime authors, starting with Mant[20] on the experienced manager through to the reports of Professor Charles Handy and Professor John Constable in 1987.[21] Mant's report really describes the desirability and relative effectiveness of different approaches to management development. Handy and Constable are in a different but now long-standing tradition of criticising the amount of management development undertaken; Handy is also concerned with content. Although valuable in many respects, the reports do not contribute substantially to the issue of evaluation.

A report by PA[22] in 1986, which looked at formal schemes in eight countries, again confirmed the major validation problem. Only 46 per cent of respondents from 200 organisations with formal schemes thought them totally or largely successful. As a matter of national comparison it is perhaps interesting that 68 per cent of the respondents in the UK claimed to have a formal scheme, whereas the figures were only 26 per cent in France and 34 per cent in the former West Germany. Given the relative success of the economies of the last two countries, it might again be thought that evidence of the ultimate effectiveness of management development schemes is somewhat lacking. This would, however, be too harsh a conclusion to draw from a single survey.

Issues on the evaluation of courses are covered in Chapter 8.

Exercise

1 What are the greatest strengths, and the greatest weaknesses, of my organisation's processes for establishing potential?
2 What are the greatest strengths, and the greatest weaknesses in our promotion processes?
3 Do we do succession planning or resource planning? Is what we are doing satisfying the real needs of our organisation?
4 Which of the possible steps identified for evaluating our management development system would it be most sensible for me to take?

References

1 LEE R. 'The theory and practice of promotion processes'. *Leadership and Organisation Development Journal.* Vol. 6, No. 2 and Vol. 6, No. 4, 1985.

2 LONDON M. *and* STUMPF S. 'How managers make promotion decisions'. *Journal of Management Development.* Vol. 3, No. 1, 1984.

3 HIRSH W. *Career Management in the Organisation.* IMS Report No. 96, 1984.

4 SACKETT P. R. *and* RYAN A. M. 'A review of recent assessment centre research'. *Journal of Management Development.* Vol. 4, No. 4, 1985.

5 *ibid.*

6 DULEWICZ V. 'Improving assessment centres'. *Personnel Management.* June 1991.

7 WOODRUFFE C. *Assessment Centres.* London, IPD, 1994.

8 SHUTTLEWORTH T. *and* PRESCOTT R. 'The hard graft way to develop managers'. *Personnel Management.* November 1991.

9 BOEHM V. R. 'Using assessment centres for management development'. *Journal of Management Development.* Vol. 4, No. 4, 1985.

10 GRIFFITHS P. *and* ALLEN B. 'Assessment centres: breaking with tradition'. *Journal of Management Development.* Vol. 6, No. 1, 1987.

11 GOODGE P. 'Design options and outcomes'. *Journal of Management Development.* Vol. 14, No. 8, 1995.

12 MAYO A. *Managing Careers: Strategies for organizations.* London, IPM, 1991.

13 HERRIOT P. *The Career Management Challenge.* London, Sage, 1992.

14 DAVIES J. *and* DEIGHAN Y. 'The managerial menopause'. *Personnel Management.* March 1986.

15 WALLUM P. 'A broader view of succession planning'. *Personnel Management.* September 1993.

16 EASTERBY-SMITH M., BRANDEN E. *and* ASHTON D. *Auditing Management Development.* Aldershot, Gower, 1980.

17 EASTERBY-SMITH M. *Evaluation of Management Education Training and Development.* Aldershot, Gower, 1986.

18 PETERS T. *and* WATERMAN R. *In Search of Excellence.* London, Harper and Row, 1982.

19 KOTTER J. P. *The Leadership Factor.* Free Press, 1988.

20 MANT A. *The Experienced Manager – A major resource.* London, BIM, 1969.
21 HANDY C. *The Making of Managers.* London, NEDO, 1987; and CONSTABLE J. *The Making of British Managers.* London, BIM/NEDO, 1987.
22 PA CONSULTANTS. *Management Development.* PA, 1986.

Further reading relevant to this chapter is shown in Chapter 13.

6

 Establishing Development Needs

The previous chapters have looked at the range of processes used within the formal system for assessing the current performance and future potential of managers. Brief reference has been made to the issue of the definition of the required skills and competences and ways in which these formal review processes can sharpen the assessment of current skill levels.

This chapter starts by building on those formal review processes such as appraisal, potential review and assessment centres, which focus primarily on individual performance. Then we move to processes which start from a more general and external view of what development needs might be, now or in the future. This leads to some comments about what might be called the macro-learning process – the learning organisation.

Informal but immediate processes

The most extreme form of unguided identification of needs occurs when a manager identifies a performance weakness in a subordinate and immediately suggests that action should be taken on it. This immediacy of diagnosis and action is certainly realistic in terms of normal managerial processes, but is prone to the same weaknesses, in both diagnosis and solution, as many other normal managerial activities. The manager may assess as a weakness something that is not a weakness or attribute the weakness to an irrelevant cause. This kind of instant diagnosis rarely engages the subordinate in a shared discussion of either the problem or solution, which may itself bring additional problems later in persuading the subordinate to believe the statement of need or accept the proposed solution.

Examples of such statements range from 'I think we should send you on an interpersonal skills course; that last discussion with Jack showed that you use too much aggression and create opposition to your ideas' to 'I am sending you out with Jean to pick up everything she knows about this new product that you are taking over.' It will be noted that in both these examples the statement of the solution precedes the statement of the problem. This is characteristic of managers who operate in this way: they are dealing with a managerial problem, not something they define as a training or learning need.

Many Type 1 learning processes derive from this kind of statement. They are an inevitable and proper way of identifying needs, though obviously they are not formal processes of identification which would be regarded as 'good' in a formal management development process. We have created problems for ourselves in management development by attempting to replace these admittedly rough and unsatisfactory processes rather than building on them. The weaknesses of diagnosis and commitment have to be weighed against the advantages of immediacy and reality.

Blank-page processes

In Chapter 4 we reviewed the possible content of appraisal forms, particularly how much guidance should be offered on the specifics of performance and skill. Sometimes managers claim that they would prefer a simple blank-page approach, and indeed some schemes provide very little guidance, on the grounds that it is better to make managers think about the words they have to write than it is to provide organised but mechanical check-lists either of headings or of explicit skills.

I once worked with a newly appointed chief executive who, while prepared to appraise at least some of his subordinates, disliked the existing appraisal form. He thought that the headings were in some cases inappropriate for the level he was to review and in others a mental straitjacket. I redesigned the form for him so that it simply asked him to review:

- current performance against objectives
- reasons for current performance
- steps necessary to improve performance

- potential for promotion
- reasons for prediction
- development needs – current and future.

His first reaction was that he had asked for a blank page, but that he supposed that I was right to divide it up with the headings I had suggested. He used the form with two of his subordinates and came back to me. He had discovered that although he could complete the form and have what he regarded as a good discussion, it was taking him a long time to think his way into the issues. So he decided that he did want something which gave him some clues about the particular aspects he should be thinking about.

Skills- or behaviour-based individual appraisal

The appraisal form, or the document used in an assessment centre, can contain lists of desired qualities, skills, behaviours, competences. The effective analysis of needs depends on such lists being appropriate to the particular organisation rather than generalised. The ways in which such lists can be produced are covered in a later section. For the moment we need only look at the advantages of such lists. The lists may be indicative: 'Think about the following dimensions in completing your appraisal', or prescriptive: 'Give your rating on each of the following required management skills.'

Chapter 4 discussed the problems of the personal qualities approach in appraisal. It is precisely in the area of development needs that such assessments collapse. The problems of providing appropriate learning experiences in order to develop characteristics such as 'dependability', 'initiative', 'energy', and 'judgement' are massive. Most appraisal schemes therefore now try to focus on performance, behaviour and skills.

The use of objectives, key result areas, priorities

A preliminary step favoured by many organisations, both for the conduct of appraisal and for identifying needs, is to establish the achieved level of performance against major output requirements. The useful residue of the management-by-objectives movement of the 1960s and 1970s, this essentially provides a rational basis on which to make a judgement about development needs. However, it provides only the basis; it does not indicate detailed requirements. Knowing, for example, that a manager 'failed to achieve the agreed objective on quality' indicates an area for discussion rather than a development need. Is the cause of failure the fact that the manager did not know enough about quality as a subject, or enough about the technical processes necessary to ensure it, or that his relationships with other departments were bad, or that the materials coming in to the plant were substandard, or that he was under pressure from the sales department to release defective goods? The great virtue of starting from such issues is that they focus on real managerial concerns, which both parties to the discussion will usually agree are real. They are much less likely to dismiss the subsequent discussion, and any development needs which may be identified, as 'an unreal exercise about learning needs'.

Individual development plans

So far all the processes illustrated have essentially been part of the direct relationship between the manager and subordinates, with managerial judgements made about development needs. They may sit down together and draw up an indivdiual development plan, a process much encouraged by the concepts and practices of self-development.[1] An alternative is to bring in a third party. This involves an internal or external adviser in a preliminary discussion with an individual manager. The results of that discussion are then taken back into the line system; it is crucial that the role of the third party is seen as facilitating the eventual discussion and not replacing it. A skilled facilitator will draw out more from the manager involved, and probably also be aware of a greater variety of potential development solutions, than most line managers. This is a relatively expensive process and has therefore been used either for senior management positions, as described by Mumford[2,3] or to meet a substantial change in business purpose, as described by Cunningham and Leon.[4]

Generalised processes of identifying needs

So far the emphasis has been on processes which are specific to the individual and to the organisation. Of course, the indicative or prescriptive lists of skills or behaviours required are general to the extent that they are used with all managers. The methods by which such lists are produced vary between organisations. Some will have carried out a detailed analysis of required skills. A list is produced, perhaps by the use of relatively unstructured open-ended interviewing techniques, by more sophisticated repertory grid techniques, by managerial skill check-lists, by discussions among groups of managers, or by some combination of these. It may be specific to a particular unit or division or to the whole organisation. Some good ideas on these approaches, and specifics on possible resulting content, are given by Andrew Stewart.[5]

An alternative approach is to use an already existing list. One easily available example is given in the book on self-development by Pedler and his colleagues.[1]

The competency approach has been increasingly favoured in recent years. The book by Boyatzis[6] gives the full results of his research, with information from 2,000 practising managers in 41 different types of jobs in a dozen different organisations. The result was a set of 18 competency descriptors, separated into four clusters. The clusters were:

- goal and action management
- directing subordinates
- human resource management
- leadership.

I have used the full set of descriptors in working with managers to assess their required level of performance and their current level of ability. Some discussions arise about some of the language used in the descriptors, but in general I have found it a powerful tool. While a number of organisations in the UK had produced their own list of competences by the late 1980s, the decision of the Management Charter Initiative (MCI) to produce and then promote the use of generic competences gave a major encouragement to this process.

Some organisations stayed with their own lists, some adopted the MCI list, some experimented with the MCI list and then produced their own variants. The market research report of the MCI, published in 1996, state that 'Of all companies that have a formal management development method, 10% were found to use the standards. This again represents an improvement from the 1995 level of 5%.' Competences and associated standards have been produced for First Line, Middle and Senior Management. These are in turn to be associated with National Vocational Qualifications (NVQs).

The MCI has undoubtedly helped to increase visibility of, and decisions about, management development in the UK. Its approach is most closely associated with what I described in the Introduction as Strategy 1, since it clearly depends initially on a diagnosis of competence against predetermined (and national) standards. However, the associated idea of 'Crediting Competence' does provide for competence described retrospectively to an experience which may not have been planned – though the experience has to be described within the relevant standard. The MCI approach is rigorous – indeed one of the criticisms made of it is that it is more detailed and requires more work than many organisations and managers wish to undertake. But that is one of the necessities if you are to pursue, as this approach clearly does, a qualification focused route to management development.

The concept of competencies is itself one which is not accepted as valuable by all management development practitioners. Some would prefer to focus on explicit skills and behaviours, rather than attempting to imply a definition which seems to include not only skill but aspects of knowledge, accompanied by psychological aspects of 'willingness'. I share with Burgoyne[7] major reservations about the practicability and desirability of using the competency approach on a national basis. It is fair to say that a competency approach used with discretion by an organisation, ie adjusted and interpreted to suit that organisation's actual situation, could be more helpful, than simply doing nothing or starting from scratch.

A research report[8] claims not only that competence-based management development improves both individual and organisation performance but that MCI standards give additional benefits.

Generalised skills or competencies?

The problem essentially is that we want a convenient and economic answer and that at the same time we would like it to be an accurate reflection of reality in our particular organisation. Yet as Hirsh found in her major study,[9] there is not only widespread disagreement between organisations on what the crucial skills are, but significant disagreement on what the same word means. Good decision-making in one company means taking innovative decisions, whereas in another it means working from hard data and minimising risk.

What managers really do

We constantly return to the fact that managerial life and required managerial performance differ from one organisation to another; any generalised list is likely to be at least partially inapplicable. Lists of skills and competencies also suffer from the major disadvantage that they are too neat and discrete. Although it is convenient to separate things out for analysis, and to some extent also appropriate to work on individual issues such as the skills of interviewing or analytical approaches to decision-making, managerial life is not separated into neat boxes.

We can only be surprised and saddened by the apparent continuing failure of many authors, business schools and management training centres, to define and implement their offerings in terms of what managers actually do. The fundamental work of Rosemary Stewart,[10] Henry Mintzberg[11] and John Kotter[12] has not, it seems, been widely adopted by management developers, management educators or trainers. All three of these authors are descriptive rather than prescriptive. Their views are radically different from those of the classical theorists like Fayol and his successors through to Urwick, Brech and many subsequent imitators. These writers were essentially prescriptive: they said that managers *should* behave in particular ways in order to be effective. They further presumed that effective managerial processes were essentially the same for all managers in all kinds of organisations.

The contribution of Stewart, Mintzberg and Kotter is in many ways fundamental. It is central to our problem of defining what it is that we want managers to be able to do. It must also be remembered that their approach was based on reviewing the reality of how managers performed using interviewing, diary-keeping and observation techniques, rather than relying on detailed questionnaires or hypothetical constructs about how managers might behave if they were not answering a questionnaire. Their conclusions have a great deal in common, although Stewart collected data for hundreds of managers and Mintzberg and Kotter observed and interviewed only small numbers. Management development advisers should preferably read these three books (or at least the articles written by Mintzberg[13] and Kotter).[14] A convenient summary is provided in Mumford.[15]

In terms of the assessment of needs, and certainly of working on real issues subsequently, the Stewart, Mintzberg and Kotter material is very powerful and useful. The answers they give may sometimes lack clarity, but this is because they are describing the reality in which managers work. Their material is therefore particularly valuable where you may be working with an individual manager on analysing his own job. I have also found it of particular value on some management courses,[16] where the process of helping individuals to establish their own development needs is a significant requirement (see Chapter 11 for further discussion of this).

What generalisations are possible?

Even organisationally derived competences are generalised statements about managerial work in that particular organisation. Both
the content of a competence, and its level of priority might in fact
differ within an organisation, according to a specific function or
level. The first sensible generalisation is therefore paradoxical: the
most effective management development will derive from the most
specific statements of what particular managers need to be able to do
well.

The second generalisation is this: the more that individual or
group development is focused on requirements which in themselves
represent a closely drawn derivation from organisational or unit
strategy, the more effective the development will be.

A third generalisation is that there are at least some issues that are
likely to be of concern in the job of any manager:

- The manager is an individual, with accountabilities and responsibilities (preferably set down in writing).
- The manager is part of a social interaction, working with relatively permanent groups and teams and shifting occasional relationship.
- In managing resources (finance, material and people) the manager
  is a problem-solver and decision-maker.
- Managers have to make decisions about how much they will
  allow others to do without significant reference to them ('empowerment').
- Direct management of others is accompanied by necessary indi-
  rect influence on internal colleagues and the external world; thus
  the significance of being able to network effectively (and to
  understand political skills).
- In the late twentieth century most managers work in conditions of
  uncertainty and risk.
- The clear definition of those objectives and priorities which most
  managers would prefer to work to needs to be constantly updated.
- The only unchanging thing is that change will be ever-present.
- Change, and accompanying differences in priorities, may be best

coped with if there is a specific organisational understanding of mission and values.

- Some organisational cultures encourage particular management styles; however, even within one organisation several different styles may be displayed effectively.
- Peter Drucker told us many years ago that there was a difference between being efficient and being effective.
- Good management, and therefore good management development, is based on the promotion of being effective.

It should be noted that all these statements, though perhaps helpful in enabling management development advisers to determine their own approach to advising others, applied similarly to the content of the management developer's own job.

There are, of course, much more substantial descriptions of managerial skills and the context in which those skills are applied. Some management development advisers might want to pursue these issues in greater depth.

Leadership or management?

The development of the concept of leadership has been an obvious trend in the management development world, some particularly startling statements about it being made in the 1980s. The idea has moved on from the days of simple comparisons with military forms of leadership in the 1950s, through the early days of appraisal schemes which asked people to assess others on undefined concepts of leadership. We now have much more sophisticated, and indeed demanding statements, exemplified by, for example, Bennis[17] and Kotter.[18] The concept of some special form of direction provided by leadership is undoubtedly attractive to many managers. Part of the attraction lies in being someone who goes to Ascot as compared with ordinary races: it is an indication of higher-class status. The word implies other concepts such as 'vision', 'charisma' and, most recently, 'transformational leadership'. Bennis talks about the transformational leader as one who creates and articulates a vision, shaping and elevating the motives and goals of his followers.

Kotter's book is based on major research and on extended case studies. A totally different genre is that of business leaders – in effect the chief executive officer as hero. Although Lee Iacocca's reputation has declined since his book was first published, his book[19] is still very interesting as an explicit description of how a senior manager learnt. Sir John Harvey-Jones, in his first book,[20] also presents some useful insights about development processes, and he is unusual among top executives in mentioning explicitly some of the off-the-job activities he has been through.

My own conclusion about top executive books is increasingly that though they are often interesting to read, they are unlikely to be a useful part of organised management development. Perhaps we are growing weary of a succession of industrial leaders who sparkle for a time and then disappear. Not that this has happened with Sir John Harvey-Jones, who has remained very visible through his television programmes. Perhaps we conclude that focusing development on the extraordinary characteristics of particular individuals is helpful neither to the organisation nor to development processes.

If you take the view that leadership is separate and distinct from management, then it could represent a different level or type of development need. The books referred to will help the reader decide whether that is indeed an appropriate road. My own view is that it is not. To attribute to the manager only the most routine, basic and least exciting parts of the direction of his unit or organisation, while attributing all the stimulating, creative and direction-changing processes to the leader is to demean the managerial process itself.

Changing requirements

Emphasis has so far been placed on identifying real needs in existing job performance. However, this form of analysis needs to be supplemented by considering three ways in which individual development needs have to respond to more than current circumstances. The first of these is changes in skill requirements in the current job. Perhaps the most dramatic examples of this have occurred in the 1980s with the privatisation of public-sector organisations. The changed requirements in, for example, British Airways and British Telecom are referred to later in this chapter. In other areas of our life, too, there have been major shifts of emphasis even if not of ownership, as in the National Health Service and large areas of local government. Those skills which managers required under the previous arrangements may no longer be as important, and they may need to acquire other skills such as financial discipline and the ability to relate to customers.

The discussion of promotion in the previous chapter highlighted another important issue of succession. It is sometimes possible to identify a very specific job or type of job for which a manager is destined, and then to assess his or her current levels of skill and experience against the requirements of the upcoming job. It may be that the requirement is to extend, or develop further, existing skills and knowledge; but promotion often brings with it new and different responsibilities and skill requirements.

Substantial as the problems of predicting potential and establishing development needs against existing jobs are, the uncertainties involved in trying to develop skills for unknown future jobs are even more frightening. There has been no shortage over the last 20 years of predictions about changes in management skill requirements; but these have usually been offered at a general level. Inevitably, they also tend by definition to reflect informed guesswork rather than analysis of the new jobs, since these do not yet exist. The clearest examples of the creation of new jobs in the last 10 or 20 years are of course in the technological field. We are now witnessing the evolution of managerial jobs in information technology, accompanied by the need for managers to understand the technology involved and its application even though they are not directly managing it.

Since it is difficult to be precise about what is needed in these areas, the pressing issue from a management development point of view becomes that of providing processes which as far as possible give analogous experiences. An example of this would be enabling managers to cope with future change by helping them to learn more effectively from the changes to which they are currently exposed. This issue is developed further in Chapter 7.

The reader may care to test current practices and possibilities against the individual-centred methods of identifying needs:

Exercise

1 Which methods do we currently use?
2 Which seem to give greatest return in terms of willing participation of our managers?
3 Which serve the overall purposes of our formal management development scheme most effectively?
4 What changes, if any, could we consider within a particular method, or which additional methods might we consider using?

Business-centred needs identification

Some of the most powerful definitions of need have arisen in organisations using a different process. The parallel is with needs arising from individual objectives and priorities, as illustrated earlier. Needs can be identified through, and generated by, changes in organisational objectives and priorities. One kind of example has already been given, the transformations in managerial requirements in organisations moving from the public to the private sector, or substantially influenced by some organisational imperative. It may be that a substantial transformation in the perceived purpose of the business, or of its managerial requirements to meet those purposes, requires the development of a new range of skills. An interesting example is given by Bruce.[21] He describes part of the shift of attitude required in British Airways following the identification that customer service, not price, would give them a competitive edge.

The process used by myself and Peter Honey at Ford (see Chapter 7) involved managers more directly in establishing needs on a more personal basis, rather than simply participating (desirable though this is) in the identification of overall needs. As part of their shift towards a more participative style, and the use of a form of matrix management, we designed a development programme which required managers to analyse the need for changed behaviour.

In more steady-state organisations, identification of needs may still derive from the push of general business requirements as well as from individual-centred initial analysis. In its most characteristic form it nowadays derives from the organisation's formal business plan. The people who write the formal business plan are required to consider management resource and skill implications, with consequent management development consequences. This may be expressed in terms like 'We need to enhance our marketing skills in order to generate new and more effective marketing plans', or 'Our proposals for enhanced quality management mean that we will need to recruit a senior level manager, and train all our production managers to meet the new standards.'

In some organisations the requirement that management resourcing and development implications should be written into the plan itself does not exist. In those cases a concerned individual, probably a personnel director or a management development adviser, has to go through the plan and draw out the implications. In the previous chapter we looked at management resource planning in terms of identifying individuals for particular jobs; but it may be that the adviser will have to identify the skills needs arising from proposed changes in the business, rather than emphasising the processes necessary for appointing managers to new or enhanced jobs.

The plan may stimulate a shift from a national and geographic organisation to a product-based one, or a decision to devolve responsibility to identified profit centres because of projected growth in business. A few organisations even manage to plan their organisational changes sufficiently far ahead for the development of managers to occur before the change. Sadly, it is more likely that an organisation will decide to devolve more responsibility and create more profit centres, and only begin to recognise needs when weaknesses are identified in the managers in post. This seems to have been the case in the National Health Service, where the imperative of organisational change preceded the development of managers capable of operating the new organisation successfully.

In an action-learning mode, it is possible to use the process of drawing up the business plan to create an awareness of, and indeed specifically identify, the skills and behaviour required to implement the plan. This process is described by Seekings and Wilson.[22]

Needs or wants

One of the basic issues for individuals is whether what may be objectively recognised as needs actually exist as subjectively felt wants. On a macro-scale the same issue obtains for organisations. Objective, analytical, well-based statements of what managers need in order to be effective can be treated with impatience or disrespect or simply not prioritised in terms of resources.

This is a frequent experience for management trainers and educators. Managers all too often arrive on courses with no analysis at all of their individual needs having been undertaken or, where an analysis of some kind has been done, without any commitment to it. If we add to this a disbelief in the efficacy of courses in general or in the ability of this particular course to meet the need, then the likelihood of success is predictably and actually low. The ideas usually described in management literature as 'expectancy theory' have been used by Charles Handy[23] to produce what he calls the 'motivation calculus':

- the strengths or salience of the need
- the expectancy that energy or effort will lead to a particular result
- the instrumentality of that result in reducing the need shown at the first line above.

We should, however, emphasise that however sophisticated the process by which we try to establish needs by detailed job analysis, lists of competencies or skills, or indulgence in the futurology of management expertise, little is likely to happen unless we seriously engage managers themselves in the process.

Figure 6.1
Learning Opportunities

The opportunities identified here are not necessarily separate. You may, for example, think of something first in terms of something happening at a meeting – or you may think of the way in which one of your colleagues achieved success at a meeting.

Situations within the organisation	*Processes*
Meetings	Coaching
Task – familiar	Counselling
– unfamiliar	Listening
Task force	Modelling
Customer visit	Problem-solving
Visit to plant/office	Observing
Managing a change	Questioning
Social occasions	Reading
Foreign travel	Negotiating
Acquisitions/mergers	Mentoring
Closing something down	Public speaking
	Reviewing/auditing
	Clarifying responsibilities
Situations outside your organisation	Walking the floor
Voluntary work	Visioning
Domestic life	Strategic planning
Industry committee	Problem diagnosis
Professional meetings	Decision-making
Sports club	Selling
	People
	Boss
	Mentor
	Network contacts
	Peers
	Consultants
	Subordinates

It is relevant that cold-blooded, logical analyses of the kind largely illustrated here bear little relationship to what managers actually do when they are managing. It is for this reason that the approach through performance – perhaps through the achievement of objectives – is likely to be more attractive and therefore more successful than an approach through skills. It is similarly the reason why, at the large-scale organisational level, the identification of particular problems and concerns, whether through a formal business plan or simply through the recognition of a need for a major change, is again likely to be more effective than some of the more coolly considered and specifically learning-centred approaches illustrated earlier.

This is why I tend to approach this whole process from the view that managers respond to what I call 'felt hurt'. If we deal with the things which worry them we stand the risk of being superficial, it is true; but we acquire the great benefit of dealing with things that are of significant concern to them. The danger of emphasising cool, rational analysis is that it will produce needs which objectively are excellently defined, but which unfortunately fail to attract the interest of those we need to respond to.

Using learning opportunities to define needs

The model of management development offered in this book includes those informal and accidental experiences described as Type 1. The emphasis so far in this chapter on wholly formal processes of identifying needs should be supplemented by an understanding of how these Type 1 experiences themselves can create a better recognition of needs, which can in turn lead to Type 2 management development. At a personal rather than a cool analytical level, individuals recognise that they need to learn something. Such experiences can be described as 'triggers'.

Managers will tend to think of managerial activities and problems first, and recognise a learning need only as a secondary requirement, and indeed a secondary stage, in their thought processes. It is significant and sometimes hurtful experiences, or being faced with something new, or being exposed to a different kind of activity or a different boss, which helps to stimulate the recognition that learning has occurred, or could occur in a similar situation in future.

One way of using the Type 2 approach, or at least encouraging it among line managers, is to ask them to consider the opportunities that exist for learning from real management work. Figure 6.1 (which has already appeared on page 2) can create such a review, often (interestingly) without using the word 'need' at all. Managers can be helped to consider opportunities for learning that from our point of view include an implicit recognition of needs without actually being explicitly exposed to the word or concept 'need'.

The reader may like to consider how to take advantage of these various approaches to identify need from the perspective of business reality indicated here.

---

1 Do we currently have a business plan that could be used in the ways indicated here?
2 If we do not have a business plan, is there some other process of discussing major objectives for my unit in which I could be involved and from which I could help to generate management development needs?
3 What is the balance between formal analysis via skills or competencies and the kind of 'felt hurt' approach in my organisation at present?
4 How can I relate the suggestions on Type 1 and Type 2 processes to the identification of needs?

The impact of organisational culture

Since reference has frequently been made in this book to the contingent nature of management, and the fact that different organisations will need and respond to different processes, it will be no surprise that the culture of the organisation influences assessment of needs in at least two different ways. One of the purposes of management development can actually be to change that organisational culture.

The nature of the organisation can determine the kind of management development which is appropriate or acceptable. This point could have been made in the previous chapter on systems, but has been included here because it probably has its most direct expression in terms of the dual aspect of needs:

- what an organisation wants to achieve in terms of improved or changed skills
- what processes it might choose in order to determine those needs.

Handy[23] argues that some organisational cultures are better fitted to formal management development systems, or for particular elements in those systems. The suggestions here about using and developing from Type 1 to Type 2 in our model may, for instance, be more acceptable to organisational cultures which emphasise task and person rather than those Handy identifies as power cultures or role cultures. The particularities of the impact of an organisation's culture on what the needs are and how they should be identified is illustrated implicitly rather than explicitly in the articles on AIB, Ford and British Airways. Some aspects of needs in a single but changing organisational culture (building societies) are given in the article by Smith.[24]

The attitudes and behaviours in particular organisations affect the capacity to recognise learning needs and opportunities (and hence on organisational learning) – see Chapters 1 and 12.

Do entrepreneurial managers have different needs?

One of the problems here is to establish exactly what form of entrepreneurship is being discussed. Is it the entrepreneur running a small organisation from scratch of perhaps 50 people, or is it the successful entrepreneur who has moved on to run a more substantial business, like Anita Roddick of Body Shop or Steve Shirley of F International, or is it indeed an entrepreneur like Clive Sinclair, apparently unable to sustain early success? Some of the characteristics said to distinguish the entrepreneur from the 'normal' manager clearly relate to issues of size rather than entrepreneurship; one example is the need to be effective in close contact with both customers and employees at a personal level. Entrepreneurs may well need this skill; but so do managers of small companies who are in no sense entrepreneurs.

It may well be that entrepreneurial organisations have particular needs, but it is just as dangerous to generalise about these as it is about any form of organisation. The skills involved in creativity would generally be thought to be peculiarly appropriate to entrepreneurial organisations; yet creativity in business can lead to unsuccessful answers at least as often as it leads to good ones.

Innovation and change

A more useful dimension than the pure entrepreneurial issue is that of the different managerial skills associated with innovation. Here we have the advantage of the literally masterly book by Kanter.[25] The new skills required in securing successful change apply to a much wider variety of organisations than those which could be defined as entrepreneurial. These are:

- power skills – persuading others to invest information and support resources in new initiatives
- skills in managing problems associated with greater use of teams
- understanding how change is designed and constructed in an organisation.

One of the most useful aspects of Kanter's book is the reminder it offers that skills will not develop successfully without an appropriate facilitating context. Her emphasis on the nature of the innovative organisation is a reminder that innovative skills can be neither successfully identified nor developed in isolation from the organisational context.

The learning organisation

Organisations, like individuals, have to change and adapt to meet new circumstances. The processes necessary to measure the changes required are no different from those we have already discussed. An organisation that takes learning seriously may pursue any learning processes with a greater level of intensity. It may be that a strong push to change the culture might entitle an organisation to be called 'a learning organisation'. I do not think that research so far has shown that the processes of establishing these needs are any different from those set out in this chapter. (See Chapter 12.)

References

1 PEDLER M., BURGOYNE J. *and* BOYDELL T. *A Manager's Guide to Self Development.* 2nd edn. Maidenhead, McGraw-Hill, 1986.
2 MUMFORD A. 'Counselling senior managers' development'. In BOYDELL T. *and* PEDLER M. (eds), *Management Self Development.* Aldershot, Gower, 1981.
3 MUMFORD A. *Learning At The Top.* Maidenhead, McGraw-Hill, 1995.
4 CUNNINGHAM I. *and* LEON P. 'Focusing management development'. *Journal of European Industrial Training.* Vol. 10, No. 8, 1986.
5 STEWART A. 'Diagnosing needs'. In MUMFORD A. *Handbook of Management Development.* 4th edn. Aldershot, Gower, 1995.
6 BOYATZIS R. *The Competent Manager.* Chichester, John Wiley, 1982.
7 BURGOYNE J. 'Doubts about competency'. In DEVINE M. (ed.), *The Photofit Manager.* London, Unwin, 1990.
8 WINTERTON J. *and* WINTERTON R. *The Business Benefits of Competence Based Management Development.* London, HMSO, 1996.
9 HIRSH W. *What Makes a Manager.* London, Institute of Manpower Studies, 1988.
10 STEWART R. *Contrast in Management.* Maidenhead, McGraw-Hill, 1975.
11 MINTZBERG H. *The Value of Managerial Work.* Hemel Hempstead, Prentice Hall, 1980.

12 KOTTER J. P. *The General Manager*. Free Press, 1982.
13 MINTZBERG H. *'The manager's job: folklore and fact'*. *Harvard Business Review*. July/August 1975.
14 KOTTER J. 'What effective general managers really do'. *Harvard Business Review*. November/December 1982.
15 MUMFORD A. 'What managers really do'. *Management Decision*. Vol. 26, No. 5, 1988.
16 MUMFORD A. *Developing Top Managers*. Aldershot, Gower, 1988.
17 BENNIS W. *Leaders*. London, Harper and Row, 1985; *On Becoming a Leader*. London, Hutchinson, 1989.
18 KOTTER J. P. *The Leadership Factor*. Free Press, 1988; *A Force for Change: How leadership differs from management*. Free Press, 1990.
19 IACOCCA L. *Iacocca*. Bantam, 1986.
20 HARVEY-JONES J. *Making It Happen*. London, Fontana, 1988.
21 BRUCE M. 'Managing people first'. *Industrial and Commercial Training*. March 1987.
22 SEEKINGS, D. *and* WILSON B. 'Allied Irish Bank in Britain: organisational and business development through action learning'. *Business Education*. Vol. 9, No. 3, 1988.
23 HANDY C. *Understanding Organizations*. London, Penguin, 1985.
24 SMITH D. 'Organisational culture and management development in building societies'. *Personnel Review*. Vol. 15, No. 3, 1986.
25 KANTER R. *The Change Masters*. Simon and Schuster, 1983.

Further reading relevant to this chapter is shown in Chapter 13.

7

Formal Processes for Development on the Job

Chapter 4 described the systems of formal management development set up to overcome the major disadvantages of relying on accidental learning for the development of managers. The achieved learning that resulted from such systems was described there in terms of the effectiveness of the system as a system: whether job moves were actually planned and achieved, whether courses achieved some recognisable result. When we move beyond the system to the particular processes involved in implementing the systematic plans, we are faced with a dilemma.

Type 3 formal management development characteristically provides for someone to be moved into a new job, to work in a different country or on a different product, or to work for a different boss and with different colleagues. It does so because without formal planning and direction, accidental opportunities will be insufficient. Yet what happens as a result of the Type 3 initiative is that managers are actually largely placed in Type 1 learning contexts: in many organisations no attempt is made to improve the effectiveness of the learning and development process within the new job.

It is in this situation that the difficulty of judgement arises. Do we look at this with an amused smile and treat it as a characteristically British oddity? Do we argue that formal management development processes in effect stop at the manager's door, thereafter relying on initiative and drive to secure self-development? Or do we see the situation as an area of inefficiency that can be corrected?

The contention of this book is that once we have seen that the emperor has no clothes, we must look for some. It is unnecessary and intolerable that we remain aloof from the reality of how managers do and could learn from opportunities on the job. We need to provide help to managers on how to learn more effectively from these opportunities, as I have shown in detail.[1]

Not the least benefit of doing this, from the point of view of formal management development, would be that improved learning productivity from planned, on-the-job opportunities would increase the credibility of the formal scheme. Not only would individual managers benefit from an improved capacity to take advantage of the opportunities provided by the scheme, but in doing so they would be more likely to recognise that the scheme has actually produced these beneficial results.

A major cause of failures in this area has been the grotesque lack of attention paid to learning processes in institutions that provide off-the-job learning. If individuals are not helped to develop their learning processes in those circumstances uniquely dedicated to learning, it is not surprising that little is done on the job to encourage understanding of learning processes. The essential features of the learning process are discussed in greater detail in Chapter 11, but for our immediate purposes we need to recognise that:

- learning is not a single achieved/not-achieved process, but one involving different stages of learning with different achievements (the concept of the learning cycle)
- different individuals may respond better or worse, and be able to deal more or less effectively, with different stages of the cycle. Thus the concept of individual learning preferences expressed as learning styles.

Plans for development

Although learning is something that can be achieved only by the learner (ie it cannot be achieved by a teacher), in most managerial contexts and for most managerial purposes it is also a social activity. For managers it is often an activity with organisational purpose, drives and rewards. So the individual manager may be 'driven' towards learning through a formal appraisal. That may lead to a personal development plan which sets out what the individual intends to achieve and what the organisation will do to aid achievement (see Chapter 6). Some authors have suggested a 'learning contract' between the individual and the organisation. My preference would be

Figure 7.1
Planned and Deliberate Learning Processes

Changes in job
● promotion
● same job but in different function or product: job rotation
● secondment

Changes in job content
● stretching boundaries of job by extra responsibility and tasks
● special projects
● committees or task groups
● junior boards

Within the job
● being coached
● being counselled
● monitoring and feedback by boss
● being mentored

---

the term 'learning agreement'. In terms of normal working relationships between a manager and subordinates the term 'contract' is unrealistic. It is difficult to envisage them in their normal day-to-day
dealings thinking or writing to each other in these terms, whereas
agreements are put into effect, though not necessarily on paper, all
the time in the course of their managerial work.

Figure 7.1 lists the 'planned and deliberate learning processes'
which have already been set out in more detail on pages 12–13.

Changes in job

There are significant differences in the nature of the opportunities
provided by different types of change and of the difficulties involved
in taking up the opportunities. The levels of difficulty were indicated
in Figure 3.3 (see page 68).

Moving into a new job

Whether the move is planned by the manager's current employer, or whether a new organisation takes the arriving manager on, the same development issues arise. What is the new manager to learn, at what pace and through what processes?

As Figure 3.3 indicates, the most difficult move of all, yet the one with the most potential learning, is promotion into a new organisation. Some kind of induction programme will usually be arranged. The new manager will meet new colleagues, will probably be given a tour of the office and perhaps of other working facilities. There may be arrangements to meet a range of customers, suppliers and other useful contacts. In essence the manager has to learn about the nature and purpose of the organisation – 'getting to know the business'. Then there is the need to find out about internal relationships: the politics of the business, the way in which people work together, or avoid working together. Finally there is the outside world, the people and organisations serviced.

Rosemary Stewart[2] points out that acquiring the *knowledge* necessary to perform a new job is relatively unstressful. It is more difficult for the manager to understand and respond to differences in the *managerial processes* in the job. She provides a useful check-list on the nature of these differences.

Example

> A newly appointed general manager of an overseas subsidiary of a UK multinational was brought to the UK for a week. His programme included a number of visits to different people at head office, research division, several managers of similar companies. The original design of the programme filled almost the whole of the week with visits and travel, with no opportunity for the manager to review what he had learned and to check out that he had learned appropriately. Two review sessions were therefore built in, during which he reviewed what he had learned from his visits and contacts with his immediate boss and the main board director concerned.

Gabarro[3] describes in a most helpful article the stages involved
when managers move into a new job:

- taking hold
- immersion
- reshaping
- consolidation
- refinement.

The example above shows that effective action can be taken to help
with the stage Gabarro describes as 'taking hold'. Gabarro sets out
the further requirements for this stage:

- Make sure priorities are set out for the new manager.
- Provide processes by which new managers work out expectations
  with their new subordinates.
- Give support in areas of lack of knowledge or experience.
- Accept that taking charge takes time.

Gabarro says that short-term assignments – by which he means appointment to a full job but for a short period – are not likely to be
successful. He derives this view from the research that established
the five stages described above, which he found took from two to
two-and-a-half years. My own experience would support his view
that without a substantial period of this kind it is not possible for
most managers in most jobs to learn how to do the new job effectively. What some of them can do successfully is demonstrate that
they can analyse problems and requirements well and set in motion
processes of improvement. If they are moved on after a year or 18
months, they not only all too often fail to learn in depth from what
they have done so far, but the relatively short period of implementation means that they may actually have received incorrect feedback about the accuracy of their analyses. The organisation may also
make a wrong judgement about the effectiveness of the manager involved.

What is involved here is clearer recognition that the transition between jobs, whether promotion or movement sideways, involves a

great deal more than some prior training and development activities and an initial induction period. This transition frequently provides only informal and accidental learning. In part this is because of failure by formal management development processes and organisers to recognise exactly what is involved in these transitions and to provide formal development plans during the transition. It is not simply a case of waiting for the first review of the manager's performance (probably a formal appraisal) and picking out from it the learning needs that experience on the job has identified. It is quite possible to see in advance what at least some of those learning needs will be and to plan for them formally. The review would then more usefully be of both performance and the achievement of and learning from that experience. Of course those readers who have been converted to the ideas of this book will also want to encourage Type 2 learning both by initial discussions with the participants and perhaps by suggesting that powerful incidents are reviewed by the managers involved from time to time.

To summarise, moving to a new job creates learning opportunities but does not satisfy them in a 'planned and deliberate way'. The special learning opportunities arising from the new appointment merge gradually into opportunities arising within a job that is no longer recognisably new.

Secondment

I define secondment as a process of moving a manager into a job outside his employing organisation. Some organisations and writers have taken a rather broader view, so that secondment actually includes moving people across divisions or from one company to another within a group of companies. While some of the motivation for either kind of secondment move may well be the same – to provide a job for a manager – the development processes involved are likely to be considerably different. So it is more sensible to regard movement within an employing organisation when undertaken within a formal development scheme as a form of job rotation. Of course there are organisations where relationships between the different parts of a group are so tenuous that in practice the same novelty pertains!

This discussion is concerned with secondment as a development process, and not with secondment as a means of finding a possibly temporary job for a manager who would otherwise be redundant, or who is out of favour with his or her superiors. The secondment may in certain instances have a dual learning objective. For example, secondment of a manager from industry to work in the Civil Service normally has a double objective; the individual learns from exposure to a different culture, a different environment, a different way of doing things. At a secondary level the organisation sponsoring the secondee learns about how the Civil Service operates and may therefore learn how to deal with it more effectively. Indeed, there may be a very precise relationship between secondment from industry to, say, the Department of Trade and Industry and the acquisition of knowledge about the process the department goes through in considering particular issues.

As the former IPM's Code on Secondment said,[4] it provides a 'unique development opportunity for employees to learn to perform in challenging new situations'. The Code also said that 'the secondee must be debriefed to elicit what has been learned from the secondment'. Secondment may involve the acquisition of particular areas of knowedge, or the generation of particular types of experience. There are benefits to be derived from transfer to a quite different country, which may offer an experience not otherwise available within the organisation.

One of the main benefits to many of the companies who engaged in secondment during the 1980s was that of exposing a manager to a quite different sort of experience in terms of 'standing on their own feet'. Several large organisations told me that many of their managers had been brought up in an environment in which they had a great deal of professional and functional support in carrying out their jobs – sometimes perhaps more than they really wanted. To go to a small organisation where they had to do everything for themselves was thought to be a considerable development opportunity.

As this point illustrates, different kinds of secondment have different objectives. Civil Service type secondment really involves the acquisition of knowledge, whereas secondment from a large to a small company gives a different kind of experience and probably an opportunity to develop different kinds of skills. As much as anything, however, these latter secondments are about responsibility, authority and the application, perhaps, of some management knowledge not fully utilised in the sponsoring organisation.

The emphasis here is on the development benefit to the individual and to the sponsoring organisation. The prime objective of some secondments is obviously different. Secondment can be a way of getting rid of someone for a time; but it can, more generously, be the result of a decision by an organisation to put something into the community concerned. This happens when organisations send somebody to work for a charity or voluntary organisation. Although there are glowing exceptions, research by the Centre for Employment Initiatives found that this form of secondment was not usually undertaken as a method of career development, although organisations sometimes claimed it as such. Most often the people seconded were either nearing retirement or were for one reason or another 'available'. In these latter cases, of course, the end result of the secondment may have been to send back a manager who was actually better equipped or happier than when he or she left; but that seems not to have been the prime purpose or the stimulus for any planned development within the secondment.

Fertilisation within the job

Movement between jobs at the same level is job rotation. The idea is that just as an agricultural crop will extract all the goodness from one location and therefore benefit by being grown in a different one, so with managers. The agricultural analogy can be developed further by considering development opportunities within existing jobs. Instead of being moved to a different location to get development benefit, the manager can extract more from the existing location. Formal management development does this by identifying particular kinds of work that can be available within and around the existing job.

Again, all too often opportunities are provided without any effective development taking place. The formal process is only properly effective when the job is actually fertilised, rather than treated as naturally fertile ground from which useful things will grow. The fertilisation involves the construction of effective learning and development processes around the opportunities provided. We shall now look at some examples of opportunities.

Stretching boundaries and acquiring new tasks

This is the process by which a manager, without changing job title, is given additional responsibilities or a greater weight of responsibility. An example of this would be that of a sales director handing over to a sales manager responsibility for a major national account previously handled by the director. Another would be delegating to a subordinate manager the task of producing a report, visiting an important customer or negotiating with a trade union.

Committees/working parties/task forces

Line executives most frequently assign managers to special committees or task forces for purely managerial reasons. The group wants a particular expert on the subject or a representative from a particular area in the business or somebody who is known to have the ear of somebody important. Such appointments may lead to Type 1 learning.

However, the responsible executive may actually consider the development opportunity involved, either because he or she has a personal interest or because the personnel director or management development adviser suggests it. If this is not discussed between the line executive and the appointed manager, then the manager will not be aware that his or her career has been influenced by formal processes. Where someone is appointed for development reasons it is much more desirable to discuss those reasons and identify the development opportunities and ways of benefiting from them. These opportunities may arise from the exposure of a manager to a quite different process, or to a different level of management, or they may give the manager the opportunity of acquiring functional knowledge. The opportunity may also involve the development of skills, such as managing meetings, or the more subtle skills of influencing others (sometimes pejoratively called political skills).

Junior boards

Managers can stay in their existing jobs but be given experience in simulating the processes of their board of directors. They may be given the same information as the board on a particular issue. They may be asked to consider it and make recommendations to the board, perhaps against criteria that the board has set. Such 'junior boards' have obviously been set up with primarily development objectives. Perhaps because they are so purely developmental they have not really been widely accepted. The main reason seems to be that their actual lack of responsibility and accountability means that the discussions are frustratingly lacking in identifiable results. The knowledge acquired, either in terms of the content of the managerial decisions required or of the process, seems to be outweighed by feelings of psychological and managerial impotence.

Visits to customers, suppliers and others

A production director was identified through the company's resource plan as having high potential for promotion to a general manager position. It was recognised, however, that he had had experience in only two of the functions (production and supply) for which he was likely later to carry overall responsibility. A personal development plan, produced in discussion with him, identified two courses of action (among a larger number not repeated here). The first was to remedy the fact that his experience had all been focused within the plant. It was arranged he would accompany two sales managers over a period of five or six weeks. On his return he said:

> As a production director I had always thought that sales made
> life difficult for us. It took these visits to show me exactly how

the customer makes life difficult for them. It also really brought home to me that if you cannot satisfy the customer (and on some of the visits we could not), you did not sell, and if you do not sell there is nothing for production actually to have to moan about!

As a further step this individual was appointed to a working party on the development of a new product, through which he was exposed to a great deal of marketing analysis and marketing strategy. (As a final comment it is interesting to note that this particular individual declined the opportunity to go on a general management course, on the grounds that he preferred to learn in the ways indicated here.)

Other examples include a sales director who was given the experience of observing a production line; he became much more sympathetic to the problems facing a production director trying to cope with short runs rather than economical long runs. A senior manager in a growing company which had good and informally based relations with its employees recognised that it would need to review these processes and perhaps to change them. It identified a manager not currently in the personnel function to go and find out what other comparable companies did. His visits were seen both as acquiring knowledge for the company and about developing the understanding he had of appropriate practices for which it was envisaged he might be given special responsibility.

Projects and on-the-job development

Projects can be a development tool in all the processes mentioned so far. The manager in a new job can take up a major project as a development process, for example 'find out why repeat orders have declined by 28 per cent in the last six months'. A secondment can include a project or indeed be totally dedicated to one. 'We are seconding you to charity X for six months. Your project is to review their management control systems, and produce a report for the chairman of their council.' Projects can also be identified within the existing job. 'We want you to do an investigation into the forecasts actually used by sales, marketing and production. Why do they have different forecasts and what problems result?'

It will be clear from the abbreviated terms of reference that any of these projects could have been set up as purely managerial exercises, resulting at best in informal learning – Type 1. They were actually Type 3 development opportunities, because the manager selected to carry them out was chosen for development reasons as well as for managerial ones. There was also discussion with the individual about why he had been given the project as a development exercise. This was supplemented by a relatively short but effective discussion on how the manager might take the best advantage of the development opportunity. In each case a development plan was agreed and in both cases a short review session was held at the end of the project, separate from the managerial project presentation and review.

Projects provide major potential developmental benefits. They often involve managers in looking at a wider range of issues, in greater depth, across a wider range of functions than might otherwise be encountered. At their best, even within a formal development context, projects of the kind described here should be real rather than invented purely for development. In some cases they carry responsibility for implementation as well as recommendation, in which case they provide for the strongest form of development. Even projects in which the participant does not carry final responsibility can, if properly managed from a development point of view, provide good learning.

Projects have increasingly been recognised in the management development world as powerful and useful development aids. They have the great advantage of being definable and separable pieces of managerial work with a beginning and an end. The development opportunities and components can be clearly identified, and at the same time they are seen by managers as real managerial tasks with identifiable managerial benefits.

However, simply providing a process through which project opportunities are created for managers is not fully effective Type 3 management development. Unless the development opportunities are analysed, discussed and the actual processes of learning are understood and employed by the manager involved, the learning is still accidental rather than planned and deliberate learning.

The concept of action learning – learning from real managerial work on real managerial problems – includes projects as a major vehicle (see Chapter 2). It is not, however, simply 'learning by doing'. The doing element is a necessary but not a sufficient requirement. Action learning involves doing through a designed and organised approach which is explicitly intended to incorporate learning as well as managing. In its best form, action learning is the prime example of effective learning from projects. Any project potentially involves learning: but this may be informal and accidental. The action learning process deliberately aims to secure learning through a defined process: 'What have we learned from and with each other?'

A project may therefore be stimulated by the management development process as a purely individual activity involving individual reflection and subsequent discussion of learning achieved. In its action learning version it involves a wider group of people, perhaps discussing a number of projects, and certainly stimulating and fertilising each other with different ideas, different problems and different solutions. Action learning has blurred the distinctions between on-the-job and off-the-job development, which is part of the explanation for its usefulness and success.

Exercise

1 As a result of reading this chapter so far, do you see any ways in which you could make use of some processes you do not currently use?
2 Do you see ways of improving your use of the processes you do currently use?
3 In what ways does your organisation currently assist managers to learn from the opportunities created for them through the formal scheme? Could this be improved?
4 Which of the processes outlined in this chapter have been the most powerful and useful in your organisation? Why?

Readers may like to return to their answers to the exercises given in Chapter 1 on the processes used in their own organisation for on-the-job development.

Learning within the job

In this section we are concerned with the ways in which learning is assisted, as distinct from the previous section which reviewed opportunities.

Coaching

In the 1970s coaching was seen as the up-and-coming management development tool. It became a popular subject for developers and trainers, who inevitably began to run courses on how to coach effectively. It seemed a very appropriate activity, since it focused directly on the possibilities of a relationship between managers and their direct reports, through which the superior wisdom of the former could be passed on. Some people recognise that this description, however appropriate in sporting activities, was not perhaps the most appropriate way of envisioning this process in management. So the idea developed of a less directive form of coaching, in which the coach drew out from the learner a better understanding of the problems being addressed, and perhaps offered only very gently any ideas on how to resolve them.

Megginson and Boydell[5] said that coaching is 'a process in which a manager through direct discussion and guided activity helps a colleague to solve a problem or to do a task better than otherwise had been the case'. This is an admirably appropriate definition, though not all subsequent writers agree. I like it because:

- it refers to 'guided activity'
- it aims to 'solve a problem'
- it talks about colleagues with the useful indication that the manager can be working with peers as well as with subordinates.

The aspect not covered in their definition is that coaching may also be performed by a mentor or by a consultant.

Another issue is whether coaching is different from counselling. As the definition above indicates, coaching is more concerned with the overt aspects of relatively immediate problem-solving. Counselling, on the other hand, I have seen as more likely to be directed at deeper aspects of personal relationships or career direction. But, of course, helping managers to resolve their problems may involve discussion of their interpersonal relationships with other people – the cause of the problem may be the particular form of behaviour ('You come across as aggressive') which may in turn be the overt manifestation of a deeper-seated psychological issue. The latter might be what some people would see as requiring counselling.

The great attraction of coaching arises because, of all management development methods, it is the closest to what managers actually do in their normal work – they tackle problems every day. However, that in turn brings some problems. Managers as coaches primarily want the task done well and only secondarily want individuals to learn from doing it. As a formal development process, of course, it is the learning aspect that is emphasised as an objective. However, from a task point of view, managers do not just focus on wanting to resolve the problem; usually they want to resolve it quickly and, from their point of view, with relatively little fuss. Which takes them back into a coaching role more like that of a teacher or instructor, one rather different from the non-directive style encouraged by many books and courses. So there can be an incongruity between the values and processes espoused through books and courses, and the reality of what managers are actually prepared to do. The reflective, listening, analytical, objective coaching style is far removed from their normal style, and they find it difficult, not to say incongruous, to be asked to change it. Most particularly they find it difficult to be asked to change it just to do coaching. Obviously it would fit better if they changed their style totally in this direction for all their managerial activities, in order to remove this difference. But that is something many of them would not be prepared to do – though to do so would create a wonderful market for further courses beyond coaching! Non-directive coaching involves:

- an open style between participants
- a dialogue – not one-way direction
- the coach asking questions that enable learners to identify for themselves what the issues are and what the solutions may be
- some 'confronting' behaviours by the coach.

Directive coaching, on the other hand, tends to emphasise:

- explicit guidance
- statements from the coach's past experience
- instructions on 'how to'.

The question then becomes how one is best to fit coaching to the reality of management in general, and to the reality of particular managerial relationships. As well as general issues of the preferred style of the coach, from a learning point of view there is additional value, but also additional difficulty, in relation to the preferred learning styles of both the coach and the person being coached. In terms of the Honey/Mumford Learning Styles, to require an 'activist' boss to be a reflective listening coach to an 'activist' subordinate is a recipe for failure. If there is mutual understanding, there is slightly greater chance of success with an 'activist' boss and a 'reflector' subordinate, if they have actually exchanged views about the learning process involved and their own separate learning styles. On the other hand, a 'reflector' boss and a 'reflector' subordinate may well enjoy and benefit from the kind of coaching described in the non-directive form.[6]

The prescription for creating an effective coaching relationship within a formal management development system is relatively clear. It is not only necessary to assist managers to develop the skills involved in coaching, such as effective listening, observations and giving non-evaluatory feedback. It was also necessary to help the coach and the learner understand the learning processes involved in the act of coaching. Unfortunately, if one is to judge by published course syllabuses and books, many of the proponents of coaching have not fully understood these issues. Many of the books, for example, have an overaddiction to sports metaphors, an apparent belief that coaching is something that occurs on courses, and largely an absence of any understanding of the practicalities of informal, on-the-job coaching. It is this latter point that seems to me potentially so productive. Surely it is more appropriate to move away from specially arranged coaching sessions, which clearly survive all too rarely many months beyond the coaching course. Rather we should be helping managers to recognise day-to-day opportunities for coaching, not ones specially arranged or written up as such.[7]

Parsloe[7] provides by far the best guidance on coaching, though his material is very much geared to how people are developed for qualifications. The Megginson and Boydell book,[5] Megginson's article[8] and an article by Marsh[9] all provide good guidance. The latter is particularly significant because it includes some detailed research with managers.

Counselling   While the attempt to separate counselling and coaching is understandable, the fact is that in many management development systems the processes are confused – probably because they are in fact, difficult to separate. Counselling may clearly be taking place when a manager discusses issues of domestic significance and difficulty with a subordinate. It may still be counselling when the discussion centres on problems with personal relationships at work. But is it counselling or coaching if the discussion focuses on how the subordinate's aggressive instincts towards the head of another department can be reduced to a level acceptable to both sides? A discussion about an individual's career may also be counselling. 'Everything about the way you do your job tells me that you are much happier giving advice than having to scurry round implementing actions. I think your next job should be in staff function and not in the line.' But suppose the guidance is offered differently: 'What do you think about the way you responded to the need to fight a number of fires last week? Looking back, do you think you might have behaved differently? What were the causes of the ways in which you did behave? What were the things that influenced you?' Is this the launching pad for a counselling discussion on a future career, or is it the beginning of a coaching discussion about how a manager should improve his reaction to certain kinds of event?

The extremes of coaching and counselling are distinguishable, yet both of them require rather similar skills in areas of common interest. Some managers will be able to make direct statements under either coaching or counselling umbrellas, while being unable to carry out a gentler non-evaluative process under either heading.

Indeed, the whole problem of these distinct management development processes of coaching and counselling is that managers do not readily key into them. They are seen as formal management development processes which have no direct association with what happens in real life. Most managers do not see themselves as coaches or counsellors. They deal with business issues, with management problems and management activities. They provide guidance and help on these. If management development advisers choose to call the process by which the help is offered 'coaching', well, with a politely resigned shrug, so be it. When I pointed out to a manager I worked with a few years ago the 'coaching' aspects of his normal behaviour, the light dawned. 'You mean if I am helping somebody with a problem, without telling him what the answer is, that's coaching. If you want to call it that, OK. I call it helping him with his problem.' Yet again we face the issue that, all too often, formal management development processes are seen by the managers they are intended to help as separate from the world in which they live. The designation I would really prefer is 'mutual problem-solving'. That covers the reality of a normal managerial working relationship between boss and subordinate. That is why it appears as a Type 1 and Type 2 process rather than as a Type 3 process.

It is very necessary to put over the basic idea of the coaching concept to managers. They would otherwise concern themselves exclusively with improving task performance, whereas they need to draw out with subordinates, through explicit learning review, how to build on that performance.

Mentoring Clutterbuck[10] says that this was an unknown term until the late 1970s. He may well be right about its application within formal management development systems, but the essential informal process was certainly well known in management, as in other aspects of life. As a formal process it was first implemented in the

United States, and most of the research and literature still comes from there, although Clutterbuck's book provides additional UK material, as does the text he wrote with Megginson.[11] One of the American authors, Zey,[12] gives a definition:

> A person who oversees the career and development of another person, usually a junior, through teaching, counselling, providing psychological support, protecting and at times promoting or sponsoring

My own definition, which gives much greater clarity to the development relationship, is:

> A protective relationship in which experimentation, exchange and learning can occur and skills, knowledge and insight can be developed.

The idea of an older manager choosing a younger manager for whom he will act as coach, counsellor or sponsor is one that has long existed informally and accidentally. The process of nurturing the growth of another individual as a planned input within a formal scheme is newer. One of the problems with this word, as with so many others, is that organisations and authors define it differently. Most of the American literature includes the manager's direct boss as a mentor. This confuses two roles. Chapter 9 indicates the variety of roles carried out by the boss; but they are carried out precisely because the boss is managerially responsible for someone else. It is much more helpful to restrict the term 'mentor' to someone who has no direct responsibility: usually someone older, probably from another department or another division, or even from outside the manager's own organisation.

Even within that more restrictive definition there are different aspects of the role, and different ways of carrying it out. Some mentors are 'door-openers': they try to ensure that their protégés are considered for important jobs, assignments, projects. They ensure that those who make decisions about people know what their protégé has achieved, and why that level of achievement is noteworthy. The door-opening role is rather that of a sponsor; and of course the protégé may not be aware of it. How pleasant for the mentor to be able to murmur in later years that he created the opening for someone who has subsequently shot upwards in the organisation! Formal management development schemes do, however, make the relationship explicit, turning it from an informal into a formal management development process.

The other major type of mentor relationship is one in which a more experienced manager 'coaches' a less experienced one via discussions about work issues, job performance, politics and relationships. This offers more opportunity for facilitating the less experienced manager's learning, because the process is explicit. This can be especially helpful in encouraging the development of women managers. (There are, of course, very few examples of women acting as mentors of men.)

Mentoring is a highly personal relationship, which can sometimes lead to a level of dependence. Because of the potential benefits, but also the potential problems, some organisations have run formal programmes in training both mentors and protégés. These can certainly be helpful in defining expectations at both an organisational and an individual level and can take on board such problems as whether the senior male and junior female manager relationship – which can be effective in facilitating promotion – is none the less potentially harmful in its reinforcement of male/female stereotypes.[12]

As with the other processes, the styles of the mentor and the protégé need to be compatible for the protégé to learn most easily from the relationship – an issue addressed in Mumford.[6]

Modelling on boss, colleagues, outsiders   Some managers learn by observing others. The modelling may be positive – seeing someone doing something well and doing it that way yourself. Or it may be negative – seeing something done with disastrous results and deciding to give that technique or process a miss. Most frequently this is a Type 1 experience; but sometimes the formal system provides the opportunity. Formal management development ought to include help on how to observe others at work, and how to build in review processes after the observation.

Acquiring feedback   We have fortunately long passed the stage of accepting in a management development policy that a 'manager is responsible for developing his or her subordinates'. We have recognised that no one can be 'responsible' for the development of anyone else: the boss has a role in helping the development of subordinates. In the Type 3 context it is the job of the boss to monitor and give feedback on performance. (Colleagues give informal feedback.) This is required primarily for effective performance but is also essential to learning and development. Most management development systems concentrate on improving the validity of the performance review and pay very little attention to the reviewing of learning and development. The role of the boss is so fundamental that it requires more extended discussion, which occurs in Chapter 9.

Reading   Managers read a great deal; but they usually read technical, professional or industrial material connected with their work. In the UK, at any rate, they read books and articles on management less frequently. Yet articles are circulated, particularly among senior managers, 'for your interest', sometimes by the chief executive and sometimes by the personnel director. Managers buy, and quite often read at least part of, the bestsellers like *In Search of Excellence* or *Iacocca*. The formal scheme ought to integrate this kind of relatively casual reading into the planned development of individuals. This could be done by suggesting discussion meetings or, better still, by recommending that time is set aside at normal management meetings. In my research I came across a number of organisations where copies of *In Search of Excellence* had been circulated, presumably because the person responsible thought that his or her colleagues could learn from it. Yet, oddly, the book had never been discussed.

The quality of achievement

The emphasis throughout this chapter has been that management development systems have been characterised more by their attempt to provide opportunities for learning on the job than by attempts to improve the quality of such learning. It therefore becomes additionally difficult to define achievement in this area. If the opportunity has been provided but has not been taken up, then whose is the failure? Since the attempt is being made under a Type 3 banner, the failure actually lies within the formal management development scheme. Until we clarify our objectives to include actually helping with the process rather than simply providing the opportunity, then the level of achievement in relation to any particular opportunity will be no different from the lack of achievement on the equivalent opportunity provided by informal and accidental processes. The formal scheme may have increased the number and range of opportunities; but it will not have increased the capacity of the manager to take advantage of them.

The need is therefore primarily to design in additional quality by increasing the content of the formal processes. The scattered, accidental, occasionally bruising nature of the learning process which occurs in normal, informal managerial work may be acceptable because no one is pretending that the process is other than a by-product. When we start improving development through formal processes, we cannot afford to stop providing informal opportunities; these focus on the very process that we want to improve – the ability to learn.

Exercise

1 What steps have we taken to assist in formally providing opportunities for development on the job?
2 What steps have we taken to assist managers to take advantage of these opportunities, and to assist their bosses to make them more meaningful in the provision of effective learning?
3 How many of these opportunities do we in fact provide? Are there some which we do not currently use that could be suggested to some or all of our managers?
4 What steps could be taken to help on issues such as coaching and mentoring?

Methods for improving the quality of the learning process, in both Type 2 and Type 3 modes, are provided in Chapter 11. They are taken together, because of course the attention to learning and development processes recommended here for Type 3 purposes will have the great virtue of enabling managers to improve their capacity for accidental learning from experiences, converting them into Type 2.

References

1 MUMFORD A. *How Managers Can Develop Managers.* Aldershot, Gower, 1993.
2 STEWART R. 'Developing managers by radical job moves'. *Journal of Management Development.* Vol. 3, No. 2, 1984.
3 GABARRO J. 'When a new manager takes charge'. *Harvard Business Review.* May–June 1985.
4 INSTITUTE OF PERSONNEL MANAGEMENT. *IPM Code on Secondment.* London, Institute of Personnel Management, 1988. (No longer available.)
5 MEGGINSON D. *and* BOYDELL T. *A Manager's Guide to Coaching.* London, Bacie, 1979.
6 MUMFORD A. 'Learning styles and mentoring'. *Industrial and Commercial Training.* Vol. 7, No. 8, 1995.
7 PARSLOE E. *Coaching Mentoring and Assessing.* London, Kogan Page, 1992.
8 MEGGINSON D. 'Instructor coach mentor'. *Management Education and Development.* Vol. 19, Part 1, 1988.
9 MARSH L. 'Good manager good coach'. *Industrial and Commercial Training.* Vol. 24, No. 9, 1992.
10 CLUTTERBUCK D. *Everybody Needs a Mentor.* London, IPM, 1985
11 MEGGINSON D. *and* CLUTTERBUCK D. *Mentoring in Action.* London, Kogan Page, 1995.
12 ZEY M. G. *The Mentor Connection.* Dow Jones Irwin, 1984.
13 LAHTINEN H. 'Mentoring female executives'. *Executive Development.* Vol. 6, No. 3, 1993.

Further reading relevant to this chapter is shown in Chapter 13.

8

 Planned Development off the Job

The problem with development processes centred on the job is that their great strength – reality – constantly poses the risk of seduction. The manager's attention is always likely to be seduced by the reality and felt priority of the managerial activity rather than focusing on learning.

The case for taking managers away from that reality and putting them on a course is precisely that they are then able to concentrate entirely on learning rather than managing. Nor is it only a question of focus of attention. Informal managerial learning through normal work practices is insufficient, inefficient and dangerous. But even the improved Type 2 version of learning through real work is unlikely to produce a manager fully capable of operating effectively in the modern world. Although we can greatly increase the productivity of learning through real-life experiences, they will still offer learning only within the limits of those experiences. You cannot learn on the job anything that is not available within or around it. You cannot develop a skill if that skill is not actually employed currently. An even more pervasive problem is that you cannot improve your level of skill if there is no one else around capable of demonstrating, coaching or facilitating your development of it.

Two examples will help to illustrate this. Most managers learn how to conduct selection interviews through 'informal and accidental' processes; they have some experience of being interviewed, they carry out interviews themselves and they may have some discussions with other people about the process and the results they secure. These informal processes can certainly be improved by the application of the ideas given in Chapter 3. They can be improved further through an interviewing course. A well-designed course will offer an appropriate balance of knowledge about the principles of interviewing, and practical exercises. Such a course is likely to include principles such as the interviewee's air time being quadruple that of the interviewer, and the need to ask open-ended questions. Those principles are carried into effect on the course by providing exercises in interviewing. Observations, video-recording and skilled feedback will give the manager involved the chance to review the skills he has used and see how he might develop them further.

If we look at chairmanship, we shall see that the nature of the meetings that managers chair varies according to their jobs, the organisations they are working in and the purpose of the particular activity. As with selection interviewing, the capacity to run meetings successfully can certainly be shown to develop from personal experience, and can be enhanced through improved learning on the job. A formal training course, if properly designed and delivered, can develop through practice, observation, feedback and more practice the skills involved in managing a meeting successfully rather than just 'chairing meetings'.

In each of these cases – deliberately chosen because they focus on common managerial activities – it is possible to see elements of knowledge and elements of skill. The knowledge could also be put over in writing – which is why there are popular books on management techniques. But the combination of knowledge and skill offered on a course designed to give the opportunity to work out the knowledge in practice makes for a much more effective learning process. It is the combination that makes the process effective, and which may also bring into play a third element: attitude.

It is possible that attitudes, which are inevitably learned informally, can be changed via a more considered learning process on the job. But a well-designed course can achieve attitude change more effectively, through the combination of knowledge and skill reviewed through observation and feedback, which may generate new understanding and different attitudes. Whereas, for example, it is not unknown for a manager to be told that his or her attitude is wrong in the on-the-job situation, the influence of such a statement is often minimal. In a structured learning environment a manager who sees the results of his or her behaviour, either through a video or by feedback from colleagues, may be more motivated and better equipped to change.

We can take as an example one of the areas in which attitudes are most demonstrable and also very difficult to change. The male stereotype about female managers includes beliefs about the latter's likelihood of continuing a managerial career or surrendering to domesticity, beliefs that women are emotional rather than rational, that they are soft rather than hard in their managerial dealings, and that other managers – 'although not me, of course' – would have difficulty accepting a female boss. It would be proper to be modest in any claims about the influence that any course on women as managers, run for men, would have on these stereotypical attitudes. However, there is increasing evidence that whereas simply telling male managers that their attitude is wrong is ineffective, illustrating the nature and consequences of their stereotypical attitudes on a course shifts at least some managers some distance.

Effectiveness is the core

A manager is a person who gets things done. Some of those things are achieved by direct, personal and largely solitary activity; others are achieved by getting other people to do things. One of the problems in management training and education is that we tend to start by distinguishing knowledge, skill and attitudes, as we did in the previous section. Yet managers do not characteristically think that way. They think about themselves and others in terms of relative effectiveness in getting things done. They may, through analysis of their success or failure, subsequently perceive a lack of knowledge, skill or attitudes. But they start from effectiveness: and effectiveness is defined by results actually secured, not by knowledge or skill. To reiterate the point, courses ought to work initially, if not always primarily, from what managers need to achieve.

Instead of giving emphasis to the provision of knowledge and asking managers to interpret and use that knowledge in subsequent action, we should give prime attention to action issues. This is more appropriate because it is actually about what managers do; it is also more successful because the managerial learner is more likely to be interested. Knowledge and the capacity to analyse and produce solutions to problems are necessary but insufficient contributors to effective action. Even attention to managerial skills, which looks at first sight a more attractive option, both to managers and to tutors, may be misplaced. The first focus of attention should be on the desired managerial result rather than on the particular skills required for achieving that result.

Some management trainers already do what I am suggesting. Others show that although they work on managerial skills, they do so on the basis of analysis of the particular skills and specific level of skill required in their organisation (see Chapter 6). Others, in discussion, are slightly puzzled and say that since the analysis of skill requirements has already been undertaken it seems unduly long-winded to review them at the beginning of a programme, or to focus on issues of effectiveness first, when 'at the end of the day we are going to finish up with a list of skills that we knew they needed in the first place'.

It may indeed seem puzzling, if you have gone through the kind of careful analysis suggested in Chapters 4 and 6, that your first step in designing a course should be to put this analysis on one side. Yet this is a necessary step, both practically and psychologically. It is practically necessary for the reasons already suggested: managers will simply not attend to a discrete list of knowledge and skills in the way you would like or envisage.

The second reason is just as fundamental – and perhaps more difficult to accept. It is that management trainers and educators, for quite obvious and indeed quite admirable reasons, think they know a great deal more about the skills required for effective management than most managers. We have spent time reading about it, thinking about it, designing and redesigning courses on it. We finish up with an answer to which we are committed. In manufacturing industry that answer would be called a product. We become concerned to sell the product and deliver it successfully. All this is quite understandable and legitimate; and, like many products, what we offer is – up to a point – very helpful to the customer. But the elaborate analysis of skills, knowledge and attitudes we have worked through may mean that the process we recommend is product- rather than customer-centred.

My own experience has been the successful development of processes from the starting-point that managers much prefer working from their understanding of management than from a textbook breakdown. This applies even to my modern gods of managerial behaviour – Stewart, Mintzberg and Kotter.

Readers may wish to test their own position against the views expressed in the first part of this chapter.

Exercise

1 Go back to your answers to the questions in Chapter 6 about how you and your organisation currently identify needs for improved skills or knowledge.
2 How do you use that analysis at the moment in designing courses?
3 What concepts about managerial skills, behaviours and effectiveness do you currently employ in the *design* of your courses? (Note the word design, not content.)
4 By what process do you currently try to engage the commitment of managers attending a course to what you will be doing on it, again focusing on issues of design and not on issues of nomination, preparation, design and delivery?

Links

Many of the suggestions here are linked with those in earlier chapters; there is a common theme of using managerial reality rather than ignoring it. It may be useful at this stage to summarise.

Managerial reality

The focus for our development work ought to be reality not only because it is (obviously) real, but because it engages the attention of managers. The problem with processes and content that do not engage and focus on reality is that for many managers they create learning problems rather than making learning easier and more effective.

Building on experience

It is more sensible to build the design and content of formal training and education on the experience that managers have when they arrive on a course. It takes longer and may be less exciting for the tutor; but it is actually more effective.

Using familiar learning processes

Although one of the great virtues of formal training and education is precisely that it focuses on learning rather than just managing, the achieved learning of managers will be low if the process is too different and distant from what they usually do. Since managers do not customarily spend their time listening to lectures, even brilliantly delivered lecturers may not attract them. If they do not spend their time reviewing historical case-studies of managerial practices in other organisations, a learning process based on this starts with some major disadvantages. Perhaps most powerfully of all, if the learning process, of whatever nature, is seen as something that is likely to be useful only on a course, not in real managerial life, then again our achievements will be more limited than they should be. We will have achieved something by causing managers to think in a different way, by giving them opportunities to listen, study, reflect and generate new ideas. But if they see these activities as applicable only in a formal course context, then we have limited our results.

Continued learning

A follow-on from the last point is appropriate for many courses. It is desirable that the learner should continue learning after the course. This is not simply a matter of 'further reading' or individual action plans. These are partial but low-level contributions. For any but short courses on particular techniques, participants should be given such an understanding of their own learning processes that they can seek out and use appropriate learning experiences beyond the confines of the course. A successful consequence of such attention would be a vast increase in Type 2 learning as a result of these Type 3 experiences. It is not necessary that all trainers and educators should use these particular descriptions; but it is desirable that they should take on board responsibility for enhancing the capacity of managers to learn outside as well as on their courses. This means explicit sessions on learning to learn – not claims that 'it happens naturally' on courses.

Preferred approaches to learning – tutor and learner

There is quite a lot in the management development literature about how to deliver particular methods of off-the-job development, usually including either an explicit or implicit claim that the par-ticular method has special virtues. However, when I came to review the literature it was extremely weak on two very important issues. The first question in choosing any method is what need it is pre-eminently suited to meeting. Why should a case-study, a lecture or technology-based training be supposed to meet that defined need? The second issue is whether that method, whatever its general suit-ability for a defined need, will actually suit the learning preference of the people exposed to it.[1] Different individuals have a different capacity to create sense from the same elements; they prefer their learning to be presented in particular forms. Course designers and tutors need to enhance their capacity to deal with these individual preferences, difficult and time-consuming though this may appear to be. (See Chapter 11.) Consider each of the headings in Figure 8.1.

Figure 8.1
Manager-centred Learning

Managerial reality
Building on experience
Using familiar learning processes
Continued learning
Preferred approaches to learning

Exercise

1 With which of them do you agree or disagree? Why?
2 Do your current courses meet these desirable criteria?
3 Are there any of the criteria which you now think you should apply to any or all of your courses?
4 To what extent do you perceive your courses to be integrated into a total management development philosophy, and a total management development system?

Too paradoxical for trainers and educators?

It could be argued here that we are presenting a paradox. It is recommended that trainers and educators should focus on the real interests and levels of understanding of managers, rather than starting from their own understanding. This appears to suggest that trainers and educators should ignore their own preferences and adapt their interests and needs to those of managers. One answer is that this approach is likely to be more effective. Another is that we should see ourselves as marketing a service, not selling what we want to produce.

Since managers' and trainers' needs and interests do differ, it would be not merely paradoxical but hypocritical if this chapter did not attempt to meet the different levels of understanding, belief or need of different kinds of trainer and educator. So the next section gives some examples of the more traditional 'skills and knowledge' route.

Skills-directed management training

Two of the most familiar parts of an organisation's management training catalogue, or consultants' or training centres' brochures, are:

- a basic course on management
- a communications skills course.

Here are two examples (the second is phrased in terms of objectives rather than content):

Effective management 1
Course objectives and individual objectives
Motivation – group discussion and research findings
Management styles
Decision-making – alternative processes
Team and group processes
Setting objectives
Individual performance review/appraisal
Participant action plans.

Communication skills 2
By the end of the course participants will be able to:

- use questions to collect information from others
- demonstrate effective listening by monitored feedback
- be able to identify appropriate styles of chairmanship for meetings
- be able to operate conversational control behaviour as individual member and as chairman
- be able to make a five-minute presentation with a 70 per cent satisfaction rating from fellow participants.

These are examples of courses familiar to many management trainers because they respond to the kind of needs often encountered in organisations. They can be run either in company or outside (see below for further discussion). Such programmes have considerable advantages in their own right, even though they do not meet the criteria suggested earlier. The advantages are these:

- They deal explicitly with areas of skill and knowledge.
- They do so within a format and a level of understanding relatively

familiar to sponsoring managers who may have attended similar programmes themselves.
- Once managers are persuaded to look at skills and knowledge needs, programmes like this provide a clear response to those defined needs.
- They fit the relatively neat structure of the way of developing skills and knowledge that many managers will understand from experience in schools and universities.
- They provide relatively clear boundaries on what is to be covered, so that sponsors, participants and trainers are able to share a degree of comfort about 'how far the course will go'.

The second example illustrates progress over the last 25 years; increasing attention is given to describing measurable objectives rather than just listing apparently appropriate content. Although not without problems, this has the great advantage of focusing attention on what people will be able to do, and therefore offers a basis for subsequent evaluation.

Values

Skills- and knowledge-centred design seems best fitted to single-loop learning (see page 7); if the real need is for double-loop learning (which challenges current wisdom), then the apparent benefits may be outweighed by disadvantages.

In-company courses can be particularly powerful in protecting and sustaining the culture and value system of the company. Indeed, this is precisely what some courses explicitly, but more often unconsciously, attempt to do. They are really saying, 'This is a splendid organisation for which to work and here are the reasons why.' They may also say, explicitly or implicitly, 'Here is the way we want things done round here – do not expect to get rewarded or promoted if you behave differently.'

One of the problems for management trainers is that although courses can promote particular kinds of values, and attack others, the values concerned may not be those of the organisation. Some management trainers have values which they perceive as appropriate for organisations, and seek to promote change. Thus many management trainers believe that participative management processes are better than autocratic ones, that an open style of management is better than not discussing issues, that you secure better results by kicking problems around rather than imposing solutions. These may be the values of the organisation – or they may not. Even if they are the stated values they may not have much to do with the actuality of the organisation. How many organisations, for example, would accept business ethics on an in-house course? (It is, after all, a relatively new feature in business schools.) A further issue here is that the values and beliefs of trainers may take them into territory that is more comfortable for them than for participants. Learning about trust from blindfold exercises, even if valid as a process, may be more an expression of trainer values and immediate authority than a legitimate metaphor for management. Some trainers delight in 'touchy-feely' issues; are their clients free to choose not to participate?

Exercise

1 What values do you believe your courses are promoting?
2 Have these values been established explicitly within the programme because of some organisation statement, or because of your beliefs about what the organisation's values are?

The link with individual needs

One virtue of the effectiveness-centred approach is that it is more likely to secure the real participation of individuals on the course. The effectiveness approach does not necessarily mean starting with a vague session on 'Managerial effectiveness in our organisation'.

Instead the programme may start with a session on 'What is our business and what do we need to do to manage it well?' or 'What are the problems and opportunities facing our organisation and what do we need to do well to meet them?'

While this approach may mitigate, it will not overcome the different problems so frequently encountered on many management courses: failures in the nomination and preparation process. Management trainers and educators usually point to the nominator as the cause of the problem. Managers arrive on courses at short notice having been told 'it was their turn' and with no previous discussion with their bosses about why they are being sent. Some people for whom the course is, in fact, appropriate turn up but are poorly motivated; and sometimes people turn up for whom the course is not appropriate at all. When every allowance has been made for the exigencies of managerial life, which does sometimes mean that nominations have to be changed at the last moment, there are too many occasions when people who could have been given adequate notice were not. It is scarcely surprising that someone whose needs have not been discussed is at best unlikely to see how a course may help or at worst be disposed to reject the course precisely because it has been imposed without discussion.

The effectiveness approach illustrated

We return now to four examples of the effectiveness approach. The first has been deliberately chosen to illustrate how a concern for effectiveness, ie what managers actually can be helped to do, caused a change in the design of the programme. I have encountered the original design in a number of other organisations. It was in most cases clear that they had not identified the basic concept of their programme as effectiveness. They had seen this particular part of the programme as a useful culminating feature, with all the trappings of presentations to the chief executive. They also had seen it as essentially about imparting knowledge on the company strategy, which is regarded as a useful thing to do with middle or senior managers.

Both these are legitimate objectives. The change illustrated in the first case-study below followed from a different understanding about the usefulness of focusing on effectiveness, and a different view about the priority of doing so in comparison with 'handing knowledge out'.

Case 1

The final stages of a two-week management development programme were originally geared to the participants reviewing the corporate strategy of the group for which they worked. The intention of the sessions, which included a presentation to the chief executive, was that participants should be more familiar with the thinking behind the corporate strategy. It seemed to me less relevant that participants should understand the corporate strategy than that they should be encouraged to take action on strategic issues affecting their own business. So a change was made. Participants were asked to make proposals on a significant business problem currently affecting most of them. One group was asked to work on the nature of, and possible reactions to, competition from Japanese manufacturers. While they could not do anything to affect corporate strategy, except perhaps understand it better, they could do something in their own companies about the Japanese 'threat'.

Case 2

A company that had revised its sales objectives and organisation structure was concerned that the managers involved might not have the skills necessary to achieve the changed objectives. Analysis made it clear that, although a number probably were lacking in some skills, the more crucial problem was that, although apparently committed to the revised objectives, they had not fully set up the action plan necessary to implement them. The prime effectiveness concern was not therefore the skills of sales management, but the identification of action to implement the broad objectives agreed.

Case 3

A company that had changed the composition and structure of
its marketing function found that a number of those involved
would be unable to produce what was required because they
did not have the requisite marketing skills. In the course of discussion with them the emphasis was shifted from the acquisition to the implementation of skills. An in-house marketing
programme was devised which, as well as giving managers the
necessary tools, helped them identify specific marketing projects which needed to be undertaken. The programme was designed to meet the general marketing skill requirements of the
organisation, the specific requirements of the projects that had
to be undertaken and the completion of real work to meet the
needs of the business.

Case 4

MBA programmes normally provide participants with a better
understanding of the various functional areas of management
like marketing, finance and production. It is expected that managers who have acquired this knowledge will be able to manage these functions better or, through a better understanding,
improve their relationships with other departments. The MBA
programme run at International Management Centres starts at
the other end of the process by requiring our associates to
analyse the nature of relationships between their own function
and others in the business, and to make proposals for improvement. While we believe that it may be important for most managers to 'understand finance better', we see it as at least as
important that they should be helped to take specific actions
relevant to their needs in dealing with other functions.

Exercise

1 What is your experience in dealing with needs similar to those described here?
2 Has the description of focusing on effectiveness, and the illustrations presented here, given you different ideas for handling similar problems in the future?

Education or training?

In the past, education has been defined as a broadly based and broadly directed process aimed at the whole person and total career, while training has been seen as the specific process of helping managers to learn things appropriate to particular circumstances, within specific organisations or industries. The distinction also broadly followed location: education was what happened in the further education system and training was what happened in management centres.

The distinction, if ever true, seems now to have largely lost its meaning. Although training centres probably tend to focus more on issues that are practical and specifically related to organisational needs, they also often see themselves as educating a manager for his or her total life. Similarly, education centres have increasingly taken on responsibility for developing managers who meet the specific needs of their particular organisations. One of the most obvious illustrations of this has been in the attitude of the major traditional business schools. When first set up they took a distinctly lofty and distant view about the desirability of doing in-company work (except as private ventures by senior faculty). Now all of them make a virtue, as well as a great deal of money, from giving such work prominence.

Until relatively recently a different distinction could have been drawn between education and training. Education processes, particularly as exhibited on MBA programmes, were clearly

knowledge-based, whereas training was much more likely to have a
higher skill content and be more directly concerned with implementation. But, under the impact of customer resistance, there has been
a considerable conceptual and practical shift towards skills of implementation and effectiveness. Revans's attacks from outside the
system on traditional business school processes were significant
because they provided a distinctive phrase – action learning – and a
description of managerial learning processes that was intellectually
as well as practically attractive. Not that Revans was successful in
converting any existing business school, or indeed that he had a
major impact on other business schools for a number of years. Nor
did the parallel work of John Morris (at the Manchester Business
School), who showed in his *Joint Development Activities*[2] that the
essential concepts of action learning could be incorporated into at
least part of a business school. Indeed, Morris's ideas remained a
special feature rather than being incorporated into the total philosophy of his business school.

It took a privately funded business school (International
Management Centres) to go wholeheartedly for the action learning
concept. Other business schools have on the whole tried to tack
some action learning concepts and methodologies onto otherwise
traditional MBA programmes. In most cases this has meant adding
a project, a process that can take students into the area of reality and
effectiveness.

It might be thought that I am simply engaging in special pleading
for the kind of work my own institution does. We are, however, a
particular illustration of the general case I am making, of the necessity for moving business schools towards reality and effectiveness.

MBA programmes receive disproportionate attention in discussion about management education and training because they are
the longest and most ambitious attempt to develop managers by
structured processes. Measured in terms of growth of numbers since
1966, and in terms of a substantial proportion of client reaction, traditional MBA programmes can scarcely be said to have made a
major contribution in the UK. Even in the United States there are
major concerns about the actual results achieved by 80,000 MBA
graduates a year, and this concern has been expressed not so much

by concerned industrialists as by academic researchers like Behrman and Levin.[3] The proposals in the Constable Report[4] to quintuple production of MBA graduates in the UK seemed rather odd to me. This report lacked any analysis of why management training and education processes had so far been unattractive to British management. However, by 1997, 100 UK business schools were producing perhaps 6,000 graduates.

Of course, a great deal of good management education is achieved outside the major business schools. We are paying attention here to such schools and to shifts within them because those schools are inevitably in a leadership position.

It should finally be emphasised that, since it is a theme of this book that individuals differ, their capacity to learn from particular kinds of programme and their interest in doing so will also differ. The traditional business school programmes, with their heavy emphasis on knowledge, rationality and analytical skills, may well be more appropriate to some individuals than courses of the kind that I have tended to argue for in this chapter.

Figure 8.2

Comparison of 'Own Organisation' and Open Programmes

Own organisation	Open
Potentially specific to organisation needs	Likely to be general
Can make use of company-specific material	Use material from a variety of sources
Contained within organisational culture	May develop alternative views about organisation culture
Probably focuses on company issues	Operates more widely in a general context
Participants more likely to feel they are being assessed	Participants more likely to feel they are not being assessed
Experience on offer is relatively narrow	Experience available from managers and faculty likely to be wider
Economic for groups of managers	Suitable for 'single' managers
Tutors may be perceived as 'junior'	Higher quality and/or credibility of tutors

Own organisation and open programmes

This book's stress on the contingent reality of management – that what a manager needs to be able to do well in one organisation may differ significantly from requirements in another – suggests that in-company programmes are more likely to meet these needs successfully. Not all organisations will in fact have a choice, because they may not be of sufficient size for it to be economical or feasible to gather all managers together for a formal training course. Where organisations are large enough, they will probably opt for a mix of in-company and outside courses. Virtues and defects are readily identifiable, as shown in Figure 8.2 on page 175. The problem is to distinguish which apply to particular purposes and individuals. A good review of pros and cons is given in Hussey.[5]

Exercise

1 Consider an experience in your own development, where you can compare the benefits of own organisation and open programmes. How far do these match the points made in Figure 8.2?
2 Consider an experience of someone whom you may have nominated to attend a course. To what extent were the issues covered in the figure considered, and with what result?
3 What action may you take in the future as a result of these first two questions?

Line management ownership

It is preferable for nominations to arise through a well-conducted appraisal or personal development review. If managers respond to the arrival of a course brochure, and suggest it either for themselves or for someone else, this relatively opportunistic process can be successful, if there is proper discussion. The worst nomination position

is that of 'Buggins's turn'; there are still organisations where someone attends a course because all senior managers do and it is now his
or her turn to go.

There are four other aspects of the contribution of line management:

- design of internal courses
- participation
- production of case material
- counterpart role.

It is very helpful, particularly for senior programmes, to involve a
senior line manager who is perceived as the programme's main
client in its design. The line manager would not be expected to contribute in terms of method, but he or she should validate the content.

It is often easier to get line managers to participate in laying on
the course. The formal role has tended to be that of giving a talk; but
line managers are now increasingly invited as receivers of syndicate
reports or reviewers of projects. Not all of them are good at this (any
more than they are at giving a talk); but this latter role is much more
relevant to management processes. Those for whom pressure or lack
of competence make a formal role inappropriate can be invited to
contribute informally, perhaps by attending dinners during the
course. Individual managers can be asked to help develop particular
case study material to be used on the programme. This might be
gathered directly from their files or drawn out of them by discussion.

In my own organisation we have developed the concept of a
'counterpart'. This is a senior line manager or director who acts as a
twin with our faculty: for example the organisation's marketing director works closely with our marketing tutor. We have found this a
particularly helpful process in sorting out the real issues and priorities in a business; we get further reinforcement that what is done on
the course accords with organisational priorities rather than those
which we as experts might impose.

Open and distance learning

These two approaches are often coupled, although in fact they are neither the same thing nor even mutually dependent! Snell and Binsted[6] define open learning as to do with learners having:

- choice about which learning goals they pursue
- choice about sequence or depth of learning
- choice about learning processes and depth of their involvement
- unrestricted access from the educational point of view, eg no entry qualifications.

Distance learning is defined as that which:

- involves the geographical separation of the tutor and the learner
- involves the use of at least one form of media (print, video, computer output)
- is suitable for solo learners (although can be used in small groups of two or more)
- needs a delivery system
- works anywhere providing appropriate hardware is available.

Given these definitions, it is confusing that the Open University and the Open College are so called. The titles derive from the *intention* of the offer rather than the *nature* of the process. A number of the concepts involved in the description of open learning will be addressed further in Chapter 11 in relation to self-development.

It is relevant here to offer some brief comments on distance learning. The packages that were developed from the early 1980s were initiated and publicised as a flexible and cost-effective way of dealing with large-volume training requirements. Considerable sums of money were spent on the development of the major packages. The programmes were intended to cope with the fact that managers do not find it convenient to attend courses, but could be stimulated by the opportunity to learn from visually presented material at home or at work. However, evaluation so far shows considerable wastage and ineffectiveness. Mann, in an article based on her original research,[7] showed that only one-third of students actually completed their study. The article spells out the reasons for failure, some of which are not peculiar to distance learning: they relate to the now familiar issues of relevance to need and the nomination process. Packages have to be general in order to sell to a general population; but inevitably they then become less useful for some participants.

There are two further important points about the learning process. The largely solitary nature of learning means that participants often lack precisely those additional inputs, challenges and supporting behaviours that they would get in a group process. As Snell and Binsted state, preferred learning styles are also a major issue. Some learners will find the solitary, reflective, non-participative, non-action-oriented process acceptable, and others will not.[8]

Design issues

Managers' criticism of courses has often centred on the issue of reality. Sometimes the word is seen as coterminous with relevance; but strictly speaking they are different concepts. Relevance relates to a manager's perception of whether the content or some part of the content of a course engages with issues that are important in the job. As we have argued throughout this book, this is of major importance. However, reality is something different. Content could be relevant, as described above, but still be seen as unrealistic compared with how the manager perceives things actually to work.

Team-building processes illustrate the difference. Most managers work in groups, and many work in what are intended to be teams. Team-building sessions are therefore likely to have high relevance potential. (Although actual relevance will, of course, depend on whether managers perceive team issues as being actually important in current performance.) However, the particular process used for developing ideas about, and techniques for, effective teamwork might be seen as unreal. For many years trainers have used simulation exercises whose prime purpose is to promote reflection about teamwork. The construction of the tallest tower in Lego™ bricks, or the longest unsupported bridge, or outdoor training are examples. All of them deal with the 'relevant' issues of teamwork, but all of them have been criticised as unreal.

Reality becomes an inherent inescapable problem when managers do anything other than 'real' work. All processes involving exercises, whether of the kinds mentioned above or role plays, case-study analysis or business games, simulate, but are not, managerial reality. They are an attempt to provide, in a structured learning environment, something that is believed to tackle the issues or to demonstrate the skills involved in real management work. There are at least three problems with simulations:

- They are clearly designed by and in the control of the tutor. They involve games playing, and games played to rules set by the tutors, not by managers.
- They are sometimes offered not primarily as a means of best meeting a specific objective, but as a means of providing variety within a longer programme, or as a rather crude means of involving managers.
- As with any other learning process, individuals respond differently. Some are incapable of abstracting from unreality and drawing out useful lessons, while others accept the unreality and are able to generate useful learning experiences.

Effective management training and education recognises and attempts to deal with these problems. A thorough-going analysis is provided in the series of articles by Binsted and Stuart.[9] Huczynski's *Encyclopedia* illustrates the extraordinary variety of techniques available.[10] We should not abandon simulations, or any other process, simply because they are unreal. But any simulation technique should be used with a much more careful attention to objectives and learner preferences than seems often to be the case.[11] Management trainers should consider first if it is possible to use reality rather than simulate it. It is a legitimate argument that the triviality of tasks such as building with Lego™ bricks or making paper aeroplanes is necessary so that managers do not get so obsessed with the task that they avoid the learning. There are circumstances in which that argument is a clinching one. If, however, we tried to make more frequent use of real-work experiences within a programme – and a project is an obvious example – then:

- we would be less frequently criticised by managers for designing unreal situations
- we would reduce the notorious 'transfer' problem
- we would actually enable managers to go away having achieved a real managerial task, rather than having received the award for the most effective bridge or map-reading exercise.

Finally, reality may mean that we design courses more as incremental than transformational learning experiences. Managers are more likely to cope with a step than a leap.[11]

Designing learning into courses

One of the problems with management training and education has been a tendency to accept generalisations about learning and an absence of serious work on the learning process, its application in the course context and its interpretation for particular individuals. It is extraordinary that we have had only one major institutional contribution to our understanding of learning: the collection of individual and research projects conducted at the Centre for the Study of Management Learning at Lancaster University. Learning is apparently a subject unworthy of attention from our major business schools.

Some of the main aspects of the learning process were indicated in Chapter 2, and are developed much more fully in Chapter 11. The main points here are these:

- Courses can and should be designed around explicit learning concepts, not on superficial and anecdotal statements such as 'Managers like to learn by doing things.'

- The recognition that managers differ in their current capacity to learn from different types of learning experience does not need to remain at the level of a crude generalisation. It is unacceptably facile and lazy to throw a variety of processes into a course on the grounds that variety is a good thing and that this will ensure that no one is bored all the time.
- The capacity of individuals to learn from particular processes is predictable, identifiable, observable and discussable. This capacity can be diagnosed, as Mumford describes.[12]

The view that a course should consider every variety of managerial skill without attempting to discuss, let alone develop, the one common skill necessary for the development of all the others is ludicrous once stated. Yet there are still many courses where the opportunity to work on individual learning is ignored. (See, for example, nearly all traditional MBA programmes.) This is illustrated in articles about two quite different courses.

The first, by Honey and Lobley,[13] describes the intensive nature of the learning review process adopted on a redesigned outdoor management course. In view of the surge of popularity of outdoor training in the 1980s, this article is most important in showing how understanding of the learning process, and therefore learning itself, can be enhanced. A problem with all too many outdoor courses has been that the excitement over the physical activity has far overwhelmed any learning benefit. Butler's article[14] describes a different kind of management development programme, very much more in the mode of traditional three-week programmes for senior functional managers.

Evaluation

The previously traditional separation between validation – people learning what you intend them to learn – and evaluation – has what they learned been put into useful effect? – was referred to in Chapter 7. In principle both activities are much easier in relation to a structured learning event like a course. It does, however, seem to be the case that only a tiny proportion of courses is subject to either. Easterby-Smith reviews both the reasons for evaluation and some of the reasons why it is found difficult (in relation to courses and other management development schemes).[15] Reasons evaluation is rarely conducted include:

- the absence of clear objectives and standards of achievement for the course
- lack of interest by line managers, who have not forced trainers to provide clear statements of benefits achieved
- a lack of interest among trainers and educators, who are characteristically more interested in delivering the course than reviewing the results; it may be significant here that on the Honey/ Mumford learning styles scores, trainers score relatively low on the reflector score, indicating a lack of interest in collecting data
- the actual difficulty in constructing relevant analytical processes.

Many trainers and educators still use what are in effect 'happiness sheets'. These review participants' perceptions of the quality of tutors, the effectiveness of particular techniques used, the range of facilities provided and perhaps some summary of learning points achieved. Although not totally without merit, in that they assist decision-making about the future employment of particular tutors, for instance, they do not provide either validation or evaluation. They actually provide best of all something that has nothing to do with either – an opportunity for course participants to say something and to feel that they are contributing to the future development of the course.

This is an area that remains a problem. There is every logical reason for giving more attention and more resources to it, and yet trainers and educators have survived for years without. Sensible and helpful guidance in the materials indicated is available; what is lacking is the personal motivation to undertake it.

Formal learning without courses

There are a number of learning opportunities away from work, such as those spelled out in Chapter 7. Just as individuals can, through a formal management development scheme, be placed on particular task forces or committees, so they can be appointed to outside committees. They can be encouraged to join in the work of voluntary or charitable organisations. They can be sent as representatives to industry associations. The formal system can encourage the sensible choice of people in terms of development not just in terms of their capacity to represent the organisation. But just as with the analogous internal activities, these things will remain only partially used opportunities if they incorporate no process for facilitating learning.

Compared with all the other material in this chapter, the distinguishing characteristic here is that these managerial or quasi-managerial activities are not designed specifically as learning experiences. Learning is therefore less likely to occur, even if the formal system makes the individual aware of the learning opportunity, unless the steps shown in Chapter 11 are taken.

You may like to ask yourself the following questions about your organisation.

Exercise

1 Have we reviewed recently our use or non-use of courses? What, in our experience, are the most powerful reasons for using courses at all, or for not using them?
2 What system do we currently use for assessing whether to have own organisation or open programmes of our provision of courses?
3 For which purposes is one more suitable than the other?
4 What use do we currently make of the other learning opportunities outside work (see Figure 7.1)?

References

1 MUMFORD A. *How to Choose the Right Development Method.* Honey, 1997.

2 MORRIS J. 'Joint development activities'. In Beck J. and Cox R., *Advances in Management Education.* Chichester, Wiley, 1980.

3 BEHRMAN J. N. *and* LEVIN R. I. 'Are business schools doing their job?' *Harvard Business Review.* January–February 1984.

4 CONSTABLE J. *The Making of British Managers.* BIM/NEDO, 1987.

5 HUSSEY D. *Management Training and Corporate Strategy.* London, Pergamon, 1988.

6 SNELL R. *and* BINSTED D. *Issues in Management Development.* CSML, 1985.

7 MANN S. 'Why open learning can be a turn off'. *Personnel Management.* January 1988.

8 SNELL and BINSTED, *op cit.*

9 BINSTED D. *and* STUART R. 'Designing reality into managerial learning events'. *Personnel Review.* Vol. 8, Nos. 3 and 4, 1979 and Vol. 9, No. 1, 1980.

10 HUCZYNSKI A. *Encyclopedia of Management Development Methods.* Aldershot, Gower, 1983.

11 MUMFORD A. 'Putting learning styles to work'. *Journal of European Industrial Training.* Vol. 17, No 10. 1993.

12 MUMFORD A. *Learning at the Top.* Maidenhead, McGraw-Hill, 1995.

13 HONEY P. *and* LOBLEY R. 'Learning from outdoor activities'. *Industrial and Commercial Training.* November 1986.

14 BUTLER J. 'Learning more effectively on a general management programme'. *Industrial and Commercial Training.* July 1988.

15 EASTERBY-SMITH M. *Evaluation of Management Education Training and Development.* 2nd edn. Aldershot, Gower, 1994.

Further reading relevant to this chapter is shown in Chapter 13.

9

 People Who Help Development

The prime responsibility for ensuring that managers develop their abilities and potential to the full rests with themselves – and they know it. From the mid-1970s this recognition has been accompanied by a changed recognition of the nature and impact of formal development processes.

The early writers on managerial self-development were stimulated by different views and experiences. The processes and issues involved, and the general principles of what individuals should do for themselves, are covered in Chapter 11. It is crucial here to recognise that the role of all the people mentioned in this chapter is secondary to the role of the individual. While this may seem wholly obvious and acceptable in relation to informal and accidental development activities, it is also true of the role that others may play in encouraging, delivering and monitoring formal management development processes. This is a fact which it is easy to accept in principle, but which for a variety of reasons those involved often find difficult to implement in practice.

Exercise

1 Do you agree that primary responsibility for development rests with the individual, not with any helper?
2 How far do you think the management development processes in which you are involved actually demonstrate this?
3 Consider two experiences in which you may have been involved:
   - If you have been running a course, to what extent have individuals been encouraged to define their own needs, and identify their own solutions?
   - If you have been involved in counselling an individual's development, what has been his or her involvement in defining needs and identifying solutions?

It is likely that the response of some readers to this exercise will have been that 'of course it is a matter of balance'. So the next question is:

4 How far do you think the individuals you have identified

in the exercise above would feel that they were in charge
of their own development, as compared with accepting
your well-designed and helpful interventions?

A range of help and helpers

In this chapter an extensive range of people who may help is reviewed, as is a number of the processes by which they may offer
help. The chapter covers help offered within the formal processes,
but also shows how help can be given to improve learning on the job
in the Type 2 mode. Figure 9.1 shows the range of people who might
be involved. (I have noticed in some organisations an aversion to the
terms 'boss' and 'subordinate', so I have used in some cases below
a more delicate alternative.)

Figure 9.1
Potential Helpers in Development

On the job	Off the job
● direct manager (boss) ● grandboss ● professional advisers – internal ● professional advisers – external ● mentors ● colleagues ● direct reports (subordinates) ● management development committee	● tutors/trainers/facilitators ● consultants ● friends ● spouse

The actual roles of the people indicated in Figure 9.1 are clearly different; but it is useful to note that their type of responsibility is also
different.

● *The direct manager* normally has an explicit, and certainly an implicit, managerial responsibility for helping the development of
  subordinates. The responsibility is attributed, but in practice
  avoidable.

- *Professional helpers* also carry formal responsibility, which can again be explicit or implicit. Compared with the direct manager, however, they lack for most purposes direct power: they usually influence rather than make decisions about the development of individuals. In most cases their responsibility is seen as entirely concerned with formal processes. This is partly because of perceptions about the nature of management development.
- *Other helpers* are essentially volunteers. They may either offer help or respond to implied or explicit requests for help. With the exception of mentors on some occasions they are normally part of the informal and accidental processes of management development. They are a most significant part of that dominant process, but they have no formal responsibility. With the direct manager, they are the prime means of securing more effective development from real managerial activities.

The direct manager (boss)

The example of Reg Jones, chief executive of General Electric, was quoted on page 90. Here was a man at the top of one of the largest companies in the world engaging in the formal process of identifying a successor for himself. He also described the managerial work he had assigned to potential successors as part of that process. This is an example of the formal responsibility of the boss, although the actual example showed only part of that responsibility. As we have seen so often throughout this book, much formal development is about providing opportunities, but not about ensuring that those opportunities are properly utilised and understood. Perhaps Reg Jones did discuss what was involved from a learning, as well as performance, point of view; but he did not say so.

Formal management development systems emphasise the role of the direct manager. This is correct, since a unique managerial responsibility rests with him or her. While we have fortunately long passed the days when the direct manager was actually seen as 'responsible' for the development of subordinates, rather than for helping their development, the system is quite right to place the direct manager at the forefront of formal processes.

What has, predictably, been less understood and provided for is what actually happens in terms of learning from real managerial work. Formal systems have allocated formal responsibility for particular kinds of development role, because it is perceived that without the allocation of such formal responsibility appropriate action will not be taken. Proper though this is, it has left as either unrecognised or untilled the rich field of learning from normal managerial work and the day-by-day relationship between direct manager and direct report. The particularly powerful nature of this relationship in learning terms was frequently evidenced in my research with directors, although they often harked back to their days as young or middle managers, rather than to recent experiences. An effective management development process would therefore not only encourage direct managers to take up their formal managerial responsibility in the Type 3 mode, but would also encourage them to improve the contribution they make in their day-to-day informal relationships. Processes necessary for converting the direct manager's contribution from Type 1 to Type 2 are shown in Figure 9.2.

Figure 9.2
Roles of a Manager in Developing Subordinates

Within formal system of development (Type 3)
- appraisal of performance
- appraisal of potential
- analysis of development needs and goals
- recognising opportunities
- facilitating those opportunities
- giving learning a priority

Within the direct managerial context (Type 2)
- using management activities as learning
- establishing learning goals
- accepting risks in subordinate performance
- monitoring learning achievement
- providing feedback on performance
- acting as a model of managerial behaviour
- acting as a model of learning behaviour
- using learning styles
- offering help
- direct coaching

One additional gloss on the distinction between Type 2 and Type 3 offered in the figure may be helpful. Formal management development processes require the manager to take on additional managerial tasks, called management development. In Type 2 processes, the direct manager is not taking on additional managerial activities but using existing ones.

This description of the role of the direct manager has so far focused entirely on direct personal contribution. Of course the collective of managers, and particularly the board of directors, has the responsibility for actually determining the nature of management development in their organisation. Their responsibility for the total system, again usually seen purely in terms of the formal processes set up for the organisation as a whole, is also important, though different in kind from that discussed so far. The general rather than personal involvement of the direct manager in the total system will include:

- helping to determine the formal management development system, and perhaps contributing to a written policy
- giving evidence of the priority attached to management development by allocating resources, participating in decision-making meetings and courses
- giving personal evidence of interest by calling for reports on what has been done and evaluating results, by discussing development issues with managers at various levels on both a formal and an informal basis, by making achieved development of direct reports one of the criteria for selection for promotion.

Of course not all direct managers provide all the support and encouragement desirable in either of the modes described in the figure.

Here is an exercise that readers can carry out for themselves and that they could also use with other managers.

Exercise

1 Consider the items in Figure 9.2 and assess yourself on
   a scale 0 = not done well, 10 = consistently done excellently. (This obviously assumes that you do have direct
   reports.)
2 Assess your own direct manager on the same basis.
3 What conclusions do you draw for yourselves and in relation to your direct manager?
In most cases what a direct manager provides is really a
Type 1 experience. Here are two examples:
   'One of my early bosses made me swim managerially.
   He pushed me in, though I knew he would not let me
   drown.'
   'One boss taught me how to prepare a case, because
   nothing got past him unless every dot and comma
   checked out. Another boss later taught me that you
   could ask for a clear case yet show trust in the guy who
   was delivering it instead of distrust.'
4 What conclusions do you draw from these two cases
   about the kind of development being offered to the direct reports?
5 What advice might you give the direct manager in each
   case in order to improve the learning experience?
6 What advice would you give direct reports to increase
   their achieved learning from this relationship?

As these last two cases also show, the direct manager–report relationship, as far as achieved development is concerned, is most
likely to centre around achieved performance because that is how
managers assess themselves and others. It is precisely because performance is so fundamental to the relationship that it is potentially
the crux of the learning relationship; it is, however, also the cause of
difficulty in the learning process because performance so often out-
weighs the learning issues involved.

You might like to try the following exercise on a manager's responsibility for developing direct reports.

Exercise

Jack Simpson went into the chief executive's office expecting promotion. He was in charge of the largest product group in his division. His career had been one of rapid advancement, through a series of successes, usually in jobs that he held for about 18 months.

His contributions to the success of the areas in which he worked were shown by the fact that his results were usually better than his predecessors' and performance often slipped back after he had left a job.

The potential new job had many of the characteristics of those in which he had succeeded previously. At each stage of his career he had shown that he could handle bigger and tougher jobs.

1 Is there any evidence in the information given here to suggest he should not be promoted?
2 What recommendations would you make about Jack Simpson?
3 What evidence is there about either his own development or that of other people?

The grandboss

In the formal management development system, the direct manager's boss has the managerial responsibility for checking that his subordinate manager is developing his direct reports. The formal system normally requires that appraisal forms are reviewed and, if necessary, amended by the grandboss (a title I have chosen in preference to grandfather or grandmother). Of course the grandboss is expected to do more than chase, by providing personally a good example of attention to Type 3 processes.

The grandboss may often exercise a balancing role, giving, for instance, a longer-term view about the desirability of a particular job or assignment for someone further down the line. The grandboss can sometimes have different priorities about the desirability of a manager attending a course at a difficult time, or being placed on a committee or working party when he or she is not the most obvious nomination but would benefit in development terms. Finally, of course, the grandboss can help improve learning on the job by demonstrating the relevant managerial and learning abilities and by asking the right question in the course of normal managerial activity.

The principle of reciprocity

An important point, which I have often emphasised, is that the learning relationship should not be one-way – it should be reciprocal. Mentors learn more than the skills of mentoring; colleagues give *and* receive.

Internal professional advisers

Personnel specialists, management development advisers, management trainers and human resource specialists of a variety of titles are covered in this section. The personnel director ought to direct the development processes and ensure that any separate specialisms are co-ordinated. This responsibility is not always met, especially where training and development are compartmentalised. The different roles depend on the size of the organisation and more particularly on the amount of resources it is prepared to put into this whole field.

I do not provide a detailed summary of the activities of a management development adviser in this chapter. This may seem a surprising omission. I believe that to do so would duplicate the suggestions offered and the exercises included throughout the book. The following comments therefore build on issues covered earlier.

An organisation that takes formal development seriously will seek advice from internal professionals on:

- the objectives, philosophy and nature of desired management development in the organisation
- the formal schemes, policies and procedures necessary to support those objectives
- the resources necessary to put formal processes into effect – internal staffing, selection and use of consultants, the strategy for internal as opposed to external courses
- the quality of resources provided: 'Which is the best course for senior executives?', 'Which consultant has the best reputation for dealing with these particular issues?'
- establishing benefits and evaluating results.

In some cases internal professionals will act as counsellors or advisers to managers on problems concerned with effective performance. So a management development adviser might help set up a two-day event 'Problems and opportunities to 2001', or 'Clarifying relationships between our divisions.' The adviser might give individual advice on development, in terms of a total career plan or in terms of advice on a particular need or a developmental process.

The internal adviser can successfully help only those interested in receiving help. Unfortunately, the status of some internal advisers constrains their effectiveness. Their status often reflects the organisation's view about their capacity to help at more senior levels – a view that may be changed if the adviser offers help on issues of real concern. It is surprising to find that there is little literature on what management development advisers do, as compared with a significant amount on trainers.

There are two additional areas of knowledge that the adviser really ought to have. The first is a *knowledge of not only the principles, but the working practices of management.* The credibility of advisers is nearly always assisted if they have actually worked in something other than management development or personnel. The qualification 'nearly always' allows for those unfortunate circumstances where the adviser is seen as a failed manager rather than an experienced manager. Whatever their background, advisers ought to have a knowledge of what actually happens in management. This is readily available in two forms: the books by Rosemary Stewart, Henry Mintzberg and John Kotter referred to in Chapter 2, or the convenient summary in Mumford.[1] The second way of acquiring knowledge is actually to get out among managers, to talk to them, to sit in on their meetings, to go on visits with them. In my experience, requests of this kind are very generously welcomed; managers are flattered that you should be interested in how they actually work. It is important that you establish some rules of the game, most particularly stressing that there will be no formal or informal feedback to others in the organisation.

The second area relates to *understanding learning and development processes.* The adviser should clearly be in the position of being able to recommend appropriate development solutions to whatever development needs arise, and appropriateness depends on an understanding not only of general learning principles, but of the specifics of how individuals will react. This subject is covered in more depth in Chapter 11 and in the associated further reading. One of the clear roles for the internal adviser is to show why planned development is necessary and how it has the potential to bring identifiable benefits.

Some aspects of this have already been covered in Chapter 6 in which we dealt with the process of analysing needs. Where these clearly show that some formal process is necessary in order to equip managers to meet the needs of the business, then a major benefit has already been established. However, this is not an answer in all situations, since the connections may not be sufficiently clear and dramatic to convince senior managers. In such cases the adviser will have to fall back on some more or less sophisticated version of 'others do more':

- competitors
- my previous company
- other countries
- excellent companies.

External professional advisers

One of the reasons for going outside the organisation for help was indicated towards the end of the previous section. The greater the level of intimacy of the development counselling and advice, the greater the likely worry of managers about the terms under which it is offered. While the internal adviser potentially has the great advantage of knowing much more about the reality of the organisation, the problem of confidentiality inevitably arises. Can a manager really get highly personal advice from an internal adviser and trust that details of his thoughts and problems are not going to be passed on or used internally? There are more positive reasons than this for going outside. The organisation may simply lack internal people with the credibility or professional competence to provide the necessary advice. Or it may wish to test its internal knowledge against the wider view. Examples might be the review of an existing appraisal scheme or the introduction of a new one, an audit of existing management development practices (see Chapter 1 for an example of what might be covered) or the analysis of particular management problems, such as how a management team is actually operating. Advice on selecting and using outside resources of this kind is given in Kakabadse.[2]

Mentors

The process of mentoring was described in the previous chapter. There is now some doubt that the widespread use of mentors identified particularly in the American literature and followed up in the book by Clutterbuck[3] is in fact turning out to be as significant as was thought. Part of the problem is a confusion of roles: the American literature has often accorded a direct manager the role of mentor. Clutterbuck gives an excellent list of ideal characteristics:

- already has a good record for developing other people
- has a genuine interest in seeing younger people advance and can relate to their problems
- has a wide range of current skills to pass on
- has a good understanding of the organisation, how it works and where it is going
- combines patience with good interpersonal skills and an ability to work in an unstructured programme
- has sufficient time to devote to the relationship
- can command a protégé's respect
- has his or her own network of contacts and influence.

I would add to that list:

- has credibility as a manager
- has an understanding of the different learning processes available and the differing learning preferences of individuals.

The American evidence about mentoring is discussed at greater length in the further reading. It is interesting that in both my own research[1] and that of McCall *et al*[4] very few executives identified a mentor contribution. In the UK there has certainly not been sufficient time to test mentoring as a formal process. If it has existed it has been essentially as an informal relationship between a senior manager and another more junior one, perhaps not always even recognised as such by either party: 'I just like giving younger people a hand.'

Colleagues

Colleagues can give help when they are more experienced or more skilled in direct coaching and counselling. They may not offer such help but may well respond to a request. In most cases the help offered is not formal. It is something that arises from normal managerial activities: shared problem-solving, discussion of a difficult forthcoming meeting, a chat about a difficult colleague, a review of organisational necessities and political requirements. So far as the managers are concerned it is really all about how to manage effectively – it is only afterwards that they recognise that they have learned something from a colleague in the course of such discussions.

Another form of learning from colleagues is that of modelling or observation. This can be either positive or negative: a manager may base his future behaviour on what he admires in a successful colleague, or he may base his behaviour on the opposite of an unsuccessful process. It may seem obvious, but it is important to point out that managers can pick up useful behaviour even from people they do not like and/or admire. I recall a case where the manager thought that one of his colleagues was superb at asking questions which clarified problems and issues. 'Unfortunately, when he has finished doing that he cannot seem to come to a decision. I improve my own decisions a lot by watching him at work, but not by his actual decision-making.'

Perhaps the most powerful aspect of a learning relationship with colleagues revolves around the kind of feedback one offers another. Managers often have quite incorrect ideas about how they achieve what they do. Accurate feedback, particularly if presented in a helpful rather than a negative way, is the first stage of learning and a necessary precursor to learning to do things better.

Direct reports (subordinates)

It is understandable that people are much more likely to quote learning from direct managers and from colleagues than they are from direct reports. Again this is partly a matter of vocabulary. When a manager moves into a new job there is always a great deal of knowl-

Figure 9.3
Interaction in Learning

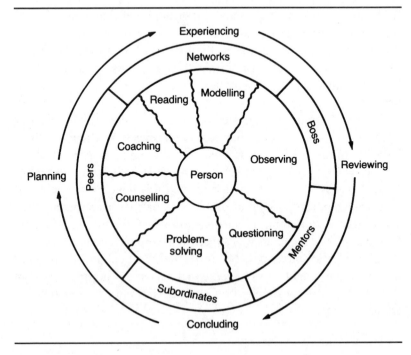

edge to pick up. This may be about the nature of the particular organisation, internal politics, how people in the organisation, particularly the new boss, behave and expect you to behave. Managers often pick these facts up from subordinates, but do not call this learning. It is more rare for them to actually pick up skills. In my own research I found just one or two directors who identified significant learning from direct reports. In one case it was in relation to a quite new function which the director had taken on. In a sense his direct report taught him the details of what was involved. In another case a director actually learned a quite different approach to decision-making – a much more surprising event.

Learning from and through others is the result of the interaction of four different elements:

- *the person's* needs and preferred ways of learning
- *particular processes* of learning on the job
- *the people involved*
- *the total learning process* – the learning cycle.

This interaction is shown in Figure 9.3. 'Networks' include the people described above as grandboss and internal and external advisers.

The traditional model of management development, with its emphasis on purely formal processes, provides a much more limited picture of the people who can help on the job and the ways in which they can help. Those management development advisers who are convinced by the alternative model of management development offered in this book will want to incorporate into their own offerings the initiation and encouragement of Type 2 processes.

Collective involvement and advice

In Chapter 5, when we reviewed the elements and processes of formal management development, we referred to the probable existence of a management development committee. The point of such a committee is to:

- generate interest amongst senior management about management development
- give symbolic significance to management development
- act as the focus for decision-making
- provide an opportunity to generate a consensus decision or corporate view.

The kind of information presented to such committees – the use of data about individuals, summaries of appraisals, information generated from an assessment centre – has been covered in earlier chapters. Such committees are usually wholly concerned with the organisation of formal opportunities, through succession planning, job rotation and nominations for courses. They are much less likely to discuss the kind of help that might be available from individuals indicated earlier in this chapter. Although such a committee therefore fills a very necessary place in the formal structure, most are stuck at the stage of defining opportunities. They do not enable managers to take advantage of those opportunities to achieve learning.

Finding help off the job

There are four types of helper away from work:

- tutors/teachers/trainers
- consultants
- friends
- partner.

Tutors, teachers and trainers have the clear formal responsibility for aiding development. The extent to which they do help development depends on:

- the needs, interests and preferred learning style of the manager being developed

- the extent to which the tutor's style and abilities relate to those needs
- the extent to which content and the process being delivered by the tutor are appropriate to the individual's needs
- the values held by the tutor, and how those values relate to those of the manager under development.

The extent to which individual tutors, or particular training centres, colleges or business schools manage to provide development appropriate to these criteria has received little attention in research. We have the painstaking and innovative work done by the Centre for the Study of Management Learning at Lancaster University, exemplified by the articles by Binsted and Snell.[5] It is sad that the articles by Margerison and Lewis[6] and Hofstede,[7] which illustrate the substantially different values held by management educators as compared with their clients, have not been followed up by more detailed research. Although not based on research, Ashton's article[8] gives a persuasive review of the values held by teachers in business schools. Like Hofstede, his primary point is that the values held by business school teachers and supported by their institutions relate neither to the needs of managers in general nor to those of individual managers. It seems likely that the debate on the number of management teachers required, generated by the Handy and Constable Reports, is at least partly misplaced. As with management education itself, we should be concerned with the quality of what is being offered rather than the quantity.

As you move away from the university-centred business schools, with their strong, traditional academic values, to colleges and independent training centres, it might be claimed that because these are less academically centred they are less likely to be drawn into overly academic processes. While this may be true, it may equally be true that no other clearly identified values have replaced the academic outlook.

It may indeed be a problem for *all* institutions that their value systems are implicit rather than explicit. Perhaps because we were a new institution explicitly confronting some of the traditional beliefs

about management education, my own institution has published its
philosophy of management development and prints this on our con-
spectus.

Values and behaviours of tutors, teachers, trainers

Exercise

1 Does your institution have a published formal statement
   of its philosophy of management education and training?
2 What do you perceive to be the values explicitly held by
   your institution, or implicit in its reward system?
3 Do you perceive there to be an actual or potential conflict
   between meeting immediately performance related
   managerial needs, as compared with broader development for the individual?
4 By what process of analysing needs has your institution
   established the programmes it runs?
5 Does your organisation insist on formal training for its
   tutors?
6 What learning theory, or what beliefs about learning,
   apply in your institution? When were these last discussed, and where are they set out?
7 If you put the last question to your colleagues, do you
   believe they would answer it in terms of learning, or in
   terms of teaching?

Consultants

External consultants can offer help in a range of ways. They can run
courses, in which case the comments made in the preceding section
apply. Their other roles include:

● carrying out a management development audit, surveying the
   practices and policies of an organisation

- carrying out an analysis of management development or training needs
- acting as a personal counsellor or mentor to individuals or to a group of managers.

The objectivity, and perhaps the heightened professionalism, of the external consultants are reasons for bringing them in. The issues are similar to those discussed for tutorial roles. The actual values of the external consultant – why he or she is carrying out the role – may actually differ from the organisational requirements. For example, some consultants believe in the desirability of openness and confrontation; you may indeed seek to challenge some existing organisational norms. If this is an explicit and clear part of the contract between you, well and good. If, however, the consultant's style is not related to a clear request from you of this kind, then problems will occur. These can be avoided by open discussion and by the internal selector doing a sensible job in asking for and following up references from people for whom the consultant has carried out similar work. Casey[9] is very helpful on these issues.

Partner

Some senior executive programmes now contain days on which the spouses of participants come for a mini-version of the programme. This kind of involvement is obviously something that affects only a tiny proportion of spouses. Much more frequently, the partner is involved in informal processes of discussion at home. There has in past decades been a considerable change in the way partners discuss careers and career moves. The advent of dual-career families is one obvious cause; but in general the trend has been towards a less clear-cut, less autocratic process of decision-making on the managerial career of one partner (usually male).

Most partners carry out a range of roles as listener, prompter, or commentator. While some managers want to leave their work at the office and not discuss it at home, others find it at least therapeutic and sometimes positively helpful to do so. This is another largely unstudied area, and there seems to be little available other than Mumford.[10]

Friends

Friends outside work sometimes carry out the role of the mentor. Like the partner in a marriage they can provide helpful guidance on questions about career or about particular problems. Just as managers often look for someone at work who can act as a sounding-board, so they may look for someone outside who carries out a similar function. Because of increasing loneliness as you move up the managerial hierarchy, the availability of such a person can be very important. This is not an aspect that has been considered in formal management development schemes, but it is one that we perhaps ought to take more seriously. We ought to provide more advice on how to identify and use potentially helpful friends, who can give advice unsullied by direct managerial responsibility (the direct manager or boss) or competitiveness (colleagues). The identification of a friendly ear – my term for this relationship – could make a major future contribution to the development of managers. Many managers do use friends in this way, but informally and accidentally, perhaps as a result of a meeting on a course. Useful though those accidental processes are, they could be improved. I am not suggesting a further column in a formal management development scheme, but rather that individuals should be encouraged to think in terms of how someone outside the organisation might help them identify or meet development needs. Or for those people for whom this would be too analytical and formal a process in itself, it might be enough to suggest that simple identification of a friendly ear is sufficient.

The process of helping

We need to revisit constantly the question of what a manager needs or wants (and to recognise the difference between needs and wants). We need to question what we are trying to provide and why, not only at the level of objective analysis of needs for those we are trying to help, but in terms of understanding our own purposes and motivations. Reg Revans's view of the place of consultants, lecturers or trainers in 'helping' is encompassed in his description of 'the inveterate hankering of the teacher to be the centre of attention'. (As with some other aspects of Revans's work and life, there is the profound irony here that he is actually a superb performer as a lecturer.) This is a central point: does the offerer's help really help?

As the earlier discussion in this chapter showed, there is much too little available about the beliefs of those who are offering help. There is the article by Casey,[9] and two important contributions, particularly for the management trainer, by Honey[11] and Nixon.[12] Another expression of values can be seen in the response of trainers to the Honey and Mumford learning styles questionnaire. The norm is for trainers to be Activists (only sales managers score more highly on this dimension). Discussion on the implications of this for what trainers are offering to their clients is a powerful way of showing the values that they are probably putting over. It is even more valuable for the individual trainer to review his or her own style. (See Chapter 11 for more detailed discussion of learning styles.)

A detailed review of the actual processes through which help is offered is given in Chapter 11, since it fits more appropriately into a general review of how managers learn.

Exercise

Developing Senior Managers
You have been appointed as the first group personnel director for a group of companies operating worldwide but based in London. The group has a very small corporate staff and a small main board. The executive directors comprise chairman, chief executive, finance director and four directors responsible for the main product areas of the group.

The group has had a strongly decentralised culture for 15 years. It has a substantial record of profitable organic growth and a mixed, but largely successful, record of acquisition. Apart from yourself, all the main board directors have more than 10 years' service in the group. Most, but not all, members of the main board have agreed on the need for the appointment of a personnel director. They have accepted the case for a better-organised process of remuneration for the top hundred managers in the business (which employs 20,000 people worldwide). They have also decided they wanted in-house help on top-level recruitment instead of relying purely on headhunters. Finally, several of them have been concerned about the development of successors to themselves and the development of people capable of taking more responsibility as the group grows.

The chairman has told you privately that he believes that a successor to the current chief executive needs to be identified and developed in the next two or three years. He hopes that the current chief executive will retire at 60 if a successor is available, although the incumbent believes he will retire at 63.

The group has for many years had a successful history of managing its growth by promotion from within, with some additional resourcing from successful acquisitions. In the last 18 months, however, it has proved increasingly difficult to fill senior vacancies. Only a small number of names seem to be available for each appointment. As a result the group has had to go outside to recruit six managers from profit-centre companies with turnovers ranging from £25 million to £60 million.

You have spent your first month in the group visiting senior managers in many different locations around the world. You have had individual discussions with your colleagues on the board both about the priorities for your activities as they see them, and their views about what has happened so far. All of them agree that there needs to be a major push on the development of senior managers. Most of them believe that the potential is there but that it needs to be developed in some way. All of them agree that proposals for management development should be your top priority – and first submission to a forthcoming meeting of the executive directors.

Discussion with your colleagues has established that appointments to senior management positions are made by each director, subject only to agreement with the chief executive. There is no formal planning process to review top management appointments. The group has a policy of encouraging an appraisal process based on management by objectives. The chief executive does not carry this out with the other directors, but some of them follow this with their own staff. The chief executive and two of the product group directors attended the senior management programme at Henley some years previously. You have encountered one major profit centre manager who has attended the Harvard Advanced Management Programme, and he has presented to you a proposal for extensive use of business school programmes at senior level. There is no process for identifying which people should attend such programmes, nor is there so far a clear view on the utility of any such programme, except that the three main board directors value their Henley experience.

You have had a further discussion with the chairman, during which he has repeated that his main concern is to identify and develop a successor for the chief executive. He has, however, thrown in a new topic: he has asked you to look at the possibility of developing a cadre of MBAs among the middle managers in the group. He has suggested that you visit a number of business schools and select the one offering the most suitable approach.

1 How do you propose to deal with the open and hidden agendas described here?
2 What priorities would you follow and for what reasons?
3 What kind of systems and processes for management development would you recommend?
4 What arguments would you deploy for the expense and time involved in senior development?
5 Would you recruit a management development specialist to help you, or call in help from a business school or a consultant?

(This exercise is an amended version of one originally published in Personnel Management; *this author is grateful for permission to reprint it here.)*

References

1 MUMFORD A. *Developing Top Managers.* Aldershot, Gower, 1988.
2 KAKABADSE A. 'How to use consultants'. *International Journal of Manpower.* Vol. 4, No. 1, 1983.
3 CLUTTERBUCK D. *Everyone Needs a Mentor.* 2nd edn. London, Institute of Personnel Management, 1991.

4 McCALL M., LOMBARDO M. *and* MORRISON A. *The Lessons of Experience.* Lexington, 1988.

5 BINSTED D. *and* SNELL R. 'The tutor learner interaction'. *Personnel Review.* Vol. 10, No. 3, 1981 and Vol. 11, Nos. 1, 2, 4, 1982.

6 MARGERISON C. *and* LEWIS R. 'Management educators and their clients'. In Beck J. and Cox R., *Advances in Management Education.* Chichester, John Wiley, 1981.

7 HOFSTEDE G. 'Businessmen and business school faculty'. *Journal of Manpower Studies.* Vol. 15, No. 1, 1978.

8 ASHTON D. 'Are the business schools good learning institutions?' *Personnel Review.* Vol. 17, No. 4, 1988.

9 CASEY D. 'Some processes at the consultant/client interface'. *Leadership and Organisation Development Journal.* Vol. 3, No. 1, 1982.

10 MUMFORD A. 'Learning at home'. *Programmed Learning and Educational Technology.* Vol. 22, No. 4, 1985.

11 HONEY P. 'What I believe about management training'. *Industrial and Commercial Training.* April 1982.

12 NIXON B. 'In search of excellent management development'. *Industrial and Commercial Training.* July 1984.

10

 Special Needs, Different Solutions

Women managers – a natural disproportion

Figures about the number of women managers vary somewhat according to the source. It seems likely that at least 40 per cent of the
UK workforce are women, yet the proportion of women managers is
much lower, somewhere between 25 and 30 per cent. (The proportion of women directors is somewhere between 5 and 8 per cent,
which illustrates the point even more dramatically.) There can,
broadly, be two views about this disparity. One would be that the
disproportionately few women managers and directors reflect
women's actual competence or their own 'natural' career choices. A
second view is that this disproportion is inappropriate either ethically or in terms of effective use of resources.

Attention to this subject is a relatively new phenomenon. Tom
Roberts's book,[1] in many ways an excellent guide to orthodox management development, does not mention women at all, even in the
1974 edition. I remember the disbelief of many readers when a survey of which I was the lead author[2] suggested that the training needs
of women managers might be different from those of their male colleagues. We have moved on a long way since then in terms of recognising the issue, and to some extent in terms of understanding; but
we have perhaps moved less far towards effective action. One of the
problems is recognising precisely what the issues actually are, and
then what objectives might be appropriate for the development of
women managers.

I can already sense the objections forming in the minds of two different types of reader. One group may be feeling that there is a
simple explanation for the lower proportion of women managers,
and that a more detailed analysis of the issue is unnecessary. Others
may feel that to give a special section to women managers is to place
them in a ghetto. In this group will be the 'cream rises to the top'
sub-group, which will include some successful women. Such people
tend to argue that although there are special problems for women
leaders, it is the successful overcoming of those problems that

209

demonstrates that you are special as a leader and not as a woman. They therefore deprecate any special measures to redress the balance on the grounds that they lead to tokenism or to reducing the value accorded to achieved success.

The proposition that the lower proportion of women managers is in some sense 'natural' appears in its most respectable form in terms of career choice. It is argued that women as child-bearers actually leave employment at a crucial time in terms of their possible development as managers, and that many of them neither want nor expect managerial careers. Organisational attitudes which mirror that expectation are therefore thought to be understandable and proper. This view is deeply engrained in some women and in many male-dominated organisations.

However, the major shift in women's views about their own lives and the change in their expectations and wants about their careers have created a considerable 'push' for a change of attitude. This has been matched by 'pull' in some organisations, notably by some of the major banks. To some extent encouraged by national debate, if not action, generated by the Equal Opportunities Commission, and to some extent fuelled by recognition of their own needs, organisations are gradually becoming less accepting of traditional views about women's careers. The word 'expectations' is extremely important here. A small minority of people who are prepared to fight hard and push has gradually been augmented by a larger number whose previous negative expectations have to some extent been changed by the apparent success of the pushers.

Formal management development action taken to change both the actuality and the expectations about career opportunities for women includes:

- developing a clear policy statement directed at increasing the number of women managers and accompanying it with procedures and monitoring processes
- reviewing selection processes and selection criteria in order to control, if not eliminate, bias against women
- developing special arrangements such as extended maternity leave, career breaks with accompanying fast-track training pro-

cesses to enable women to return to work more quickly or more effectively.

The second type of 'it is only natural' response to the lower number of women managers is more difficult to define and counter. It essentially revolves around questions of how women perform as managers and how their performance is perceived by their surrounding male colleagues. This already difficult issue is then complicated by a second question. Should women managers behave like men managers anyway, or should they behave differently? Or should more male managers try to employ the supposedly characteristic female processes evidenced by some successful women managers?

Both men and women tend to agree that women managers behave differently from their male colleagues. While women who accept the 'difference' argument will tend to say 'different but as good as', men will, more characteristically, say 'different and less effective than'. Some women managers, of course, do not accept that there is a difference in how they carry out their work, and an American article[3] based on a matched study of 2,000 managers showed that women do not manage differently from men. This research evidence might seem to support the views of those successful women who tend to argue that there is no basis for claiming that women managers are different (although it says nothing about the proposition that they are actually held back).

We are faced with a number of stereotypes: of men about women, of women about men, of women about themselves. Some men point to the success of a small number of political leaders. There is, indeed, a small group of highly successful women politicians, some of them coming from even more unlikely environments than our own Margaret Thatcher. The success of Golda Meir, Indira Ghandi, Sirimavo Bandaranaike, Benazir Bhutto, and some lesser known Scandinavian politicians (such as Iceland's Vigdís Finnbogadóttir, the first woman in world history to be elected head of state), may seem to support the stereotype 'it shows what can be done without laws on equal opportunities'. Yet senior women remain a tiny minority in politics, in the judiciary, in the civil service and local government.

Unlike a number of male knights, no woman in industry or commerce has run a huge organisation and received the equivalent damehood. Such female role models as there are in industry and commerce, like Anita Roddick of Body Shop or Steve Shirley of F International, tend to be important but atypical. As Marshall[4] points out, much of early discussion of women managers concentrated on the belief that men and women managers operated in essentially the same way in order to facilitate a more positive view of women's potential. She argues that these similarities have been overstated at the expense of legitimate and useful differences:

> Women tend to emphasise people management over task structuring, whilst men have opposite priorities; women are often inhibited in exercising position power because other people reject or undermine their use of authority, [or] stereotype them in devalued female roles.

Like other authors, she comments on the male emphasis on individualism, competition and control (in contrast to interdependence, collaboration and acceptance) as defining the values to which women managers are supposed to adhere if they wish to join the managerial club.

Writers who have highlighted these competing styles and values between men and women have not made the task of management development any easier; but they may have made it more effective. They have also helped to persuade some men to view some of their own values differently. If women have the capacity not only to be different but to be usefully and effectively different by bringing to the party some female styles and values as well as some effective male attributes, might not the reverse also apply? The article by Simmons[5] shows what can be achieved by causing men to question whether breaking gender bounds will lead to more effective management.

There has been a shift among organisations and women themselves about careers and managerial jobs. There has also been an accompanying shift in the expectations of a minority of men about the women with whom they share their lives. Women will no longer necessarily surrender their careers either to the demands of childbearing or to their husbands' careers. The issue of dual-career families is the sharpest instance of this. This is particularly significant because the social circumstances of women – when they are married and have children – often make planned career development more difficult. It is understandable, although not appropriate, that the (often male) management development adviser should accept these difficulties rather than try to overcome them. Yet they are difficulties that will increasingly need to be overcome for men as well. Cavalier assumptions that men will go where they are sent, and that wives will go with them, have ceased to be tenable – for men or women.

Up till now women managers have coped with the difficulties involved in a different way from men. According to one UK survey,[6] 39 per cent of women managers were unmarried, divorced or widowed, as against 8 per cent of men (the difference is slightly larger in the United States). The appropriate inference is not that more men ought to be similarly lonely or 'available', but that this should not be an apparently necessary requirement for so many women.

The personnel function and the management development specialism point to another special feature of women managers. There has been a tendency to push them into 'caring functions'. To some extent this process is a reflection of social stereotypes of desired female behaviour, of the failure to provide effective choice at school and of subsequent early career choice. The fact that we are more likely to find a female personnel director than production director is much more likely to be the product of these earlier factors than later career development in any particular organisation. Although in some respects the role model offered by Margaret Thatcher as 'the toughest man in her cabinet' is unfortunate, her success in carrying out her chief executive role is important. What is needed is some more role models of women moving not through the caring departments (as they used to be considered) of Education or Social Services, but through the Department of Trade and Industry, the Foreign Office and the Treasury.

Women managers – different development needs?

Women managers actually face a different situation from men managers. The predominant managerial style is most likely to be male in orientation. The woman manager is therefore faced with the issue of whether, and how, to adopt managerial forms of behaviour that may contradict or conflict with her existing style of behaviour. Some women have obviously long since adopted male forms of behaviour and have no problems of such adaptation. For others the need to adapt may include:

- coping with competition
- adopting at least some of the behaviour of male clubs (post-work socialising, discussion of predominantly male sports)
- the use of personal and role power
- developing individual self-awareness
- acquiring a positive self-image as a woman manager
  — self-confidence and assertiveness skills
  — dealing with stress.

The real issue for most women managers is how to handle the fact of being a woman within what is likely to be a majority group of men managers in an organisation which has little sympathy for and understanding of the contribution that women might make, let alone their potentially different contribution. It should also be emphasised that at least some women managers will choose to follow the line indicated by Marshall[4] in which adaptation to male domination is not seen as the only recourse.

Women managers – different development processes?

It is not surprising that male attitudes and behaviour on courses tend to follow the stereotypes about women found in the real world outside. Behaviour which is seen by men in men as normal, such as managerial assertiveness, is seen by men in women as aggressive and strident. Women who do not behave according to the other kinds of stereotype are similarly pushed towards the supposedly 'feminine' behaviour corner. Women are expected to be concerned about the comfort of the group, to pour out the tea, and to express emotion rather than to conceal it. They are treated with a form of superficial gallantry which emphasises the fact that they are being treated as a woman, not as a manager. Alternatively their capacities are belittled by reference to their sexuality: 'I bet it's difficult having a serious discussion with a beauty like Jane in the group.'

Because of the difficulties women have in largely male managerial training and education situations, and because of the view that they have special needs anyway, women-only training groups were developed. There are two conflicting arguments over this. One says that since women have to survive in a predominantly male environment, it is unreal to provide them with women-only management training. Whatever else this may achieve, the absence of men will create a future problem of transferring any learning achieved. The alternative view is that the absence of men removes some unnecessary obstacles to learning, and opens opportunities for more women to be more experimental with behaviour which may be helpful to them subsequently in the male environment. I am not aware of any research that provides a clear basis for deciding which of these views is true. There is evidence that a number of women feel they have benefited from women-only courses, in the ways indicated above. It is also the case that since some women nowadays are less prepared to accept inappropriate male behaviour towards them on courses, mixed courses can sometimes become a battleground for male/female issues rather than a learning experience related to the original objectives. It is argued on the other hand, by both men and women, that emphasising differences by setting up women-only experiences is unhelpful.

It may be that the most useful process is to create special learning experiences for women to help them define and deal with the male world. So strategies for working co-operatively together, for understanding their relationships with men, and perhaps creating processes for challenging stereotypes all provide an appropriate focus. It is not so clear that women-only courses dealing with general management skills and requirements are desirable. Perhaps here the argument of enabling women to behave differently is less clearly dominant, as compared with the requirement for them to work even in a training context with male colleagues.

It will be noted that I am writing as a man who cannot possibly have the same recognition of the balance of feeling and requirement that a woman adviser might have. So an additional point might well be that the choice of whether to make an activity women-only should depend not only on the adviser (whether male or female) but on whether the prospective female participants actually want it that way. The case for women-only groups is well set out by Marshall.

The presence of men may be an inhibitor both to achieved learning and the expression of it by women. A related issue concerns whether women's learning processes differ from those of men. The common stereotype of the emotional and intuitive woman can be expressed in learning terms by saying that women are less responsive to hard rational approaches to learning but more responsive to particular situations and feelings. The view of women as intuitive certainly implies that their learning processes will be different from men's. One part of the answer may rest in those characteristics which women are said to share – the preference for a supportive, co-operative environment in which to learn as compared with the more competitive environment characteristically favoured by men.

However, this environmental point does not deal with the basic issue of whether women as a whole differ from men in their learning processes. On the Honey/Mumford Learning Styles Questionnaire (LSQ), the norms for 174 women differed scarcely at all from men on the Reflector and Theorist dimensions, and by only one point on the Activist (higher for women) and Pragmatist (lower for women) scores. These differences are not at a level of significance to suggest that women characteristically learn differently from men. The admittedly small sample of women in my director research similarly did not differ from their male director counterparts. The information on our LSQ is, however, different from that found by David Kolb in his Learning Styles Inventory (LSI).[7] On his dimensions, women have a much higher preference for what he calls 'abstract conceptualization', as compared with 'concrete experience'. The male scores are almost exactly opposite to the female on these dimensions. The difference in results from the LSQ may be related to the fact that the LSI brings in 'feelings' in a more overt way. My conclusion is that learning experiences should not be designed according to a stereotyped view that women will learn differently; they should be designed according to the nature of the particular group or the particular individual.

Nor is there any evidence that women learn better or worse than men from any particular kind of learning opportunity. They are just as likely to learn or not learn from real tasks, projects, bosses, courses, as men are. The only area in which there may be some significant difference is that of the use of boss, colleagues or mentors. Here learning opportunities may be influenced by the stereotypes and actualities of male/female behaviour. In the scarce literature on learning from boss and colleagues there is no reference to women learning differently from men, nor is it my experience that this is so. But there may well be extra inhibitions and difficulties. The only area in which this has been researched has been that of mentors. For some time it was thought that women could only get on in an organisation dominated by men by having a mentor; inevitably the mentor was most often a man. More recently, of course, female mentors have become available. Again the evidence slowly coming to hand conflicts with stereotypes. The assumption that a male mentor and a female protégée will inevitably provoke jealousy in others, and particularly the suspicion that the relationship has a sexual side, has been examined by Bowey.[8] This article shows that, comparing male and female mentors of females:

- the sexual issue was not significant and was quite manageable
- resentment was created irrespective of whether the mentor was male or female
- there are positive benefits for both male and female mentors and their protégés both at and outside work.

Kram[9] offers rather less comfortable evidence. In her view 'collusion in stereotypical behaviours encourages women to maintain feelings of dependency and incompetence'. Clutterbuck[10] gives a useful review of the particular problems of male/female mentoring.

You may wish to test your own position, and your organisation's, on a number of the issues raised here about women managers.

Exercise

1 What are my beliefs about why there are proportionately fewer women managers than there are women at work?
2 What do I believe my organisation's beliefs to be?
3 Does my organisation have any clear policy about women managers, and procedures to implement those policies?
4 What is my view about the existence of differences between the way in which a woman manager and a male manager will work?
5 Are there different management development needs for women?
6 What is my view and practice on the provision of women-only groups?
7 Do women learn differently from men? If so in what way?

Multinational needs

There are three major aspects which make management development in multinational organisations different from those which have a single national base:

- *differences in national culture*, with consequent differences, required styles and behaviours of managers
- *mixed management teams*, which require the effective integration of different cultures and styles
- *different management development systems*, involving a recognition that a system which works in one country may not work at all, or in certain respects, in another.

The major work of practical value on cultural issues in management development is still Hofstede.[11] Because his research was conducted in one major organisation with a strong managerial culture, the differences in national style that he drew out were identifiably national rather than influenced by organisational structure, techniques or processes. Hofstede described culture as 'a collective programming of the mind'. In his research he found that value patterns differed along four main dimensions:

- large or small power distance
- strong or weak uncertainty avoidance
- individualism versus collectivism
- masculinity versus femininity.

The details of his definitions of these dimensions, and the attribution of them to particular countries, can be found in his book. We need only note here that he provides a research-based process for enabling managers to move beyond simply recognising that people from other countries are different – and because they are different necessarily inferior or less effective! Working abroad, or working in your own country with managers from other countries, creates culture shock because your expectation of the right way of doing things differs from those of other nationals. Those difficulties are, of course, exacerbated by language. The old joke about the United States and England being countries separated by a common language has the major merit of reminding us that it is all too easy to believe that another person has understood you. When the other person's language is not English, the difficulties that arise are often clearer, although equally the subject of horror stories and jokes.

The ethics of managers are another aspect of cultural belief. Some years ago I took part in a television programme and was fascinated to see how British-based managers attempted to defend the operation of ethical practices outside the UK different from those they would use at home. An interesting analysis of this kind of issue occurred on some courses run for the Swedish airline company SAS. Participants were asked to list the values most important to them. An overwhelming majority of Swedish participants chose honesty as the most important; the value of honesty was not mentioned in the top 15 by North American participants. Instead they listed competition, liberty and freedom. Competition is not an important value for Swedish or Japanese managers. Different views about such issues were also found in Weinshall and Raveh.[12] Even more explicitly, they found that, in a case study about management failure, 2 per cent of French managers said 'Fire him'; but 80 per cent of the American managers offered this solution.

The research studies here are important not least because they sometimes contradict stereotypes, or perhaps provide clarification of the existence of a stereotype. As throughout this book, however, it is necessary to warn against generalisation. Of course the casual informality of many American managers demonstrates the truth of a stereotype: but informality in personal relationships does not necessarily go with informality in communication within the managerial hierarchy. In a study I did of German and English managers, one group complained that the other was far too bound by rules of precedent and hierarchy. The British managers were astonished to find that it was the Germans who were making this complaint about them!

The question of the tightness of structure and responsibility, and the degree of openness in managerial relationships, is especially important in management development. Many UK and American books nowadays advocate much looser managerial relationships and concepts of teamwork which other countries, particularly in Asia and Africa, find quite bewildering and unusable.

It is therefore a major problem to adapt to the culture of a country when you are the expatriate manager. It is additionally difficult to manage cross-cultural relationships when you are participating in a mixed team of managers from several different cultures. I have worked with an American director working in England for an American multinational. Members of his team were predominantly British, but he also had several Germans, two other Americans and a solitary Frenchman. It so happened that he was extremely competent and flexible in his way of dealing with people; but even he had problems in trying to adapt his approach to the differing demands not merely of individuals, but of individuals with quite strong national characteristics. These factors affect the design and implementation of management development systems and influence perceptions about that implementation.

The comments about different cultures and management styles is significant for the design of systems. An appraisal scheme built on free and open exchange, including self-appraisal, may be well accepted in the United States, partially accepted in the UK and not accepted at all in some other countries. Furthermore, there has been a major change in the patterns of job movement. The opportunities that used to exist in multinationals to send people abroad for a desirable period of experience in other countries are now much reduced. Understandably many countries prefer, and need, to develop their own managers instead of creating vacancies for managers from the parent organisation. Desirable as it is that other countries should look after their own needs, this has substantially reduced certain kinds of management development opportunity for people from the parent company. An unfortunate consequence of this is that parent company senior managers may increasingly have had only visiting experience of the countries for which they may have senior responsibility at corporate headquarters. As Laurent[13] has shown, perceptions about careers and what it takes to develop careers may differ. American managers relate career to 'ambition and drive', while French managers see it as 'being labelled as having high potential'.

From a systematic management development point of view it may well be that the opportunities for posting abroad are diminishing at exactly the time when there is greater understanding of what needs to be done in order to make for a successful management appointment abroad! The advantages of distance and greater automony, which in many respects provide a good test of management competence, have to be balanced against the more solitary and isolated nature of the manager's work. There may well be greater risks, both political and commercial, involved in working abroad. And domestic problems can contribute to failure at least as often as they contribute to success. There is also the re-entry difficulty, which is now more problematic than it is for spacecraft. Finding the right slot at the right time for the returning manager, or even promising to do so before his departure abroad, can cause major headaches.

The main problem is the ethnocentric view of the world held in the corporate headquarters of a multinational in the UK. It is not only that other countries and other cultures may respond negatively to the UK style: they may well have a substantially different view of appropriate management development practices. It is true that some British managers are as tired of hearing about the more effective Japanese practices as their predecessors were of hearing about the United States in the 1960s. It so happens that the Japanese processes described by Handy[14] are very close to the Type 2 processes described in this book. However, his report also helpfully describes practices in France, West Germany and the United States, and is clearly an important source for any adviser in a multinational.

There is one further aspect of cultural differences to be discussed. We have yet to see in the UK large numbers of managers from minority ethnic groups. In proportion to the population they are fewer than women, who have already started on the journey that will lead out of the ghetto. The main steps taken by ethnic minorities seem so far to have been into local government rather than in industry or commerce. Cheap laughs are available to anyone on the occasional excesses of programmes on anti-racism. But the issue cannot be laughed away, since it involves ethics and the allocation of managerial resources. One report[15] about Afro-Caribbeans shows them half as likely to be high-ranking managers as white people.

Graduates

A number of organisations recruit graduates primarily to fill immediate technical or functional needs. After time, experience, and achieved performance they merge into the totality of the unit they have joined and their development as managers follows the normal path for that organisation.

Other organisations recruit graduates less for such immediate technical or functional purposes than to create a pool of intelligent people with high potential as a means of providing for management of the future. The difference in objectives and immediate location for these two different kinds of graduate recruitment illustrates the problems that arise. Whereas the first group go into a proper job, if below their intellectual level or ambition, the latter group often go into no clear functional stream.

The problems experienced by management trainees over the years recur, although they do seem to have diminished since the awful days of the 1950s. The problem of the Cook's tour, where graduates were hurtled around a number of departments for a few weeks or months at a time with no proper job at any staging-point were well known by the early 1960s. Few organisations now fall into that trap. More frequently organisations will put graduates or management trainees into departments for more substantial periods, or will employ them on specific tasks or projects. Not only is this something that intelligent graduates now demand, but it is something that organisations themselves have come to recognise as necessary if they are to make any judgement about the actual capacity of the graduates recruited.

There is no mystery about what to do with graduates. There needs to be a formal development programme for them which will include appropriate courses; they need to have assignments in particular units or departments long enough to establish that they have done a definable piece of work. If sharp distinctions are made between themselves and others of equivalent age but with no degree the expectations and motivation of non-degree people will be reduced.

Of course, one of the prime issues here is the same as for more experienced managers: whether the process of learning from the experiences offered to graduate entrants is actually effective in learning terms. Barrington's book[16] is an excellent guide to some aspects of this whole graduate training process, precisely because it focuses on issues about learning and not simply on issues about moving people between jobs.

Reference was made in Chapter 8 to MBAs. Some stereotypical thinking about MBA recruits has become firmly entrenched in a number of organisations. They are seen as expensive recruits who want to do the managing director's job before they have shown that they can manage a department. They are characterised as arrogant, as possessing intellectual and analytical skills rather than the practical skills on which so much effective management is believed to be based. Of course, if all organisations believed this then no business school would be able to run a traditional MBA programme. So the traditional picture is partial rather than complete. (Although some criticisms of the content and learning processes of traditional programmes are valid.) Current developments in MBA programmes emphasise relevance and reality. It does seem likely that the associated development of programmes that focus on particular organisational needs, whether on a consortium basis or an individual organisation, will provide both greater demands and greater opportunities for effective management development. There is undoubtedly a group of young managers who want the discipline and structure of a formal MBA, but who also want it conducted in terms of more appropriate general management processes and more specific relevance to their own organisation. The future growth of MBA programmes is more likely in this area than in that of providing open programmes offering a career break to middle managers.

Senior professionals

The term 'profession' has been applied increasingly widely. Some of the professions with the longest life have been relatively slow to enter into a world in which their professional activities are 'managed'. While used to the idea of perhaps some kind of professional development, they have not considered the idea of management development applicable to them, not least because many of them would not see themselves as managers. This has been most obviously true in areas such as medicine or the law, though it is no longer seen to be true in professions conducted within social services, for example. The initial issue here, as I discovered myself in projects with lawyers and trade unionists, is whether the people who are actually carrying out managerial functions see themselves as managers. The possibility of being developed for a job – ie manager – that you do not recognise yourself as occupying is obviously low. There are specific features about trying to engage in management development for senior professionals. Many of them are discussed in the book by Raelin.[17]

References

1 ROBERTS T. *Developing Effective Managers*. London, IPM, 1974.
2 TRAINING SURVEY UNIT. *Survey on Management Training and Development*. London, Department of Employment, 1971.
3 FRAKER S. 'Why women aren't getting to the top'. *Fortune Magazine*. April 1984.
4 MARSHALL J. 'Women managers'. In Mumford A., *A Handbook of Management Development*. Aldershot, Gower, 1991.
5 SIMMONS M. 'Undoing men's gender conditioning'. *Industrial and Commercial Training*. November 1986.
6 ALBAN METCALFE B. *Career Development of British Managers*. London, British Institute of Management, 1984.
7 KOLB D. *Experiential Learning*. Hemel Hempstead, Prentice Hall, 1984.
8 BOWEY D. 'Were men meant to mentor women?' *Training and Development*. February, 1985.
9 KRAM K. 'Phases of the mentor relationship'. *Academy of Management Journal*. Vol. 16, No. 4, 1983.
10 CLUTTERBUCK D. *Everyone Needs a Mentor*. 2nd edn. London, IPM, 1991.
11 HOFSTEDE G. *Culture's Consequences*. Beverly Hills, Calif., Sage, 1980.
12 WEINSHALL T. D. *and* RAVEH Y. A. *Managing Growing Organisations*. Chichester, John Wiley, 1983.
13 LAURENT A. 'The cross cultural puzzle'. *Human Resource Management*. Vol. 25, No. 1, Spring 1986.
14 HANDY C. *Making Managers*. NEDO, 1987.
15 FOUNDATION FOR MANAGEMENT EDUCATION AND WAINWRIGHT TRUST. *The Cement Roof*. FME, 1996.
16 BARRINGTON A. *Learning about Management*. Maidenhead, McGraw-Hill, 1985.
17 RAELIN J. A. *Clash of Cultures*. Cambridge, Mass., Harvard Business School Press, 1986.

Further reading relevant to this chapter is shown in Chapter 13.

11

![chess icon] Continuous Learning and Development

We have examined the reality behind the management cliché 'I learned from experience.' Another cliché might almost have been invented specifically about learning: 'You can take a horse to water but you cannot make it drink.' The provision of a greater range of opportunities, and indeed the generation of a greater awareness of the opportunities to learn from real management experiences, may turn out to be rather like taking the horse to water. Those of us guiding the horse may be very well aware that we are offering splendid refreshment; if the horse does not want water but oats then we have both had a wasted journey. This chapter is concerned with how to help managers not only recognise but make better use of formal and informal opportunities for learning. The wide variety of influences on learning is indicated in Figure 11.1.

Figure 11.1
Influences on Learning

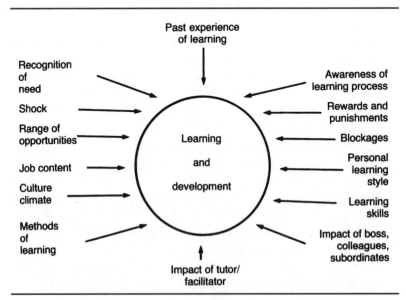

The experience of the reader so far

The introduction offered readers options about the sequence in which chapters might be read. The options were based on a view about the possible preferences of readers for particular aspects of management development. That was a small-scale attempt to recognise individually different needs. The book has also attempted to demonstrate the learning cycle illustrated in Chapter 2. Most of the books and articles I have read about management development essentially concentrate on the final two stages of that cycle:

- a statement of the author's conclusions
- a series of statements of practical things to do, with the suggestion that the reader should plan action on them.

There are practical workbooks which give individuals practical exercises in various aspects of developing themselves. Pedler *et al*[1] is an excellent and widely used example of this.

It seemed to me necessary that this book should attempt to cover the whole learning cycle. The introduction of practical exercises at various stages in each of the chapters was intended to meet two objectives:

- to give readers the opportunity to test out the propositions and statements against their own experience and beliefs
- to provide a practical demonstration of the application of the learning cycle to reading the book – a learning experience.

So in each chapter readers:

- have had the particular experience of reading the book
- have reviewed the information they have about their personal approach to management development, and that of their organisation. They have then been able to compare those experiences against the material offered in the book
- have been invited to draw conclusions from this comparison
- have been invited to prepare action plans following the sequence of review and conclude.

You may also have tested the second proposition in Chapter 2, that individuals differ in their interest in the different stages of the learning cycle. Some readers will have enjoyed the exercises precisely because they give opportunities to pause, reflect and review. Others will regard the intervention of exercises as a nuisance which holds up understanding of the mental system or model being presented. Others again would have preferred a balance much more heavily weighted in favour of lots of practical examples which could be picked up and applied. Such readers would, for example, have preferred more examples of appraisal forms, succession plans and more examples of particular types of training course.

The stage we have now reached is that of helping to make some readers more aware of some of the reasons for their reactions to the book. The result of that increased awareness will, it is hoped, be not only an improved ability on the part of the reader to understand his or her own reactions, but an understanding of the different reactions of people with different learning styles. This book itself is potentially a proof of the theme of individuality which it has so strongly emphasised.

Theories of learning

It is predictable in terms of learning styles that some readers will want more evidence about the basis for the statements about learning processes made so far. Those who do want this should look at the work of three people: Malcolm Knowles, Reg Revans and David Kolb.

Malcolm Knowles[2] has had a major influence on people who are interested in adult learning. His model of the learner is that:

- the learner is self-directed but has a conditioned expectation to be dependent and to be taught
- the learner comes with experience which means that, for many kinds of learning, adults are themselves the richest resources for one another and that there is a wide range of experience in most groups of learners

- people are ready to learn when they have a need to perform more effectively in some aspect of their lives
- for the most part adults do not learn for the sake of learning but in order to be able to perform a task, solve a problem or live in a more satisfying way.

The work of Reg Revans and his definition of action learning were summarised in Chapter 2. He has contributed two theoretical statements. The first he described as 'System Beta', which involves the assembly of data, the development of a theory, experimentation, the comparison of results derived from experiment and the final evaluation of the theory. This theory stems from his scientific background and will be seen to strongly resemble the learning cycles proposed by Kolb, and Honey and Mumford. The other major aspect of his theory is the one which has really generated action learning. Revans identified a difference between what he described as 'programmed knowledge' and the 'questioning approach'. Programmed knowledge (P) is learning from what somebody else has learned, this information being provided in the form of books, papers, studies and lectures. Questioning (Q) is learning from your own processes of action and reflection. This latter process is called action learning.

David Kolb's contribution[3] was first in the design of his version of the learning cycle, which is still used by some management educators and trainers. Its original neat representation was supplemented by his major theoretical contribution, which was that of translating the relatively common acceptance that 'people learn differently' into the concepts of different learning styles, each related to a stage on the cycle.

Is an understanding of, and a commitment to, some theory of learning necessary for effective management development? As far as many managers are concerned, clearly not. Some, who score highly on the Theorist style (or as abstract conceptualisers on the Kolb model), would probably want this sort of background if they were being introduced to their own learning processes. A significant number of them, however, would not miss an explanation of the theory, simple though it is. They would be much more concerned with the practical implications and applications. The point is more arguable for management development advisers, educators and trainers – see Burgoyne[4] on this. They too will have preferences in terms of learning process. But as people giving advice on, and constructing events involving, conscious learning they must surely have at least the small degree of theoretical knowledge offered here.

Exercise

1 What is your reaction to the statements about learning theory given above?
2 How do your practices relate if at all to these theories?
3 Do these statements help to explain your personal experiences of learning?
4 Do they help you to analyse and understand what is being offered by other management developers, educators and trainers?

The application of learning theory and learning styles

The effective use of learning opportunities depends on a conscious attempt to improve the design of the opportunities on the one hand, and the understanding of the learner about learning processes and skills on the other. This means working through a diagnostic instrument, or alternatively through a structured exercise of some kind as giving learners a better understanding of their own learning processes. The early exercises in Chapter 1 are one version of this. Some advisers prefer not to work through the formal categories of learning styles, regarding these as potentially inhibiting. The arguments for and against explicitness are set out in Mumford.[5] (Kolb's work has already been mentioned.) The Honey and Mumford *Manual of Learning Styles*[6] shows how specific material about individual learning preferences can be used for the following purposes:

- helping individuals to review their approach to learning, to select opportunities related to their preference, and for some, progress to building learning skills outside their existing preference

- for the general design of courses so that they take account of different learning styles more effectively
- for the specific design of particular events to meet any preponderant needs that may exist, which may mean designing an event to take account of any particular majority preference. If through the LSQ you know you are going to encounter majority preference for the Activist style, you should design the event differently from the way you would design an event where you find you have a majority of Theorists.
- the better design of on-the-job learning opportunities in relation to individual preferences. For example, there is little point in throwing somebody in to observe another manager at work if the observer is very low on the Reflector score (unless you give major help on how to reflect).

It should be emphasised that the prospective power of these diagnostic processes is not only to improve the capacity of the designer of learning experiences. It is to enable the learner to understand his or her own learning processes, not only in relation to that particular event, but for future learning opportunities.[7] It ought to be a major imperative that such processes are built into many of our formal learning events. Not only is it our responsibility to help managers to learn better during those events, but we ought to be helping them to learn more effectively outside them. It is a sad commentary on some major management education programmes that no such attempt is made. Apparently the priorities of many business schools and training centres relate entirely to traditional management skills or functional knowledge, not at all to the skills of learning that are actually required in order to improve those skills and that knowledge!

Learning from experience at work

The majority of learning experiences are not created and structured through a course. They are the informal and accidental experiences that provide partial and inefficient learning, or they are the improved version of this, which I have called Type 2. One feature of managerial experience as a learning process is that since the major element is the management experience, and not learning, the manager has less choice. The manager can reject a course but he cannot put aside a task, a project or a meeting. The manager may have no choice about the managerial experience; but failure to learn from it satisfactorily is not the result of deliberate and conscious avoidance but simply a failure to recognise the opportunity or ignorance about how to learn from it most effectively.

Most such opportunities are seen and used in retrospect: a manager looks back on a particularly powerful managerial experience and more or less consciously registers learning from it. Improving the informal and accidental processes requires a better understanding of what managers actually do when they say they 'learn from experience'. In our further research with directors[8] we established that while most of them learn by looking back over events consciously, the extent and depth of such reviewing varied. There were circumstances in which learning was thought about in advance, as a prospective experience, or where learning could be envisaged as arising from a future managerial activity. We identified the four different approaches to learning from on-the-job experiences as follows:

- *intuitive*, where managers learn, but unconsciously from experience. Learning occurs through some natural process of osmosis. 'I suspect you are doing it all the time without realising you are doing so.'
- *incidental*, where learning emerges by chance from activities that jolt managers into conducting a *post mortem*. Difficulties, mishaps and frustrations often provide the spur for the incidental learner. In such circumstances learning is conscious but it happens in an unstructured, informal way. 'It is the originality of the experience that makes me think about what I've got from it.'
- *retrospective*, where learning occurs much more consciously by thinking about what has happened and reaching conclusions. In addition to the mishaps and mistakes from which the incidental learner learns, retrospective learners are more inclined to draw

lessons from routine events and successes. The conscious process involves thinking things through in the head, in conversation and sometimes on paper. 'Reviewing is essential to put things into perspective.'

- *prospective*, involving planning to learn before an experience. This means seeing future events not merely as management requirements, but as events from which it is possible to learn. 'Sorting out what you want to get in advance increases your chances of getting something worthwhile.' Of course the prospective approach is then combined with the retrospective, since the effective learner later reviews what he or she has actually learned from the experience identified in advance.

The four approaches are not mutually exclusive. We have found that some managers more characteristically learn from one approach in preference to another; but most carry out at least the first three. Managers can make more effective use of learning opportunities by being helped to expand their recognition of opportunities and identification of learning processes. The powerful process of completing a learning log, increasingly advocated and used in management development, is found by a number of managers to be unreal and therefore unusable. Those particularly geared to the retrospective and prospective approach keep such a log; but others will not. For this latter group it is much more sensible to propose processes that gear themselves to existing managerial processes, like adding a few notes to a list of work activities or to a weekly summary of priorities. These ideas are further developed in the booklet referred to above written for directors but of value also for managers.[8]

Other influences on learning

Clearly, individual learning preferences, or different approaches to learning from experience, are not the only influences on whether somebody learns from a particular opportunity. These have been emphasised because they are the features on which learners can themselves act most directly, either by choosing to learn in accordance with their existing preferences or by trying to develop them. The issue of the applicability of different methods of learning, which again may be an issue about compatibility with the learner, but also as indicated in Mumford[9] by ensuring that the method actually fits the learning need.

The impact of an individual's direct manager, colleagues and direct reports has been mentioned in many of the previous chapters. These play a crucial role in providing the environment within which an individual develops. So important is this issue of the environment that it is given special attention in the following chapter. The idea of a learning culture, or a learning organisation, is one that managers need to take on board, both to assist their own development and to facilitate the development of others.

Life-long learning

The need for individuals to learn and develop throughout their working life has become a cliché. Whereas 20 or 30 years ago managers might have presumed that they were in relatively stable jobs which required familiar skills, this is today much less true for most managers. Indeed, the idea of a 'career' in management presumes that people will move from one job to another, which will obviously require additional knowledge and skills. The career may be achieved in a single organisation, and have an unchanged focus, or it may be achieved through several organisations. The manager's eventual destination may be clear at the outset or be the result of a series of changed decisions about appropriate focus – a zig-zag rather than steady upward movement on a graph. The zig-zags may represent changes of focus – a move from one function to another, from one size or type of organisation to another, from one view of a desired destination ('I want to get to the top') to another ('I want a fulfilling job which enables me to spend time with my family').

The organisational input to career choice is made through the processes described in Chapters 4–6. But a great deal of formal career planning necessarily assumes a substantial element of a steady-state organisation. But the career that is on offer through the planned process may not be available when the time comes to put the plan into effect. Most dramatically, an organisation may cease to exist because it goes out of business. In less dramatic form mergers or acquisitions may affect the availability of particular jobs. It is therefore absolutely appropriate that we should emphasise life-long learning as a major theme in management development.

Career development

Some organisations attempt to plan careers; life provides opportunities; and individuals choose what they want to be. It is the interaction of these three which creates careers. Schein[10] has given by far the best analysis of this interaction. He describes an individual's 'career anchor' as consisting of:

- self-perceived talents and abilities
- self-perceived motives and needs
- self-perceived attitudes and values.

The career anchor emphasises evolution, development and discovery through actual experience. It is the result of an early interaction between the individual and the work environment. Characteristically career anchors involve:

- technical or functional competence
- managerial competence, especially the ability to analyse and solve problems, interpersonal skills and emotional competence
- security and stability
- creativity
- autonomy and independence.

Schein's book also includes a self-analysis form enabling individuals to identify their own position. A book by Francis[11] provides a greater variety of suggestions, check-lists and questionnaires, and is very much a workbook rather than the analytical model that Schein's is.

Paul Evans has contributed to our understanding of two different aspects of career development. With his colleague Bartolome he looked at the impact of career choices on home life. They particularly showed that it is the feelings generated by work that determine the quality of private life. In their view, problems were caused by inappropriate, random and ill-considered processes for selecting and developing careers.[12] Evans has also suggested that careers should not be seen as purely hierarchical processes, but that managers and organisations should think more of opportunities for steady-state or spiral careers.[13] He argues that there are three stages in patterns of concern in career development:

- *exploration*, particularly when young (Evans suggests this is a time for self-discovery and that too much planning is neither feasible nor desirable)
- *establishment*, the stage at which people become fully aware of what they want to be (as a result of the opportunities they have taken at the exploration stage)
- *mid–late career phase*, in which being on a plateau does not necessarily equate with less development

Self-development

Action learning and self-development merged as major concepts in management development in the 1970s, and have some features in common. Behind Revans's insistence that managers learn most effectively by working on their own real problems is a resistance to the idea of the formal tutor. Self-development took on board the growing awareness that management development was not effective when it was a process 'done to' a manager. The view of a manager as a passive recipient of processes which other people had designed, according to needs that had not been established with the individual (if indeed they had been established at all), was recognisably one cause of failure in management development.

The main authors who have identified the meaning of, and the processes involved in, self-development have been Pedler, Burgoyne and Boydell. Their first book, essentially a workbook, has deservedly gone into a third edition.[14] In this they define self-development as 'personal development, with a manager taking primary responsibility for his own learning and for choosing the means to achieve this'. They define a large part of the difference as being to do with treating managers as agents in their own development processes, rather than patients receiving treatment from experts. As shown earlier, they also distinguish between learning and development, and they are especially concerned with the development of the whole person rather than with discrete, job-centred aspects of learning.

Self-development is not an activity analogous to particular techniques like role plays, case studies or lectures. Nor is it simply a collection of relatively untraditional approaches to learning through biography, self-assessment, questionnaires, development workshops or counselling. Self-development represents a dramatically fundamental and difficult shift of thinking, in that:

- responsibility for learning is taken on by the learner, and not seen as the responsibility of the provider of learning opportunities
- the focus is on the individual and his or her particular needs rather than on large groups of managers with general needs
- the manager is not simply the recipient of judgements by other people on his or her learning needs and their solutions, but is instead involved in the analysis of the needs and the discussion of solutions
- because of the process of involvement, responsibility clearly rests with the learner, leaving fewer excuses to complain about lack of relevance or inapplicability of solutions to supposed needs
- the combination of involvement and responsibility generates commitment to personal action, instead of acceptance of the need to follow someone else's prescription
- because individuals work on defining their own personal needs they have already begun to engage in not only the generation of

solutions but work on the solutions. The sometimes unhelpful distinction between analysis and action is reduced
- while all of the reasons offered so far can be seen as pragmatic statements of how to secure more effective individual management development, an even more fundamental issue at least whispers in the background and occasionally shouts in the foreground. The more we insist that managers are responsible for their own development, the more we also imply that they have the right to choose not only pragmatically but also ethically. This closely relates to the associated point of whether we are developing or seeking to develop the whole person, or are operating at more immediate managerial levels of particular skills.

Just as most managers are not astonished to read that learning from experience is important, necessary and underemphasised in management development, so they are not at all surprised to be told that they are responsible for their own development. Whatever the contribution they recognise may be made by a relatively benevolent employing organisation, most of them would recognise that 'When you come down to it, my development is really up to me.' The philosophy of self-development fits very well with other ideas already identified in this book. A process that helps managers to see that they can define and use their own opportunities, instead of being responsive to someone else's identification and provision of opportunities, is entirely in tune with one of the major themes of this book.

However, many self-development processes focus on off-the-job activities and seem less concerned than I would think desirable with issues of how to carry learning forward into the real world. There has been a concentration on the assessment of needs through self-development processes such as a workbook, a workshop, an assessment centre, or individual counselling. The range of such activities is well set out in two collections of articles.[15] The latter collection is particularly interesting in terms of the themes of this chapter, because it gives much more emphasis than earlier works to the central significance of how a manager learns. Much of the earlier literature fell into the error of supposing that learning would naturally be enhanced by self-development.

The major omissions in the literature are suggestions about how to decide which processes will best meet the objectives of self-development. As always, the temptation is for the people designing the process to propose that things are done in the way which the designer finds most comfortable. I am optimistic that most managers can engage successfully in some kind of self-development process; but it is still clear that spraying all managers with the same holy water is unlikely to be successful. The willingness to engage in some degree of self-analysis is essential if you are to engage in self-development. This does not extend to a necessary acceptance by every individual of exactly the same kind of process through which to engage in that self-analysis. My own experience, operating mainly on issues of job effectiveness rather than the whole person, has been that I have been much too optimistic over the years about how far managers are prepared to go in learning about themselves and about group processes.

Finally, there is the continuing problem of taking self-development as a philosophy and as a collection of processes back into the organisation. It is wrong to design and run self-development activities that do not devote a very substantial proportion of energy to the identification of the positive and negative contributions made by the boss and the general working environment.

The other major issue of difficulty is that of the role of the adviser. The idea of giving up the role of expert tutor and direct leader of learning in favour of being a facilitator of other people's learning is not one that all management development advisers can manage or accept.

It would be wrong to leave this major topic with an expression of reservation and uncertainties. Pedler et al[15] show that there are problems of definition for precisely the reasons that also make the philosophy attractive. They ask whether self-development groups and distance learning for a higher degree are really part of the same philosopy. The fact that the words have been stretched in this way is probably a compliment to the essential idea, although worrying in terms of clarity. The idea of managers choosing to meet their own needs in their own way is entirely correct. Enabling them to do so successfully has very much been a theme of this book. (A more extensive review of materials on this very important field is given in Further Reading.)

Using others to help

Chapter 9 spelled out the variety of people and the variety of organisational and personal responsibilities involved in helping an individual to learn. This section concentrates on the ways in which other people can help on the job. The people involved are identified in Figure 11.2. An excellent description of the kind of activities involved is given by Stuart.[16] As he points out, one of the most useful steps is actually to draw up a map showing the people who may be able to help, and then identify which are already being used, and which are not. Stuart shows that individuals may help in three primary ways:

- clearing the way for learning
- tooling up for learning
- direct learning interventions.

The primary issue is probably the extent to which any individual manager is able to make his or her learning needs and strategies clear to others. One of the ways in which formal training and educational processes can help is in giving people explicit experience of this. I frequently use pairs and trios on management courses for this purpose. This is not only helpful in the immediate sense of developing learning plans, it is also helpful in giving people experience in a relatively supportive environment of the process of sharing and developing plans. It is possible to extend the whole process to the full group in an off-the-job situation, and this is an option particularly likely to be available in an action learning set or a self-development group. As Stuart points out, one of the issues is whether individuals look for help from others who have similar learning styles, or whether they use others to compensate for their preferences. It is one of the achieved benefits of organised discussion of learning styles and learning processes that individuals, pairs and groups can use each other's strengths and compensate each other for weaknesses.

Figure 11.2
Interaction in Learning

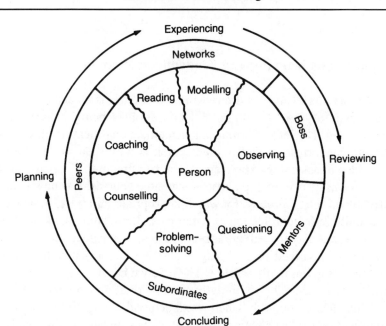

One of the prime sources of help ought, of course, to be the direct manager (or 'boss'). For reasons indicated in Chapter 7, this is easier to state than it is to achieve. It will undoubtedly be the boss who has the greatest input on the effective conversion of Type 1 into Type 2 learning experiences. It is the direct manager who knows what kind of managerial activities a direct report (or 'subordinate') will be involved or has been involved in, and who can encourage the direct report to engage in the reviewing processes indicated earlier in this chapter. The process of shared problem-solving, for example, is a prime source of potential learning. Naturally it is most comfortable for the direct report if the manager takes the initiative in using such experiences to assess or confirm learning; but it may be necessary for the direct report to take the initiative in seeking such a review. The prime issue is stimulating an awareness of learning opportunities arising from real-work experiences, and then creating a discussion of those experiences.[17]

Continuous learning and academic assessment

The crucial relevance of direct work experience as an academically valid part of formal training and education is being increasingly recognised. The idea of basing a management qualification purely on traditional forms of academic education is now seen as unhelpful. The idea of assessing experience developed first in the United States as a means of opening up entry to academic courses; it is now being developed into a process by which appropriate current experiences are built into qualification programmes. Innovative work in this country was largely led by Norman Evans. A succinct summary of the issues involved in assessing experience before entry to a programme is given in his article.[18] The practice has been developed by the Management Charter Initiative with 'Crediting Competence'.

This idea, particularly when continued within a qualification programme, represents a major shift of emphasis towards reality. It also reinforces a point frequently made during this book. If people are to be asked to review their past experience and what they have learned from it, then they need to understand the learning process in which they have been involved, and to have some structure for reporting on it. The provision of such a structure is not, however, primarily going to give better results in terms of achieved literacy about learning. It will bring about a transformation in the *actuality* of learning. My own institution gives explicit encouragement to precisely this process. We require that people who have completed our MBA programme should, five years after graduation, show that they have continued to learn during that period. Thus the practice of learning is built into their continued membership of our institution which they will have acquired initially with their MBA.

Exercise

1 What processes do we currently use to help managers understand and develop their learning processes?
2 Which of the ideas in this chapter might we pick up and use, and for which purposes?
3 Does our organisation, and the processes it offers, concentrate on the formal training input, or is it also concerned with an effective learning environment on the job?
4 Which of the influences on learning given in Figure 11.1 score highest in my own experience?
5 Taking an overall view of the organisation, which influence is most important?

Not an end but a beginning

So we finish this chapter where we started in Chapter 1 – with the recording of learning experiences, brought about by questions designed to elicit the nature and results of that learning. We also finish with the statement of things that have occurred as a result of a process – work – rather than with a statement about inputs. I hope that readers will by now be fully convinced that management development is indeed about learning.

References

1 PEDLER M., BURGOYNE J. *and* BOYDELL T. *A Manager's Guide to Self Development.* 3rd edn. Maidenhead, McGraw-Hill, 1994.
2 KNOWLES M. *Andragogy in Action.* San Francisco, Calif., Jossey-Bass, 1985.
3 KOLB D. *Experiential Learning.* Hemel Hempstead, Prentice Hall, 1984.

4 BURGOYNE J. 'Managing by Learning'. *Inaugural Lecture.* Lancaster, Lancaster University, 1985.

5 MUMFORD A. 'Learning to learn for managers'. *Journal of European Industrial Training.* Vol. 10, No. 2, 1986.

6 HONEY P. *and* MUMFORD A. *Manual of Learning Styles.* 3rd edn. Honey, 1992.

7 HONEY P. *and* MUMFORD A. *Using Your Learning Styles.* Honey, 1986.

8 MUMFORD A., HONEY P. *and* ROBINSON G. *Developing Directors: Using experience.* London, Institute of Directors, 1989.

9 MUMFORD A. *How to Choose the Right Development Method.* Honey, 1997.

10 SCHEIN E. *Career Dynamics.* Reading, Mass., Addison Wesley, 1978.

11 FRANCIS D. *Managing Your Own Career.* London, Fontana, 1985.

12 EVANS P. *and* BARTOLOME F. *Must Success Cost So Much?* Grant McIntyre, 1980.

13 EVANS N. 'New directions in career management'. *Personnel Management*, 1986.

14 See note 1.

15 BOYDELL T. *and* PEDLER M. (eds). *Management Self Development.* Aldershot, Gower, 1981; and PEDLER M., BURGOYNE, J. *and* BOYDELL T. (eds). *Applying Self Development in Organisations.* Hemel Hempstead, Prentice Hall, 1988.

16 STUART R. 'Using others to learn'. In MUMFORD A. (ed.), *Handbook of Management Development.* Aldershot, Gower, 1986.

17 MUMFORD A. *How Managers Can Develop Managers.* Aldershot, Gower, 1993.

18 EVANS R. 'Assessing prior experiential learning'. *Industrial and Commercial Training.* January 1989.

Further reading relevant to this chapter is shown in Chapter 13.

12

 The Environment for Learning

Readers were given the opportunity in Chapter 1 to do an exercise through which they could assess the learning culture of their organisations. Subsequently, references have been made to the idea of the learning organisation, and particularly to the impact of those who influence individual learning. This chapter links together ideas about the two strategies for development identified in Chapter 1, the learning organisation and the Investors in People Award.

A learning organisation?

The concept of the learning organisation has attracted both a lot of attention and an increasing level of concern, tending towards cynicism. Part of the problem is that the concept itself may be one more easily recognised and valued by human resource professionals than by line managers or other professionals. Another problem, for at least some line managers and human resource people, is that it seems easier to make statements about what a learning organisation would be like than it is to identify the concrete action necessary to turn a desirable objective into reality. This chapter offers a view about the nature of a learning organisation, and how to achieve it.

Exercise

Here are four statements for readers. Read each one and give yourself a rating on a scale 0 to 3 on how frequently you carry out the action described.

● I explicitly review my experiences and decide what to do better/differently in the light of lessons learned.
● I actively encourage people to adopt learning behaviours such as asking questions, experimenting, and reviewing successes and mistakes.

● I set up meetings where my people swop experiences and share learning.
● I broadcast (beyond my work area) pertinent 'lessons learned' from a variety of sources eg from research reports, problems solved, projects.

After this self-rating, readers might like to pause further and consider how these statements relate to their current understanding of what is required to create a learning organisation.

Definitions of a learning organisation

Chris Argyris (sometimes in combination with Donald Schon) has provided much of the intellectual stimulus for discussions about the learning organisation. His ideas about the 'defensive routines' employed by people to avoid raising or discussing issues of significance is particularly important. Also very significant was the identification by Argyris of 'single-loop learning', as contrasted with 'double-loop learning'. This brings out the view that too much learning has been oriented to maintaining things as they are, whereas 'double-loop learning' enables you to challenge and transform what you need to learn (Argyris[1,2]).

Peter Senge, who has done most round the world to stimulate a recognition of the possibilities of a learning organisation, explicitly acknowledges the influence on him of the experience of working with Argyris. Senge[3] defines learning organisations as those:

> where people continually expand their capacity to create the results they truly desire, where new expansive patterns of thinking are nurtured, where collective aspiration is set free, and where people are continually learning how to learn together.

Unlike Argyris, Senge has already collected a group of people not only within his own learning centre but outside it who have used and developed his ideas (Senge et al[4]).

In the UK, the famous trio of Pedler, Burgoyne and Boydell have stimulated attention through articles, books and conferences. Their definition[5] is this:

> A learning company is an organisation that facilitates the learning of all its members and continually transforms itself.

I have had increasing difficulty in accepting these definitions as appropriate sole guides for management developers. A detailed review of their books and articles reveals a number of characteristics:

- They offer a very wide view about the nature of the learning organisation, which often seems to embrace every conceivable aspect of good managerial practice.
- They see the learning organisation as one that is constantly probing at its own values and mission.
- The thrust of their thinking is towards 'transformational learning', rather than 'incremental learning'.
- Although Senge recognises the crucial significance of effective individual learning, Pedler and his colleagues seem almost to take this for granted in the pursuit of more ambitious declarations about organisational learning.

Discussion with developers has, however, revealed that many of them have concerns about what could or should be attempted in trying to create a learning organisation. These include the following:

- the general reaction of many line managers, who see this as, in practice, another training and development initiative
- the reaction of some managers who see the wide-ranging definition and statements about learning organisation practices as being a full-frontal assault on the nature of the organisation they run
- a view by many practitioners that they simply do not have the access within their organisation to enable them to initiate, promote

or sustain approaches that require 'expansive patterns of thinking' or an organisation that 'continually transforms itself'

- a view that the wide-ranging demands of some definitions of the learning organisation make elusive, both in concept and in practice, the explicit behaviours required for effective learning
- the practitioners' wish to provide explicit guidance on concrete behaviours and practices focused on learning, rather than working from a wide-ranging diagnosis of a range of managerial and organisational behaviours.

Recognition of such concerns does not necessarily carry with it a dismissal of the major contribution made by people such as Argyris, Senge, Pedler *et al*. It suggests, rather, that practitioners want to have available alternative tools for approaching the desired goal of the learning organisation. We can, and should, recognise the crucial and particularly challenging concepts and ideas of these authors, and acknowledge a debt to them, while recognising the possibilities offered by a different view and approach.

Developing a different view

The ideas advanced in this chapter have come through two primary sources. The first has been my own experience in working with individuals and groups to try to identify, and enable them to carry through, a variety of learning and development opportunities. The prime features of that experience (including a recognition of my mistakes) are reviewed in my most recent book.[6] The second source was my continued involvement with Peter Honey. Our concern about existing definitions of the learning organisation caused us to offer an alternative:[7]

> Creating an environment where the behaviours and practices involved in continuous development are actively encouraged.

It will be seen that, like many practitioners, our focus is on 'behaviour and practices'. Also our definition covers all kinds of learning and development, and is not geared to a necessary requirement that individuals, groups or organisations commit themselves to transformational learning. There are at least two good reasons for this.

The first is that it seems entirely inappropriate to dismiss 'incremental' or 'single-loop learning' as irrelevant, or indeed as positively disadvantageous. Learning is not a simple process, to be engaged in lightly. It is a thoughtful process which requires careful building. We do not see a dramatic transition from 'incremental' to 'transformational learning'. It must be the case that unless you recognise the ways in which you need to be effective on 'incremental learning', you are most unlikely to be able to tackle the more demanding 'expansive patterns of thinking' explicitly required in Senge's definition – or help to transform the organisation.

The second reason for this approach has been largely recognised earlier – the practical solution of many of those who would like to encourage learning organisations. What is true for individuals, ie that they need to move step by step from one form of learning to another, must surely, logically and pragmatically, also be true for groups and the organisation as a whole.

Models for the learning environment

One oddity in the Senge books is that despite the overwhelming attention to 'systems' (100 pages in the *Fifth Discipline Fieldbook*, compared with two pages on learning), his work and that of others have not fully defined a learning system. A system implies not only a connection of processes, but a complete series. Senge's admirable attention to teams and his recognition of individual learning fail to take account of one other major feature of how learning actually occurs in organisations. A great deal of learning occurs, and in managerial policy and practice is required to occur, through relationships between individuals. Most frequently this is described as a manager's responsibility for developing others, but it does of course also

Figure 12.1
The Learning Pyramid

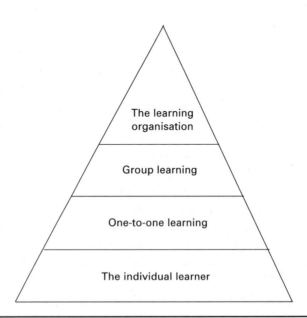

include a variety of other person-to-person relationships, as described here in Chapters 6, 9 and 11. Figure 12.1 adds different dimensions to those relationships.

The 'learning pyramid' will help to explain the term 'learning environment', which I have used but not previously discussed in this chapter. The model represents the learning organisation as being the peak of achievement. The other three levels are steps up the pyramid, each of which needs to be taken before you reach the peak. The term 'learning environment' enables management development advisers and line managers to see all the elements together, but also requires them to envisage action at all four levels in the pyramid, rather than being focused on the broad set of values or behaviours that many people seem to understand by the learning organisation. This model, through its sequential steps, provides a statement of a learning system more complete than that envisaged by other authors.

The model arrived after a particular experience.[8] A group of executives actually worked at the first three levels. The senior executives in one division of a company produced (with my help) 'personal development plans' (the first time such senior people had attempted this), discussed the issues involved with their director, and then got together as a group to discuss needs for further development both as individuals and as a group. The group then looked at how it would extend to the managers who worked for them the practices it had taken on for itself in terms of recognising and using learning opportunities. We used a variety of exercises, including several that focused on their own experience of helping others to develop, and also of being helped.

The discussions and workshop subsequently produced some actions that I was particularly pleased to hear about. The divisional director posed at the bi-monthly management meeting a question: 'Who have you been to see and what did you learn?' Thus learning and task were integrated in this group's normal agenda. What neither the client nor I recognised at the time was that these three levels of action could be articulated as actions that would help to justify the title 'learning organisation'.

Why should managers bother?

The 'learning pyramid model', and even more of course the actions that can be identified and suggested at each level, is important because it focuses attention on the particular situations in which managers ought to take action to generate learning. However, one of the problems identified earlier for practitioners was the continuing prevalence of the view of many line managers that learning and development are not a priority managerial action. The 'learning pyramid model' will be attractive to some managers, but not to others. Many will want justification along the lines of 'What is in it for me?' The following list has been developed from discussions with line managers, ie it is not a management developer's view of why managers should be interested in creating an effective 'learning environment'.

In essence they think that a 'learning environment' is created in order to:

- ensure the long-term success of the organisation
- make continuous improvements a reality
- ensure successes and best practices are transferred and emulated
- increase creativity, innovation and adaptability
- attract better people and retain your best people
- ensure people are able and willing to meet the current and future needs of your organisation.

How managers can create a learning environment

The four statements presented at the beginning of this chapter illustrate one aspect of the approach we use. Honey and I have created, tested and used a diagnostic instrument, 'The Learning Environment Questionnaire', and placed it in a resource which enables managers to look at and then develop 'the behaviours and practices involved in continuous development'.[9]

We take the view that it may not be particularly helpful to ask questions about what the organisation is doing or not doing to encourage learning. Nor should the initial focus be through even what your manager is doing to encourage learning. Just as developers and trainers began to recognise 20 years ago the crucial significance of self-development, rather than development apparently provided by someone else, so Honey and I argue that the first need in diagnosing what is actually happening in the 'learning environment' is to enable managers to look at their own behaviours and practices – certainly before they look at what anyone else is doing. Our view, of course, has echoes of the famous John F. Kennedy inaugural address: 'Ask not what the organisation is doing for you, rather what you are doing for the learning organisation.'

So the focus we provide is on the active roles of managers or senior professional people, and the explicit behaviours required to carry out those roles. Figure 12.2 sets out our second model, describing those four roles. The four items placed at the beginning of this chapter each represent in sequence one of the 12 questions representing each of the roles in 'The Learning Environment Questionnaire'.

Figure 12.2
Four Roles in Building a Learning Environment

If you are serious about making learning a priority you need to do a number of things, all of which fall into one or other of the following four categories:

1 Role model
You need to be a role-model by explicitly demonstrating in your behaviour and actions that you are an enthusiastic learner/developer yourself.

2 Provider
You need to be a conscious and generous provider of learning/development opportunities for other people, and an active supporter/encourager whenever those opportunities are taken up.

3 System-builder
You need to build learning into the system so that it is integrated with normal work processes and firmly on the conscious agenda.

4 Champion
You need to champion the importance of learning for other parts of your organisation and the organisation as a whole.

© Honey and Mumford 1

Exercise

One of the crucial behaviours in a learning organisation is the encouragement of questions. Here are some illustrations of the kind of questions readers may wish to ask at this stage.

- How far do I agree with the comments concerning leading definitions about the learning organisation?
- What is my actual position in relation to the problems raised by other practitioners about these definitions?
- What is my position on the primacy of transformational learning as a necessary feature of the learning organisation?
- What are the opportunities available to me for stimulat-

ing discussion on the learning organisation – or the learning environment?
● What do I think of the two models – 'The Learning Pyramid' and 'The Roles of the Manager'?

The learning organisation and management development

Clearly all definitions of the learning organisation describe implicitly the working situation in which managers as individuals develop. In addition to the general points I have made about those definitions, however, in terms of their practical application, the particular reason for including the 'learning environment' model and questions here is that it maps very well onto ideas presented in earlier chapters. The questions, and particularly Figure 12.2, emphasise the significance of the direct contribution of managers in developing each other. Even more strongly, they indicate that managers have to lead the attempt to create a learning organisation, of which management development is, it might be argued of course only one part. But the one part is by definition clearly the most significant aspect of the learning organisation. Managers, that is, have to lead the development of a learning organisation not just for their own personal development, but because without their leadership a learning organisation will not be created.

It may also be clear that there are links between learning organisation themes and the concept of Strategy 1 and Strategy 2 identified in Chapter 1. Strategy 1, with its emphasis on building development through planned analysis and diagnosis of the needs of an organisation, and the development of a formal management development strategy would equate to a deliberate strategy to create a learning organisation. That management development strategy might, indeed should, involve explicit leadership from the top. (Thus the importance of the role model element in Figure 12.2.)

Strategy 2 with its emphasis on the opportunistic use of learning experiences which have not been planned also fits very well with the learning organisation idea. Fundamentally, the learning organisation attempts to create a situation in which all experiences are reviewed so that learning may be drawn from them.

Investors in People (IIP)

The IIP Award launched by the UK government in 1991 does not, of course, distinguish between managers and other staff – it is concerned with the effectiveness of the whole workforce. It is therefore in some respects a part of the 'learning organisation' philosophy. To gain the award, organisations have to meet IIP national standards:

Commitment	● a public, top-level statement
	● a business plan
	● communication to all staff.
Planning	● regular reviews
	● specified resources
	● training needs agreed between managers and staff.
Action	● continuous training
	● involvement of all employees
	● employees contributing to their own development.
Evaluation	● assessments for effectiveness
	● reviews against business goals
	● top-level involvement.

Again there is a strong link to Strategy 1, since there is an explicit requirement that the training and development targets set should be linked to the achievement of national vocational qualifications (NVQs). Achievement on the Standards has to be demonstrated to an external assessor, usually a training and enterprise council (TEC). They will look for evidence of development processes on the job as well as off the job. A very important feature is that organisations have to renew their case for recognition every three years. However, a survey conducted by Cranfield School of Management suggested that a three-year review was too infrequent.[10]

Life-long learning

An Institute of Management report[11] forecast that one consequence of an increased number of career changes would be the need for managers increasingly to manage their own development. This gives a rather different emphasis to the original ideas behind the self-development movement identified in earlier chapters. It is saying that managers need to look after their own development either because organisations may not want to develop them at all or because successful development does not necessarily mean prolonged career achievement in a single organisation.

The idea of, and the need for, life-long learning has become part of the rhetoric surrounding training and development in recent years. Part of the case for it has been not only the probability of more frequent moves between organisations as suggested above, but the change in job content even within a single organisation for any particular person – in our case here, managers. It will surprise no reader who has reached this stage of the book to know that, while (of course) entirely in favour of the concept of life-long learning, I wish more was being done to convert rhetoric into a more substantial reality. It is not simply a case of acquiring pieces of learning that may convince an assessor and thereby acquire credits under the MCI 'crediting competence' approach – useful though that may be for people going down that route. Life-long learning for managers, as indeed for anyone else, must involve conscious understanding of opportunities and a review of what learning has been achieved through them. As people move around between jobs, the portfolio of learning they take with them becomes more important. Whereas a manager staying within one organisation and perhaps moving largely within one function can rely on learning experiences that have not been articulated, thought through and properly understood, this 'unconscious' learning on which so many managers in practice rely will increasingly be recognised as insufficient. This will be true whether they stay within one organisation or move outside it, but is emphasised if they move. Learning must be recognised more consciously in order to be able to be used more effectively. 'Learning to learn' will remain rhetorical for many managers unless they have been equipped to 'learn how to learn'.

References

1 ARGYRIS, C. *Reasoning, Learning and Action.* San Francisco, Jossey-Bass, 1982.
2 ARGYRIS, C. 'Teaching smart people how to learn'. *Harvard Business Review,* May/June 1991.
3 SENGE, P. *The Fifth Discipline.* New York, Doubleday, 1990.
4 SENGE, P., KLEINER, A., ROBERT, C., ROSS, R. *and* SMITH, B. *The Fifth Discipline Fieldbook.* London, Nicholas Brealey, 1995.
5 PEDLER, M., BURGOYNE, J., *and* BOYDELL, T. *The Learning Company.* Maidenhead, McGraw-Hill, 1991.
6 MUMFORD, A. *Learning at the Top.* Maidenhead, McGraw-Hill, 1995.
7 MUMFORD, A. *Management Development: Strategies for action.* 2nd edn. London, IPM, 1993.
8 MUMFORD, A. 'The learning pyramid', in K. Watkins and V. Marsick (eds), *Creating the Learning Organization.* Vol. 1, ASTD, 1996.
9 HONEY, P. *and* MUMFORD, A. *Managing Your Learning Environment.* Maidenhead, Honey, 1996.
10 ALBERGA, T. 'Time for a check-up'. *People Management.* 6 February 1997.
11 CANNON, T. *and* TAYLOR, J. *Management Development in the Millennium.* London, Institute of Management, 1994.

13

■■ **Additional Resources and Further**
Reading

Institutions

Association for Management Education and Development
14 Belgrave Square
London SW1X 8PS

This body draws together management educators, management developers and trainers in organisations and training consultancies.

European Women's Management Development Network
Rue Washington 40
B1050 Brussels, Belgium

or

Ashridge Management College
Berkhamsted
Hertfordshire HP4 1NS

This forum gives special voice to women and women's issues.

International Foundation for Action Learning
Dept of Management Learning
The Management School
Lancaster University, LA1 4YX

This small group spreads the message of action learning.

Institute of Personnel and Development
Camp Road
Wimbledon
London SW19 4UX

This professional association not only provides literature, as this book attests, but provides through its national and regional conferences and branch meetings further opportunities to discuss management development issues.

European Foundation for Management Development
Rue Washington 40
B1050 Brussels, Belgium

This organisation draws together consultants, in-company advisers and management educators from the whole of Europe. It has a particularly strong emphasis on and membership in business schools.

The Management Charter Initiative/National Forum for
   Management Education and Development
10 Russell Square
London WC1B 5BZ

MCI is responsible for promoting a competence-focused approach to management development.

Suppliers of consultancy and resources

It is really necessary to turn to specific books in order to find what you might need here.

Mike Abrahams has written a very useful guide to the choice of consultants in the *Handbook of Management Development*, edited by A. Mumford, 4th edn, Aldershot, Gower, 1994.

Specific reference books include the *AMED Directory of Consultants*.

A number of books describe particular processes such as films, case studies and business games. It is best to access the most recent of these by approaching the library of your professional institution. In addition to those mentioned above, the Institute of Management (Management House, Cottingham Road, Corby, Northants NN17

1TT; telephone: 01536 204222) has a very good and helpful library service, which can be used either by individual members or by individuals from member organisations.

Department of Management Learning
University of Lancaster
Lancaster LA1 4YX

This has been the one organisation specifically dedicated to improved understanding of teaching and learning processes. It remains the central focus for a great deal of research and associated practical work. It publishes a newsletter and runs annual conferences.

Journals

People Management has the biggest circulation of any of the journals dealing with this field. Since it deals with the whole personnel field, articles on management development obviously do not come up every month.

MCB University Press, based at Bradford, has a number of specialist training and development journals, to which it adds regularly:

Career Development International

Industrial and Commercial Training

Journal of Management Development

Journal of European Industrial Training

Management Development Review

Readers would be well advised to get the latest list of journals in this field by writing to MCB University Press at 62 Toller Lane, Bradford, West Yorkshire, BD8 9DY.

Anbar Index: Anbar, also published by MCB, provides an abstract and copy service in paper and CD-Rom of articles on management development.

Further reading

The following comments are intended to indicate books or articles that I regard as of prime significance, or that offer a different view from the one I have emphasised in the relevant chapters.

Chapters 1 and 2

The essential question here is what you consider an appropriate definition of management development.

Christopher Molander, in *Management Development*, Bromley, Chartwell-Bratt, 1986, focuses entirely on formal processes in his definition. His analysis of content, however, usefully brings out the possibility of three types of focus: individual, group and organisation.

This kind of analysis is taken much further by Robin Snell and Don Binsted in their *Issues in Management Development*, published by CSML in 1985.

Gordon McBeath's *Practical Management Development* (Oxford, Blackwell, 1990) also focuses almost entirely on systems and structured organised processes (described as Type 3 in my model in Chapter 2). Although he presents no model of management development, his implicit beliefs about the nature of it come over clearly. To him, it is about systems, structures and the completion of forms, a view which I regard as representing a well-delivered version of *formal* management development.

In contrast, Charles Margerison in *Making Management Development Work* (Maidenhead, McGraw-Hill, 1991) has more in common with the ideas expressed in this book. He is largely concerned with learning from and within real work. He has a particularly valuable chapter entitled 'What Do Managers Want From Management Development?' The focus of his ideas is on defining and meeting the needs of the organisation – a process covered in detail in Chapters 4 to 6 of this book.

John Storey has reviewed the literature in two articles, 'Management development: a literature review and applications for future research' (*Personnel Review* Vol. 18, No. 6, 1989; Vol. 19, No. 1). These two articles would assist anyone wanting to survey the whole field and needing help on identifying the issues.

On action learning I chose to refer to the most usable of Revans's many writings. The whole field is surveyed by A. Mumford in *Management Bibliographies and Reviews*, Vol. 11, No. 2, 1985, and Vol. 20, No. 6, 1994.
   Of the growing number of books, try:

A. Mumford (ed.), *Action Learning at Work*, Aldershot, Gower, 1997.
M. Pedler (ed.), *Action Learning in Practice*, 3rd edn, Aldershot, Gower, 1997.
K. Weinstein, *Action Learning*, London, HarperCollins, 1995.

Chapter 3

My own book *Developing Top Managers* is the most extensive study so far of how senior managers learn to do their jobs and why informal processes are so paramount. The American book given below similarly focuses on real managerial experiences, and also shows why work-based experiences are so powerful. It does not, however, describe the learning process so well:

M. McCall, M. Lombardo and A. Morrison, *The Lessons of Experience*, Lexington, 1988.

The article by Stuart referred to in Chapter 3 is an excellent short and clear statement.

David Megginson in 'Planned and emergent learning', *Management Learning*, Vol. 27, No. 4, 1996, has developed an interesting model and themes around the issue of how far learning can be planned for and recognised in advance.

Chapter 4

The flow of articles and books on appraisal has diminished in recent years. The book by Long is fundamental.

A paper by Bill Braddick and Peter Smith of Ashridge Management College (Berkhamsted, Herts JP4 1NS; telephone: 044284 3491), 'The design of appraisal systems', includes a most valuable review of the different purposes of different participants in appraisal. Although not referred to in this chapter, the work by Ed Schein quoted in Chapter 11, *Career Dynamics*, should certainly be read.

Assessment centres were reviewed in a special issue of the *Journal of Management Development*, Vol. 4, No. 4, 1985.

Chapter 5

An alternative view to the one I have presented on levels of career development is given by:

C. Margerison, 'Achieving capacity and competency to manage', *Journal of Management Development*, Vol. 4, No. 3, 1985.
C. Margerison, 'Managing career choices' in A. Mumford (ed.), *Handbook of Management Development*, Aldershot, Gower, 1994.

The issue of plateaued managers is addressed in two articles:

Paul Evans, 'New directions in career management', *Personnel Management*, December 1986.

For the career patterns and work attitudes of both plateaued and non-plateaued managers, see C. Orpen, *International Journal of Manpower*, Vol. 4, No. 4, 1983.

Important research showing the ineffectiveness of much planning was provided by:

W. Hirsh, C. Jackson and C. Jackson, *Careers in Organisations*, Institute for Employment Studies, 1996.

An interesting article balancing the normal view of dual-career families by looking at the man as the second feature is:

L. Greenbury, 'Move over, darling', *People Management*, December 1996.

Chapter 6

Business strategy is increasingly seen as a major cause and vehicle for management development. In addition to the articles quoted, it is worth looking at:

W. P. Nilsson, *Achieving Goals through Executive Development*, Reading, Mass., Addison-Wesley, 1987.

This gives some useful insights on this particular issue, although it is dominated by courses and has remarkably little to say about associated development and learning processes.

David Hussey, *Management Training and Corporate Strategy*, London, Pergamon Press, 1988.

J. F. Bolt, 'Tailor executive development to strategy', *Harvard Business Review*, November 1985, A. Mayo and E. Lank, *The Power of Learning*, London, IPD, 1994.

The competency thrust in the UK is encouraged by the publications of the Management Charter Initiative. Critical views can be found in:

J. Burgoyne, 'The competence movement', *Personnel Review*, Vol. 22, No. 6, 1993.
G. Currie and R. Darby, 'Competence based management development: rhetoric and reality', *Journal of European Industrial Training*, Vol. 19, No. 5, 1995.

An Ashridge Research Project on *Management for the Future*, published in 1987, presents some interesting views about likely changes in skill and competency requirements.

G. Salaman in *Managing*, Milton Keynes, Open University Press, 1995, provides an excellent introduction to what managers do, and links this to learning.

Fascinating insights into what a development adviser does, especially the political issues, are provided by:

E. Moorby, *How to Succeed in Employee Development*, Maidenhead, McGraw-Hill, 1996.
G. M. Robinson, *Managing after the Superlatives*, Tudor, 1992.

The issues of 'leaders are different from managers' was first identified in substantial form by Abraham Zalezink. Many years after his innovative Harvard article he produced *The Managerial Mystique: Restoring leadership in business* (London, Harper & Row 1990). The impact of his ideas does, however, depend on the reader's acceptance of a great deal of psychological theory.

Chapter 7

The development issues arising from job moves, on which I have
used Gabarro as my main source, are also usefully covered in:

Peter Smith, 'The stages in a manager's job', in V. Hammond (ed.),
Current Research in Management, Frances Pinter, 1985.
C. Parker and A. Lewis, 'Beyond the Peter Principle', *Journal of
European Industrial Training*, Vol. 5, No. 6, 1981.

The main works on action learning have been mentioned earlier.
John Morris, while coming from the same philosophical base, describes his own approaches very well in:

J. Morris, 'Joint development activities in practice', *Journal of
Management Development*, Vol. 1, No. 3, 1982.

The literature on mentors is largely covered in the book by
Clutterbuck, mentioned in the chapter. Additional material is to be
found in M. G. Zey, *The Mentor Connection*, Dow-Jones Irwin,
1984; D. Hunt and C. Michael, 'Mentorship', in *Academy of
Management Review*, Vol. 8, No. 3, 1983; K. Kram, 'Phases of the
mentor relationship', *Academy of Management Journal*, Vol. 6, No.
4, December 1983; and D. Megginson, 'Instructor, coach, mentor:
three ways of helping for managers', *Management Education and
Development*, Vol. 19, Part 1, 1988.

Chapter 8

D. Binsted and R. Stuart, 'Designing reality into management learning events', *Personnel Review*, Vol. 8, No. 3, 1979 give the best conceptual analysis of this.

A useful integrative article is:

G. Prideaux and J. E. Ford, 'Management development: competencies, contracts, teams and work-based learning', *Journal of Management Development*, Vol. 7, No. 1, 1988.

On business schools and particularly of MBA programmes:

G. Wills, 'Business school graffiti', MCB University Press, 1976; 'Creating wealth through management development', MCB University Press, 1988. J. N. Behrman and R. I. Levin, 'Are business schools doing their job?', *Harvard Business Review*, Jan/Feb. 1984.

J. Forrester, *A Study of the Practical Uses of the MBA*, BIM, 1984.

R. Boyatzis, S. Cowen, and D. Kolb, *Innovation in Professional Education*, San Francisco, Calif., Jossey-Bass, 1995.

Peter Bramley has written frequently about evaluation, most fully in:

P. Bramley, *Evaluating Training Effectiveness*, Maidenhead, McGraw-Hill, 1991.
P. Bramley, 'Evaluation' in A. Mumford (ed.), *Handbook of Management Development*, 4th edn, Aldershot, Gower, 1994.

There are two 'curate's egg' books (good in parts) on management training:

A. Pepper, *Managing the Training and Development Function*, Aldershot, Gower, 1984.

This is good on the organisation of training, but not on learning or on management development in total.

J. E. Jones and M. Woodcock, *Manual of Management Development*, Aldershot, Gower, 1985 also has good guidance on courses and does actually address the processes of learning.

A positive view on the possibility of transformation is given in:

G. Robinson and C. Hurley, 'Management development and transformation in the Guernsey public sector', *Industrial and
Commercial Training*, Vol. 28, No. 3, 1996.

Chapter 9

Many of the relevant books here have been mentioned in earlier
chapters.

In addition to the books by Mumford (*How Managers Can Develop
Managers*) and McCall (*Lessons from Experience*) mentioned
earlier, an article by M. London, 'The boss's role in management development', *Journal of Management Development*, Vol. 5, No. 3,
1986 is worth reading for its specific cases.

An article by T. Garavan is also particularly helpful:

'Promoting natural learning activities within the organisation',
Journal of European Industrial Training, Vol. 11, No. 7, 1987.

The article by Roger Stuart, 'Maximising managers' day-to-day
learning: framework for the practice of learning interventions', is, as
often with him, both thought-provoking and practical (published in
Management Development: Advances in theory and practice, edited
by C. Cox and J. Beck, Chichester, John Wiley, 1984).

The work by Pepper mentioned above is the prime source of material
on trainers and advisers here. For quite a different perspective, but
dealing very much with the kind of activities in which developers
and trainers may get involved, see:

A. Huczynski, *Encyclopedia of Management Development Methods*,
Aldershot, Gower, 1983.

See also R. Bennett, *Improving Trainer Effectiveness*, Aldershot, Gower, 1988.

Chapter 10

Judi Marshall has contributed most to my understanding of women's development:

J. Marshall, 'Revisioning organizations by developing female values', in R. Boot (ed.), *Managing the Unknown*, Maidenhead, McGraw-Hill, 1994.
J. Marshall, *Travellers in a Male World*, Chichester, John Wiley, 1984.
J. Marshall, 'Revisioning career concepts', in M. B. Arthur (ed.), *Handbook of Career Theory*, Cambridge, Cambridge University Press, 1989.

Another substantial contribution is:

C. Cooper and M. Davidson, *Women in Management*, London, Heinemann, 1984.

A useful collection of case studies is:

Women of the 80s, publishing by Manpower Services Commission, 1987.

For issues of gender and cultural influences on how managers learn, see:

M. Hite and K. S. McDonald, 'Gender issues in management development', *Journal of Management Development*, Vol. 14, No. 4, 1995.
A. Mumford, *How to Choose the Right Management Development Methods*, Honey, 1997.

Ashton applies Hofstede's analysis of national culture to his then organisation in:

'Cultural differences: implications for management development', *Management Education and Development*, Vol. 15, Part 1, 1984.

Other aspects are usefully described in:

F. Trompenaars, *Riding the Waves of Culture*, Economist Books, 1993.
J.W. Seddon, 'The education and development of overseas managers', *Management Education and Development*, Vol. 16, Part 1, 1985.
R. T. Pascale and A. G. Athos, *The Art of Japanese Management*, London, Penguin, 1982.
T. Vineall, 'Creating a multinational management team', *Personnel Management*, October 1988.

Multicultural Management Development, Special Issues of *Journal of Management Development*, Vol. 6, No. 3, 1987 and Vol. 13, No. 2, 1994.
H. Scullion, 'Why companies prefer to use expatriates', *Personnel Management*, November 1991.
P. Evans, 'International management development', *Personnel Management*, December 1990.

Chapter 11

Self-development
A number of relevant articles and books is identified in the article by Alan Mumford: 'Self-development: missing elements', *Industrial and Commercial Training*, Vol. 18, No. 2, 1986.

A useful short book with exercises is:

D. Megginson, *Cultivating Self-development*, London, IPD, 1996.

Some useful directions for improvement in the self-development process are indicated in Honey and Povah, 'Self development: overcoming the paradox', *Industrial and Commercial Training*, Vol. 18, No. 4, 1986.

On the learning process, Kolb's book is the 'must read' theoretical book (*Experiential Learning*). The only other major conceptual work is Patricia Cross, *Adults as Learners*, San Francisco, Calif., Jossey-Bass, 1981.

I strongly recommend to both trainers and educators the major work in redesigning an MBA programme as an illustration of competences and learning:

R. Boyatzis, S. Cowen and D. A. Kolb, *Innovation in Professional Education*, San Francisco, Calif., Jossey-Bass, 1995.

The whole field of 'learning to learn' was reviewed by Alan Mumford in 'Learning to learn for managers: a literature review', *Management Bibliographies and Reviews*, Vol. 12, No. 2, 1986.

Mumford's *Effective Learning*, London, IPD, 1996 is a short guide for managers, with useful exercises.

The articles by Stuart referenced in the chapter are very useful.

Ian Cunningham offers a different approach from that of the learning cycle or learning styles; he describes this as 'patterns'. This approach could be particularly helpful for those who do not favour the structured diagnostic instrument approach:

I. Cunningham, *Beyond Distance Teaching: Towards open learning*, Milton Keynes, Open University Press, 1987.

Although misleadingly titled, Bob Garrat's *The Learning*

Organisation, Aldershot, Gower, 1987 contains some excellent work on directors, their thinking and learning processes. This should be read in association with:

E. H. Schein, *Organisational Culture and Leadership*, San Francisco, Calif., Jossey-Bass, 1987.

The idea of learning contracts is well displayed in the misleadingly titled:

G. Boak, *Developing Managerial Competences*, London, Pitman, 1991.

Some good processes are identified in:

K. Kram and L. Isabella, 'Alternatives to mentoring', *Academy of Management Journal*, Vol. 28, No. 1, March 1985.

P. Honey, *101 Ways to Develop Your People*, Honey, 1994.

Chapter 12

The learning organisation has been a major growth area for articles and books, some of which tend to repeat, particularly in the USA, the same company cases.

The most specific and rounded UK book, focused on International Computers Ltd, is:

A. Mayo and E. Lang, *The Power of Learning*, London, IPD, 1994.

A collection of papers rather more focused on concepts than particular organisational experiences is:

J. Burgoyne, M. Pedler and T. Boydell, *Towards the Learning Company*, Maidenhead, McGraw-Hill, 1994.

A book more centred on how to achieve in the sense of practical applications is:

M. Pearn, C. Roderick and C. Mulrooney, *Learning Organizations in Practice*, Maidenhead, McGraw-Hill, 1995.

The American literature is vast; the material from which I have gained most includes:

N. Dixon, *The Organizational Learning Cycle*, Maidenhead, McGraw-Hill, 1994.
K. Watkins and V. Marsick, *Sculpting the Learning Organization*, San Francisco, Calif., Jossey-Bass, 1994.
DiBella, E. C., Nevis, J. M. Gould, 'Understanding organizational learning capability', *Journal of Management Studies*, May 1996.
D. Garvin, 'Building a learning organization', *Harvard Business Review*, July/August 1993.

These books and articles would certainly provide different concepts, priorities and methods from those indicated through my own work in Chapter 12. There is, for example, a variety of different ways of diagnosing the learning organisation. Alternatives can be found in:

M. Van Buren, and L. Lucadamo, *ASTD Guide to Learning Organization Assessment Instruments*, ASTD 1996.

All chapters

There are two handbooks on management development. Reference has been made to a number of entries in the Gower publication which I edited. Particularly useful chapters supplementing the existing references are Tony Vineall's on planning management development (Chapters 5 and 6), and Peter Bramley's on evaluation (Chapter 8).

Finally, the IPD has a book on *Continuous Development* (ed. Sue Wood, London, IPD, 1988) which illustrates its own interest in combining formal and informal learning, with a number of specific cases.

Rosemary Harrison's *Employee Development*, London, IPD, 1997 is an excellent book. Although aimed at a wider population than managers, it gives helpful guidance on the design and review of learning experiences.

Significant written material

The references I have made to books and articles so far have been to produce data in order to create or support a case. In this last section I have attempted to provide some protection against a total domination of my own interests and ideas. As I worked on this book, and particularly as I produced the references in this last section, I thought that here was an opportunity for a final exercise. The book began by asking readers to describe a powerful learning experience. It ends by inviting them to carry out a similar exercise.

Which written or visual piece of material has been of most significance to you in considering, or working on, management development? (It may be a film, a case study, an article or a book.)

■🐾 Index

Other titles in the Developing Strategies series

Managing the Mosaic
Diversity in action

*Rajvinder Kandola
and Johanna Fullerton*

*Special Commendation winner at the 1995 Management
Consultancies Association Book Awards.*

Today, all organisations have to confront the challenge of diverse workforces. Yet many equal opportunity initiatives, in particular target-setting and positive action, which focus on specific groups such as women or ethnic minorities, are fundamentally flawed. To be effective, diversity strategies must tap into the talents of all staff, not just those from selected groups.

In this provocative but highly practical book, Rajvinder Kandola and Johanna Fullerton – chartered occupational psychologists at the Pearn Kandola practice in Oxford – set out to separate myth from reality. Drawing on a wide-ranging literature search, extensive experience of working within companies, and a survey of almost 300 organisations they give clear evidence that group-based equal opportunity policies are divisive and seldom successful.

Effective diversity strategies, pioneered by companies such as International Distillers and Vintners, are summed up in a detailed new model and linked to the ideal of the 'learning organisation', whose essential elements are flexibility, an empowering culture, universal benefits and business-related training for whoever needs it. Demographic changes, legislation, and increasingly globalised markets mean that diversity is now of central concern for all employers. This book provides definitive solutions to their problems.

(Managing the Mosaic) *makes a compelling case for the better management of the resources of the business: people with their wide variety of attributes, concerns, values and needs* – The judges' panel, 1995 MCA Book Awards

1994 200 pages Royal paperback ISBN 0 85292 556 5 **£17.95**

The Communicating Organisation

Michael Blakstad and Aldwyn Cooper

Internal communication is not just part of PR or crisis management but a vital strategic tool. This pioneering book explains why employers need to devote more resources to this vital area. Drawing on their own consultancy experience, the authors reveal a number of fascinating case-studies, including:

- how the technology division of the Atomic Energy Authority carried out an in-depth audit and built its privatisation programme on the perceptions of people within, as well as outside
- how Price Waterhouse turned its consultancy skills on itself, forged a new philosophy, and communicated it to every employee
- how Meridian Broadcasting recruited its entire staff, moulded them into a single unit, and was on the air within 14 months of being granted a licence.

The text is written in a way which does not talk down to the reader ... is well written and full of useful, well-grounded ideas – Organisations and People

1995 208 pages   Royal paperback   ISBN 0 85292 575 1   **£18.95**

Ethical Leadership

Stephen Connock
and Ted Johns

Today's managers are constantly faced with acute ethical dilemmas; many may feel under pressure to sacrifice personal beliefs to corporate gain. Yet most books on business ethics are obscure and over-theoretical. This bold new text adopts a considered but completely practical approach that has nothing to do with saintliness and everything to do with organisational effectiveness and management action. Topics covered in depth, with stimulating company examples, include:

- balancing the needs and perspectives of different stakeholders
- codes of business conduct and common ethical issues about gifts, hospitality, confidentiality and conflicts of interest
- establishing the values to promote the right behaviour
- implementing core principles
- the roles of training and HR.

... a practical and inspiring definition of a contemporary ethical leadership and a businesslike explanation of why and how managers and organisations should use it – Occupational Safety and Health

1995 240 pages   Royal paperback   ISBN 0 85292 561 1   **£18.95**

Leadership for Strategic Change

Christopher Ridgeway
and Brian Wallace

Effective strategic change leadership means seeing beyond day-to-day issues towards forging a new vision for the business. It means using influence to get others on board or facilitating them to achieve results. It also means choosing the right style – flexible, participative or more controlling – to adopt in specific circumstances.

This superb book enables potential change leaders to think through the issues, assess their core skills, put them into context and proceed to action. Stimulating questionnaires test for different kinds of leadership ability. Vivid case-studies spell out lessons in organisations that have undergone major change, and frank extended interviews with key players in change initiatives offer invaluable insights.

1996 240 pages   Royal paperback   ISBN 0 85292 613 8   **£18.95**

The Power of Learning
A guide to gaining competitive advantage

Andrew Mayo
and Elizabeth Lank

Corporate survival depends crucially on adaptability, driven by employees willing and able continuously to update their knowledge and skills. . . .

This bold and challenging book provides the vision and practical guidance to help all managers and directors to tap into the power of learning. Using real-life examples and a series of 'powerpoints' to enable companies to assess themselves, it shows how to:

- forge visionary, risk-taking leaders who can coach and empower others
- use the right language to promote a culture for learning
- support constant learning through people management processes – induction, performance management, career development and reward
- build an 'organisational brain' through information technology
- ensure all employees enhance their learning skills
- achieve maximum synergy in teams, networks, and communities
- break down the barriers to sharing information
- measure the added value of effective learning.

The book concludes with a practical self-assessment tool guaranteed to help companies of every size and sector set out on the journey to becoming more effective learning organisations.

1994 278 pages   Royal paperback   ISBN 0 85292 565 4   **£18.95**